Guangzhou

A Photographic Exploration

Scott Shaw

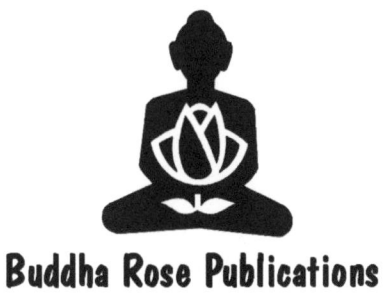

Buddha Rose Publications

Guangzhou: A Photographic Exploration
Copyright © 1987, 2014
By Scott Shaw
www.scottshaw.com
ALL RIGHTS RESERVED

First Edition 2014

No part of this book may be reproduced in any manner without the expressed written permission of the author or the publishing company.

ISBN: 1-877792-76-4
ISBN 13: 978-1-877792-76-2

Printed in the United States of America

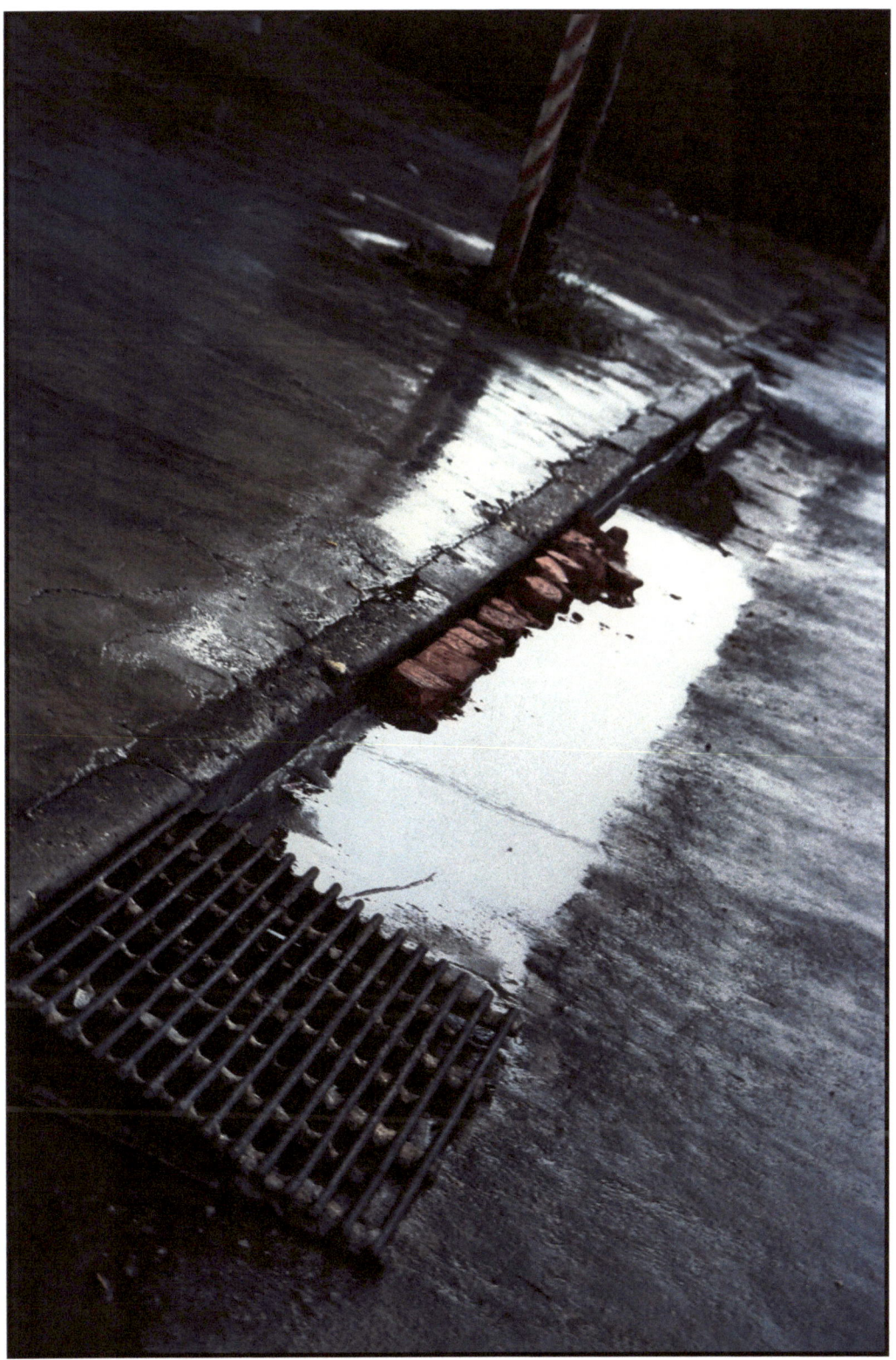

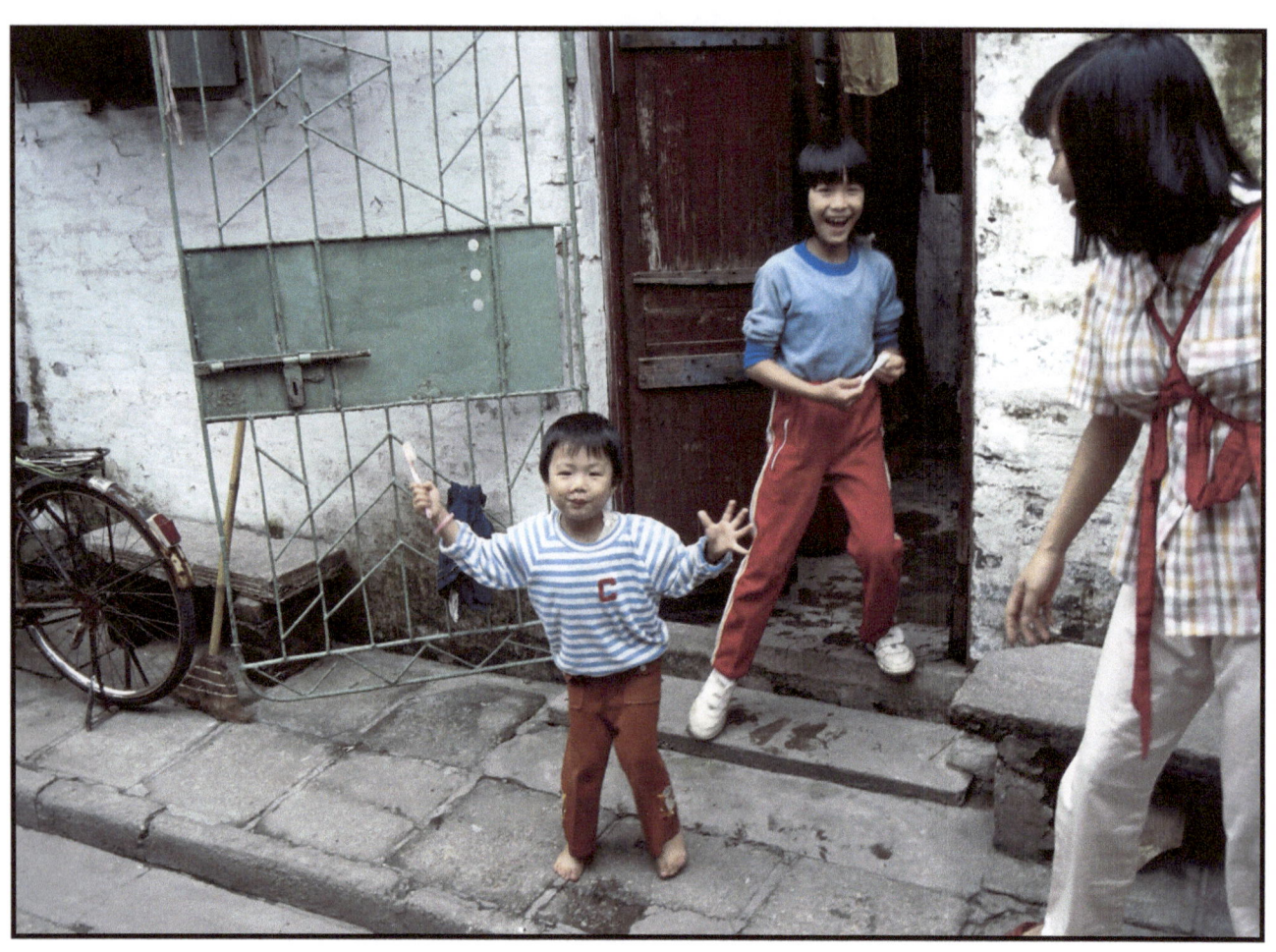

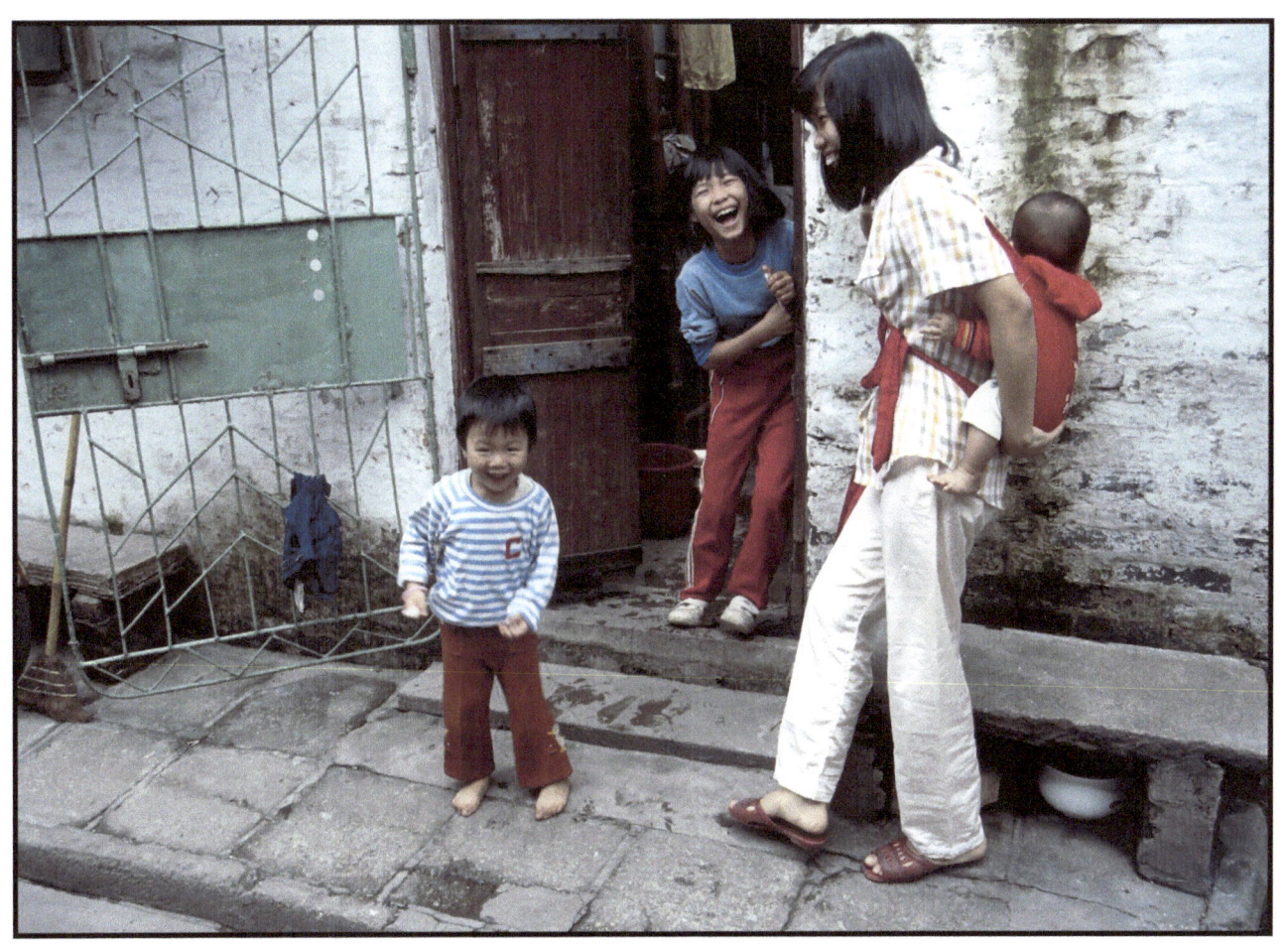

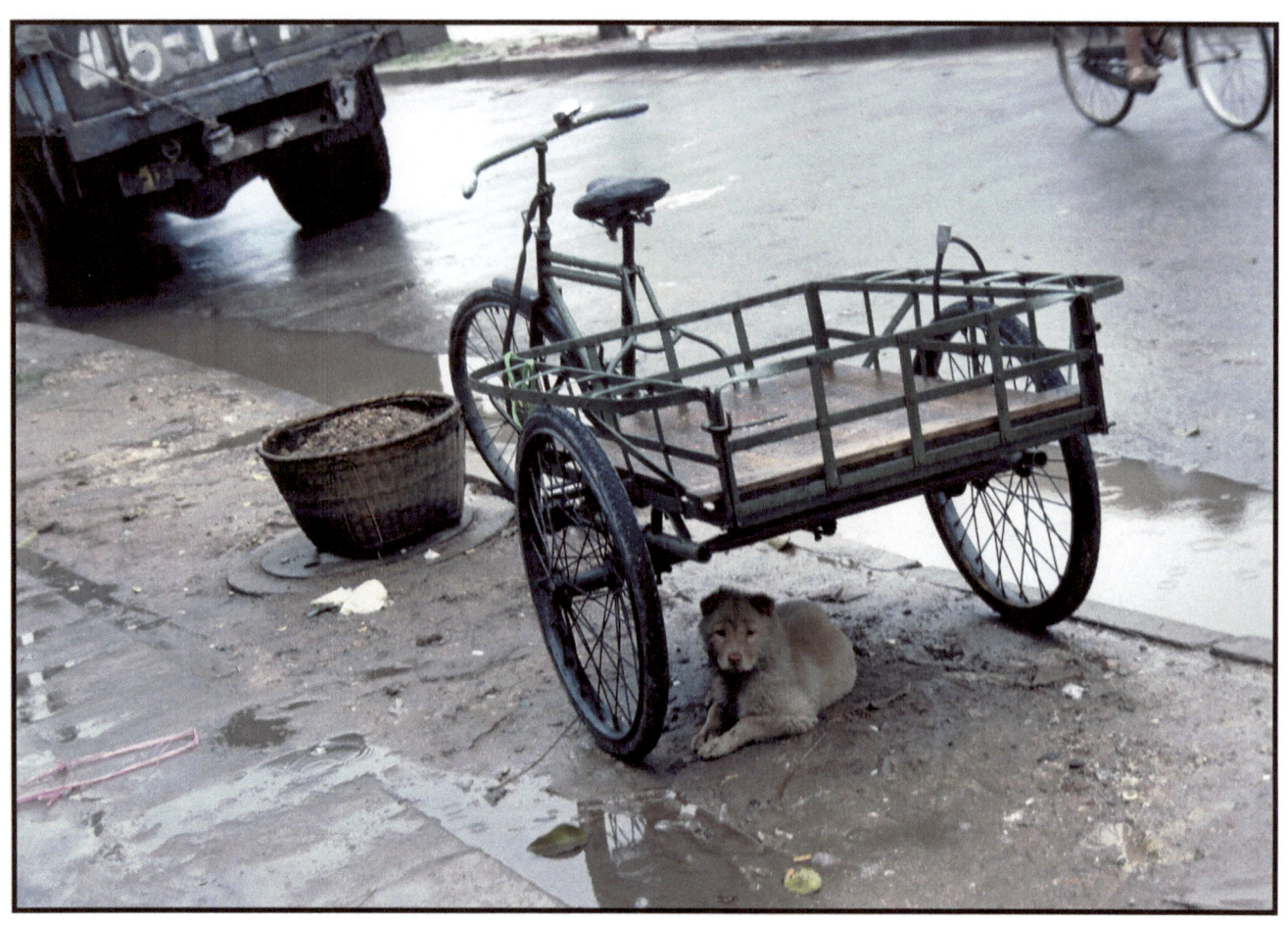

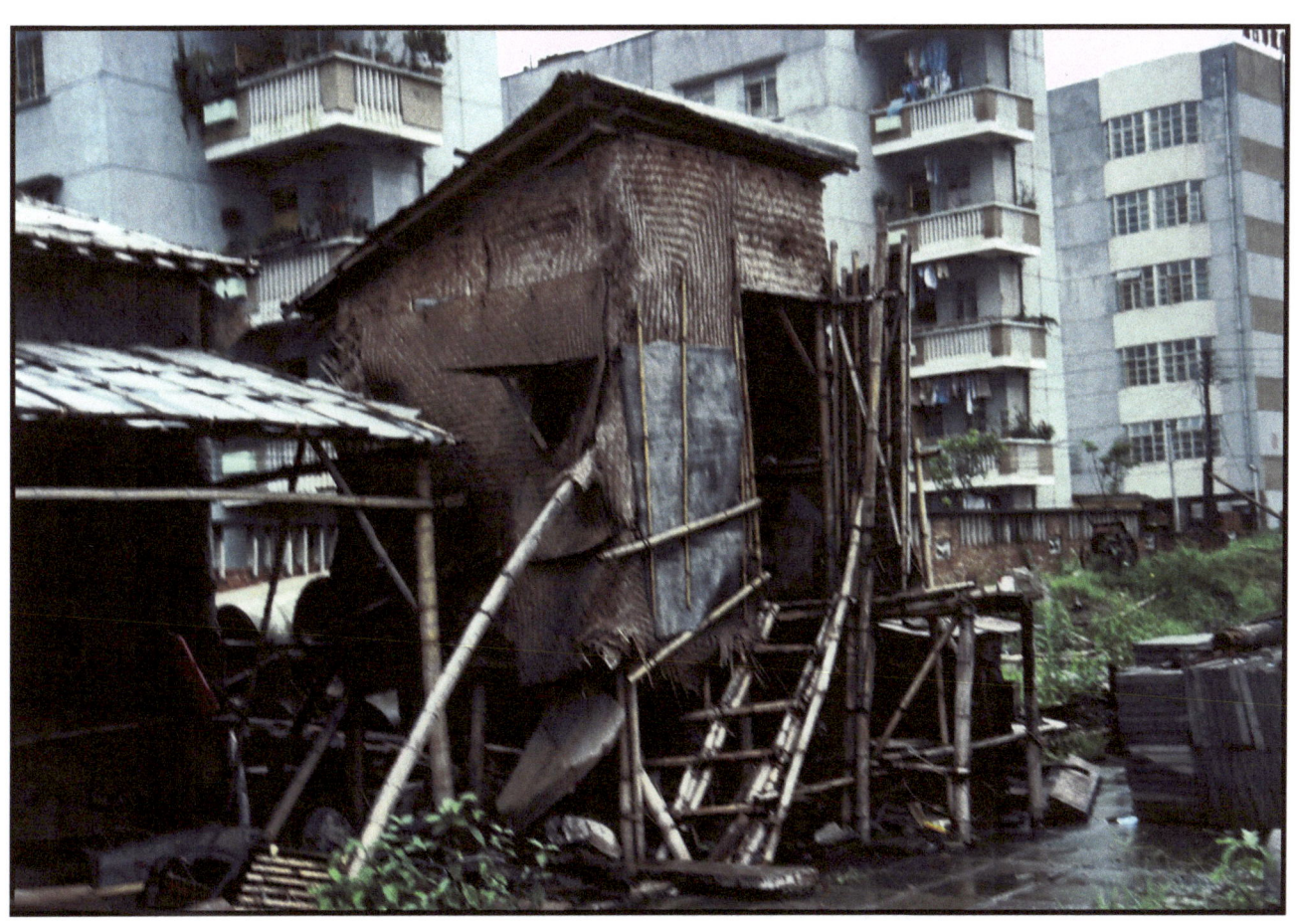

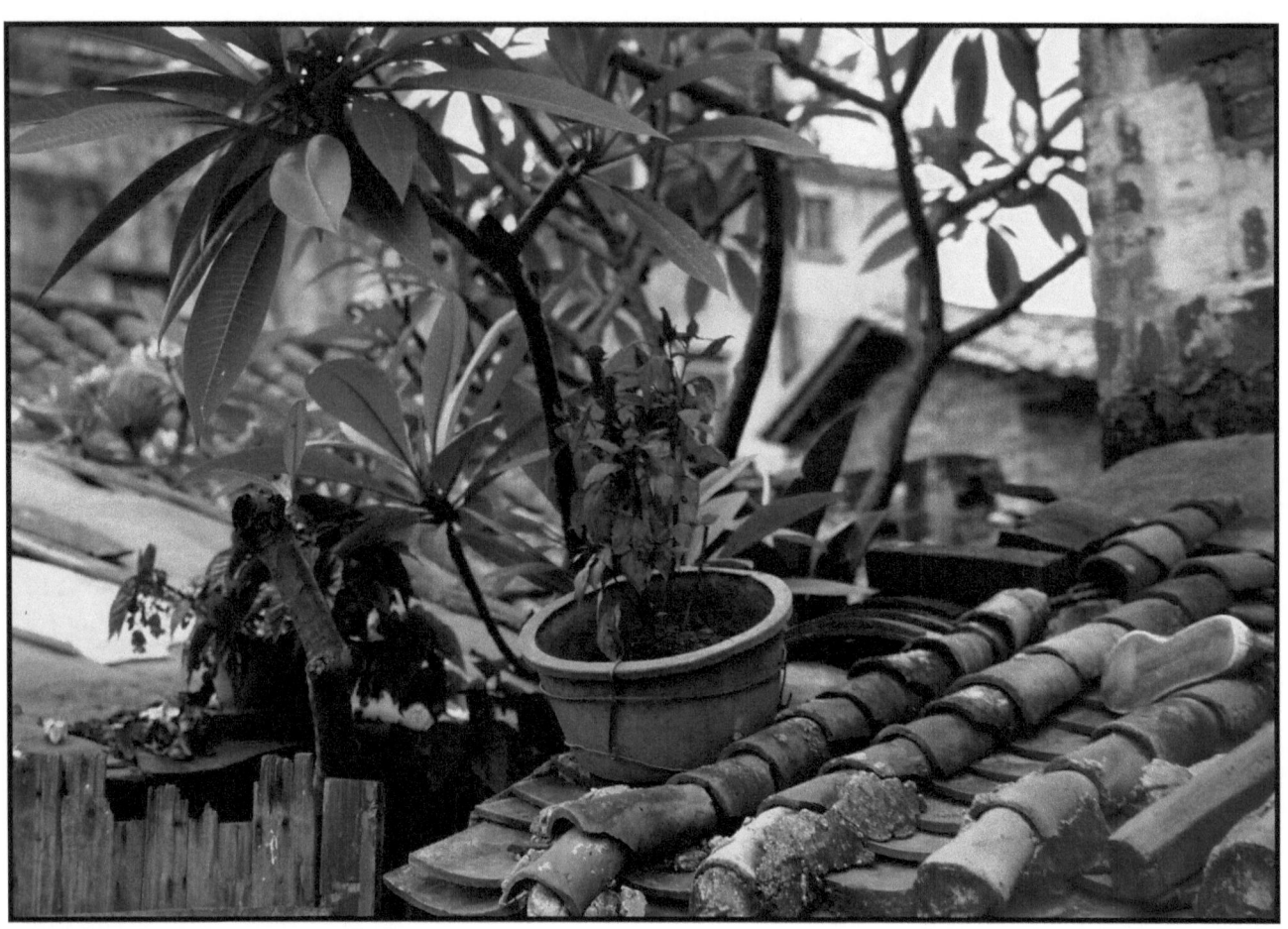

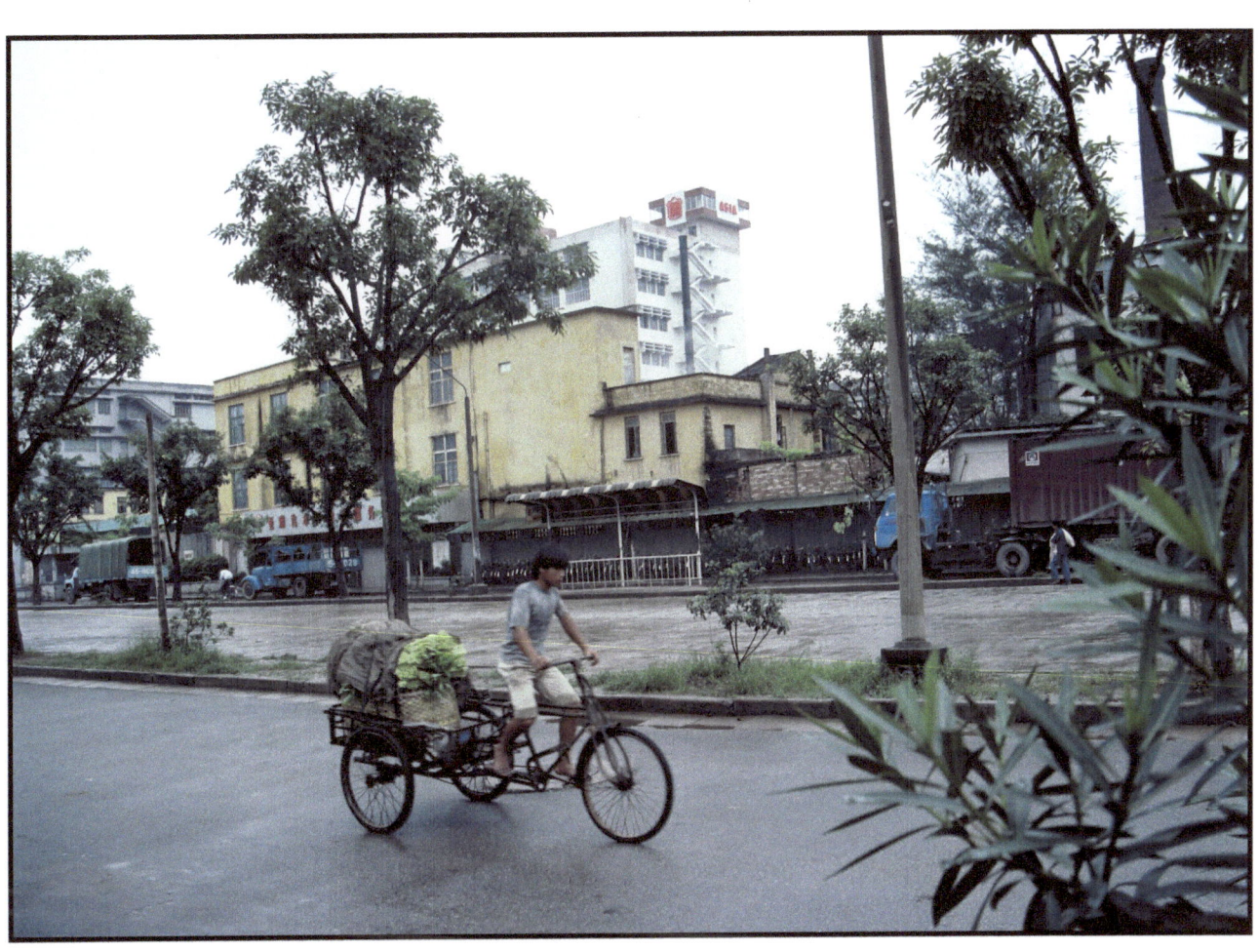

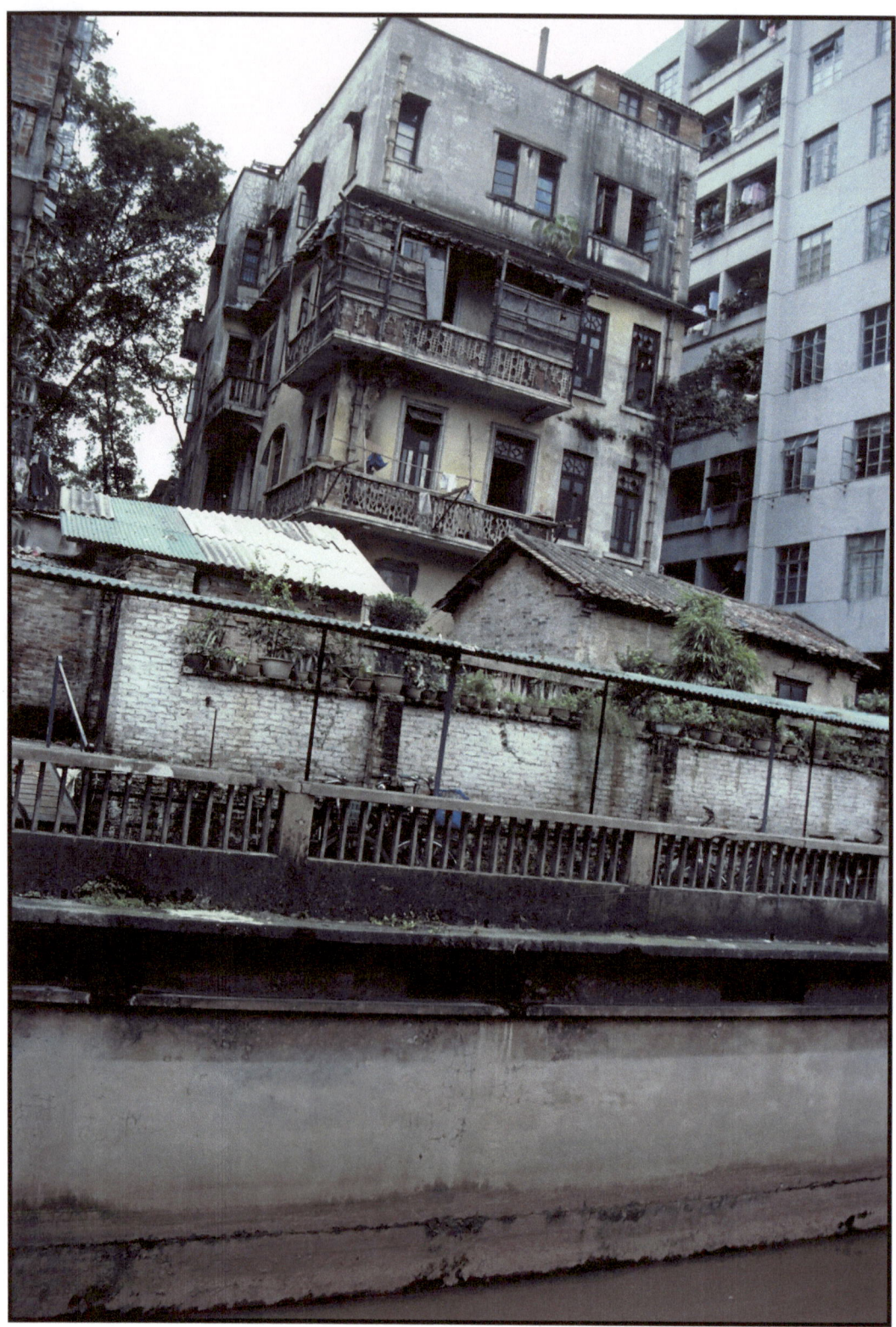

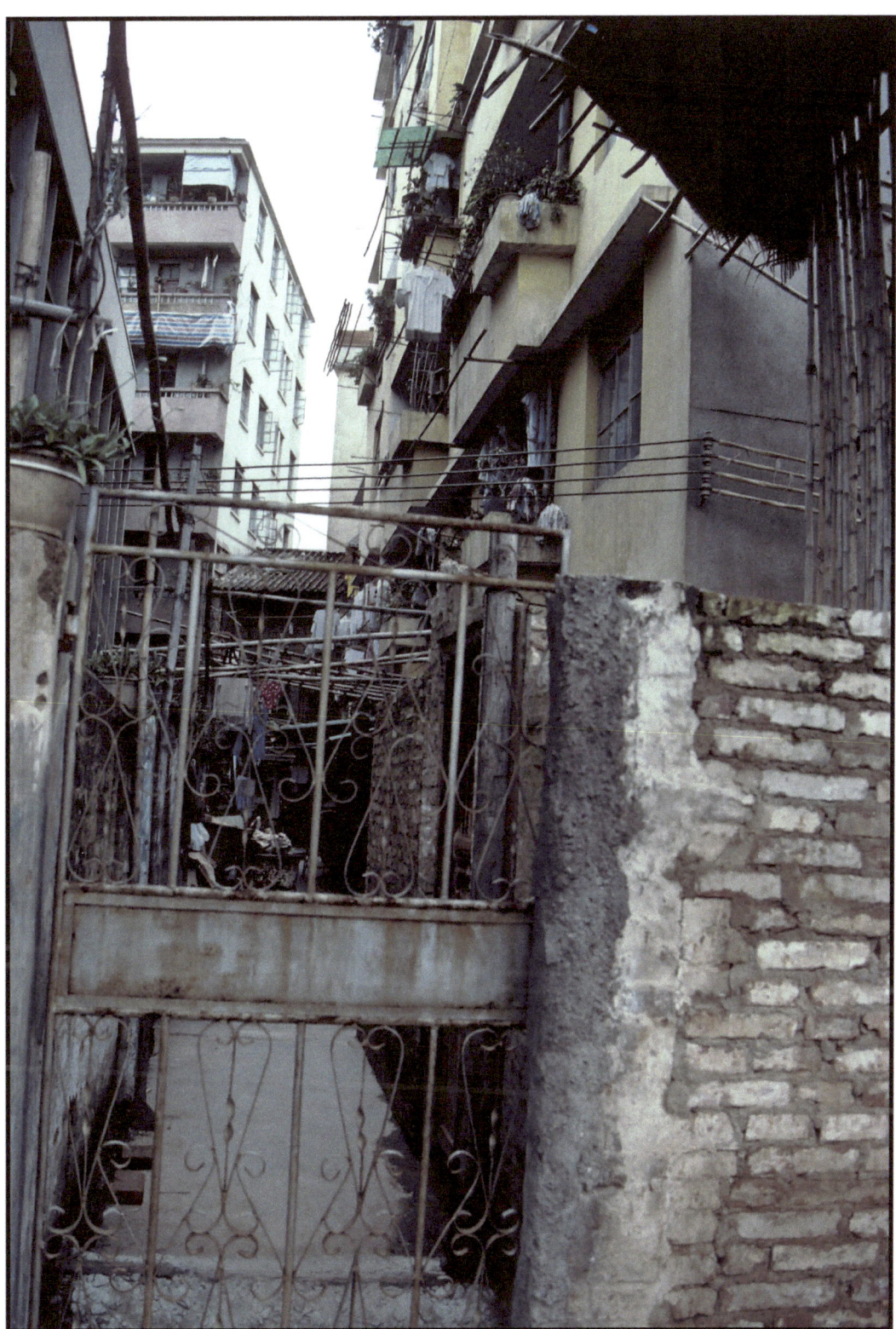

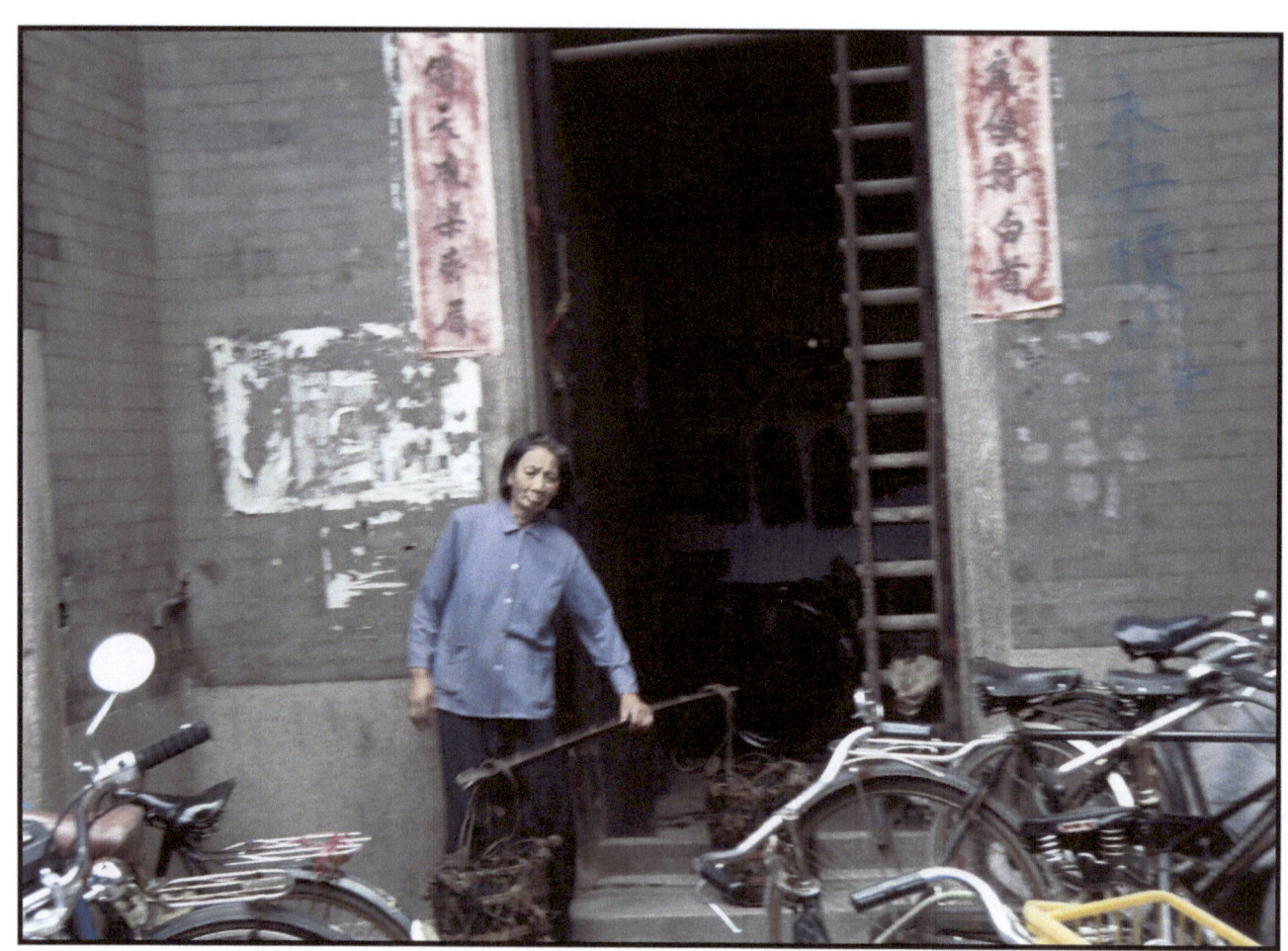

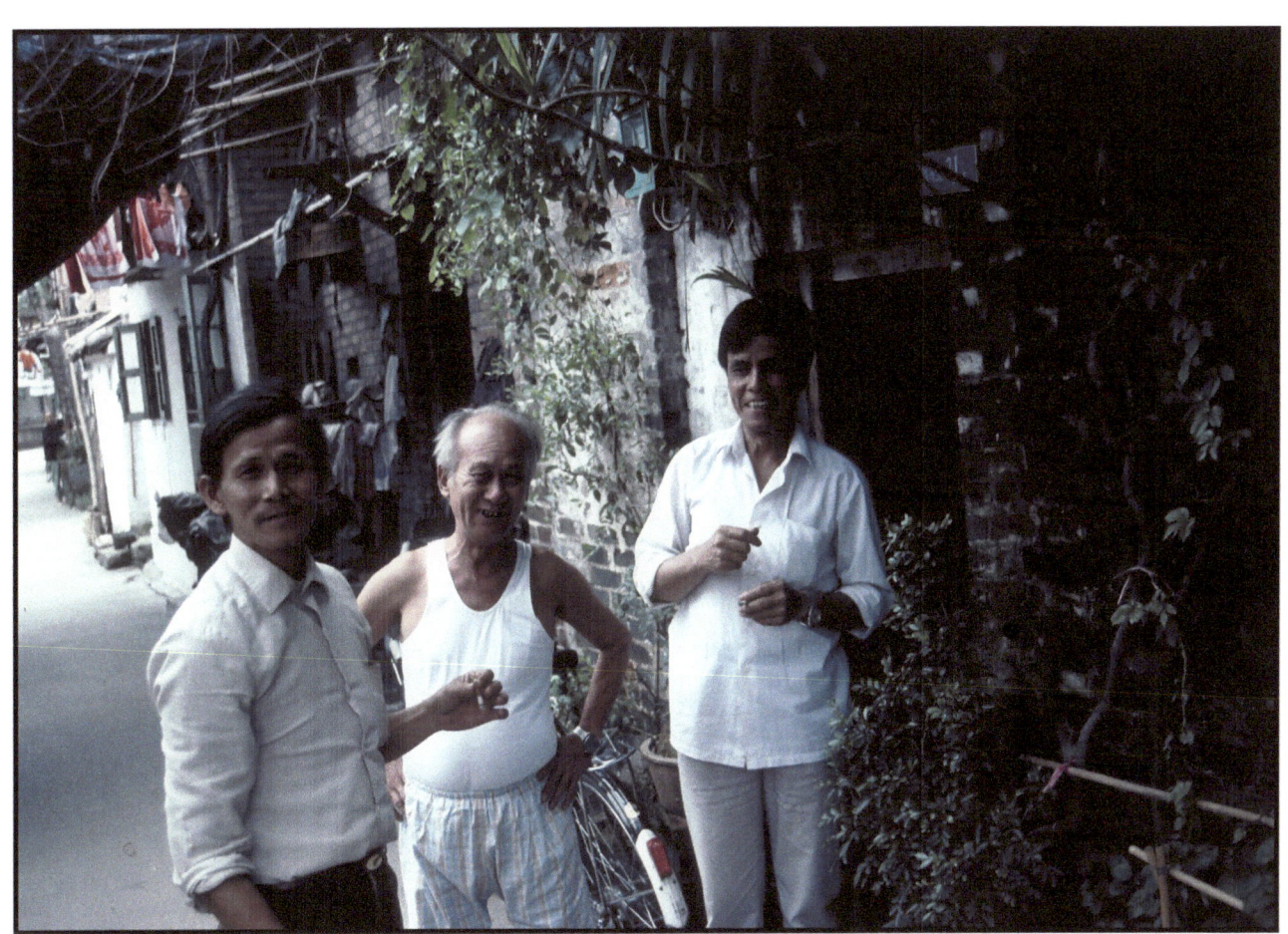

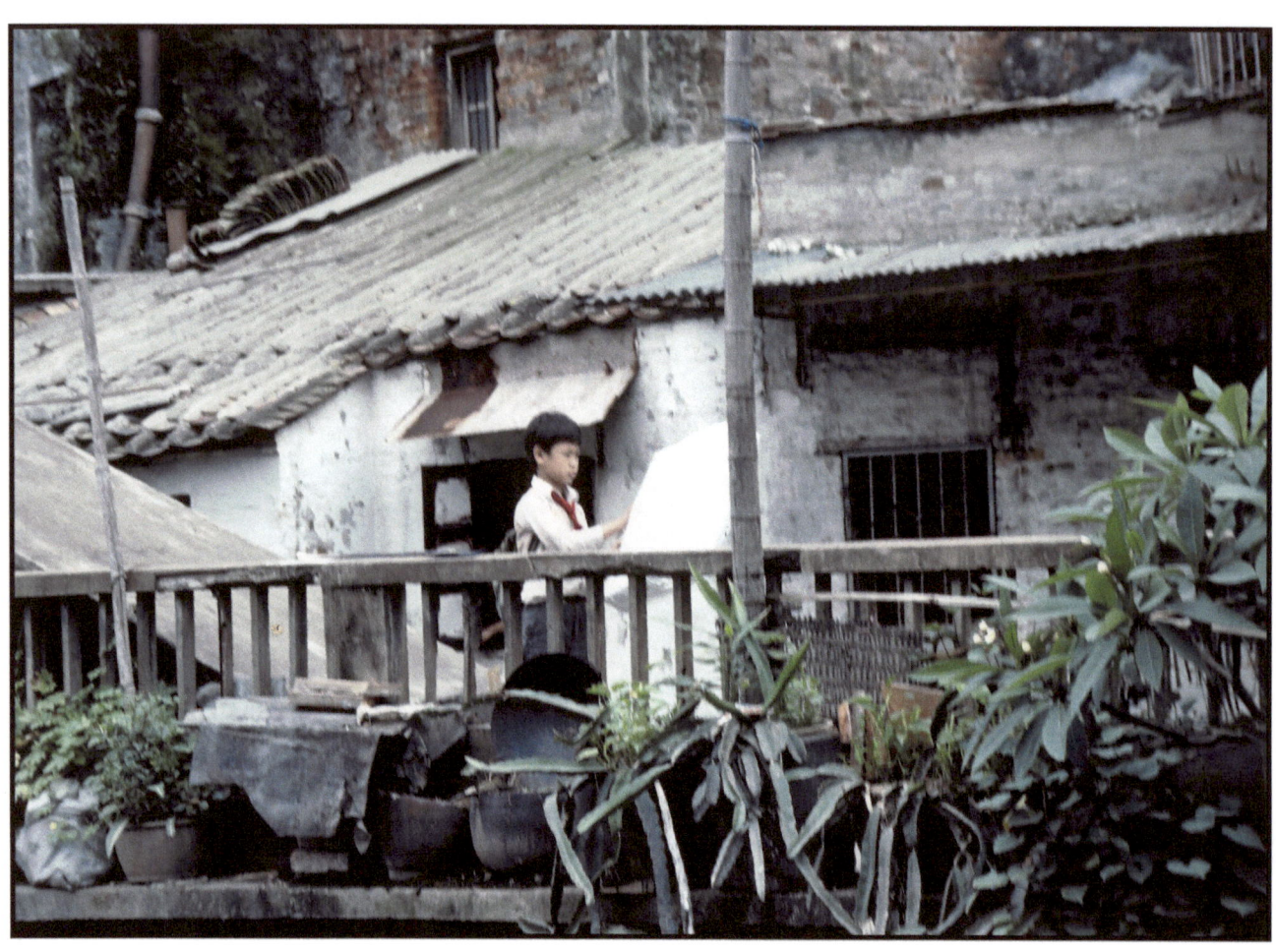

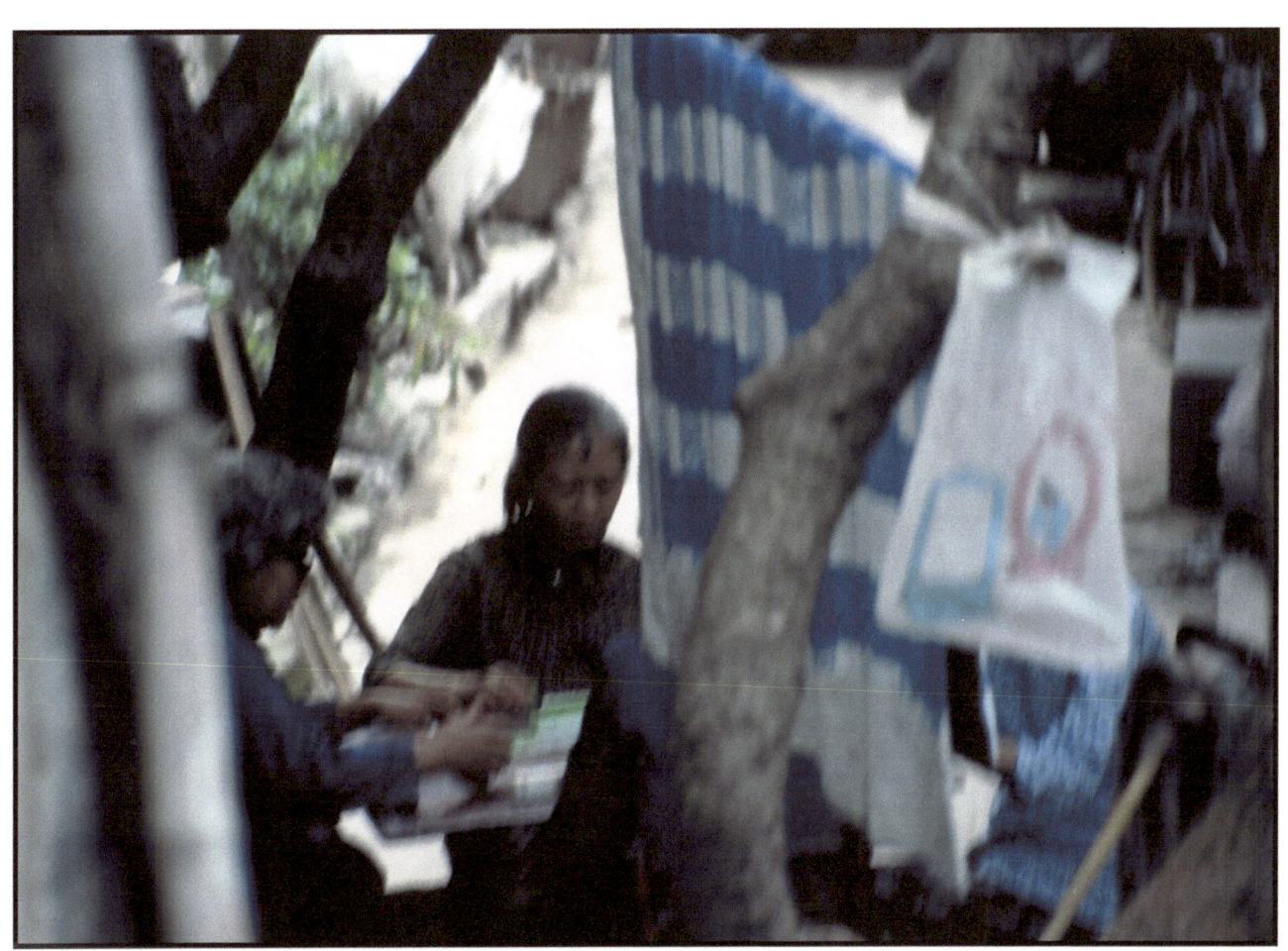

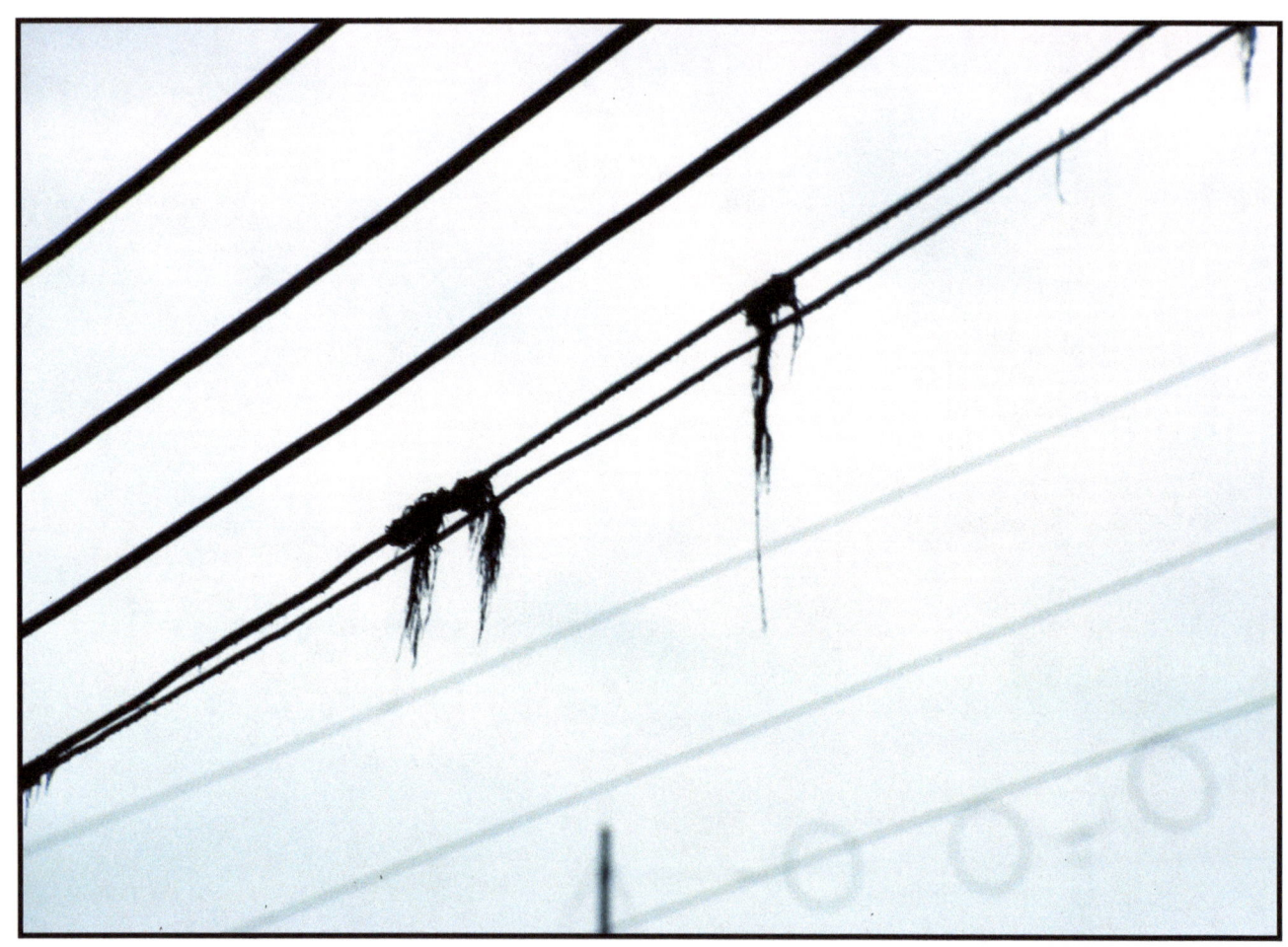

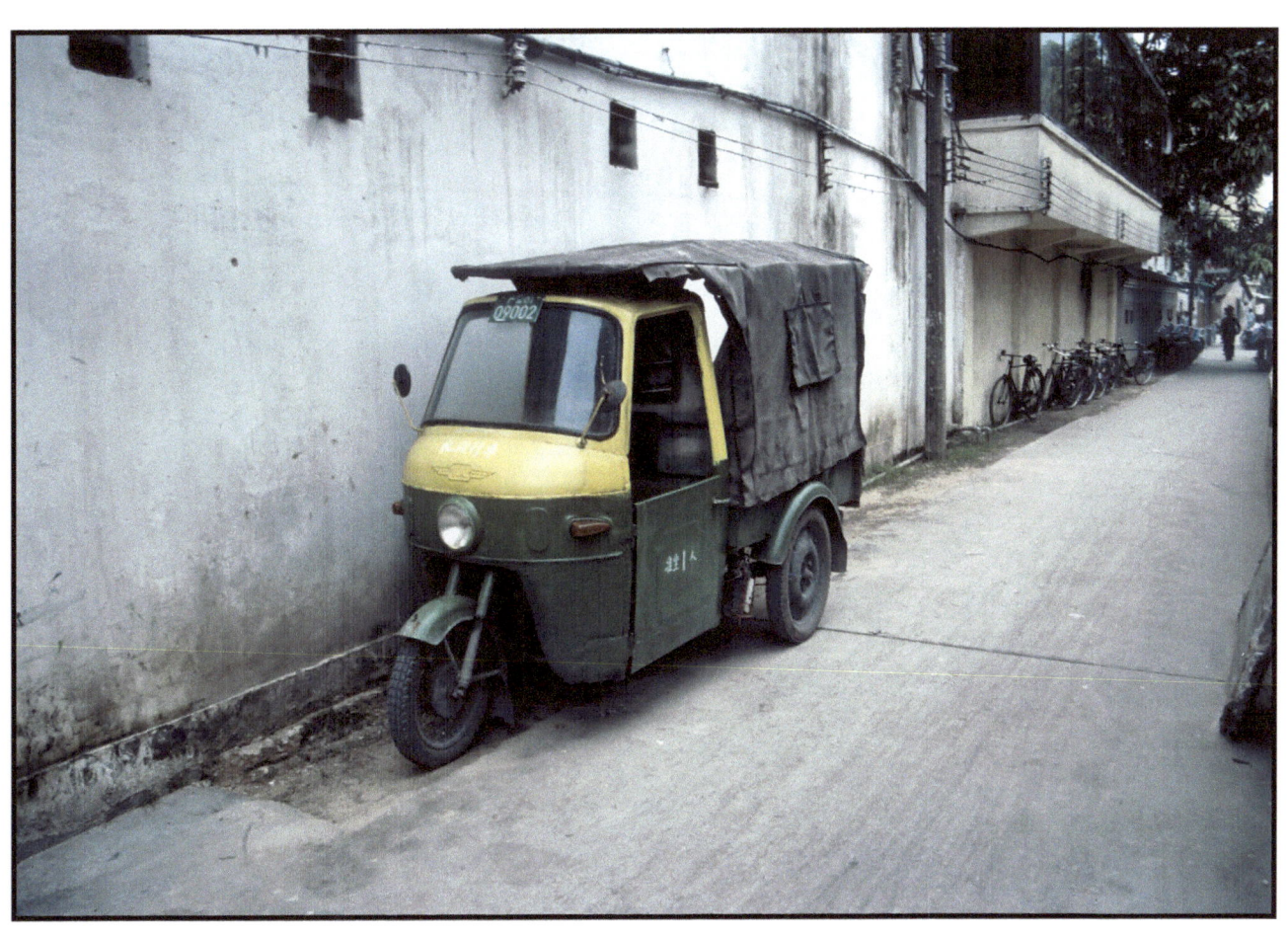

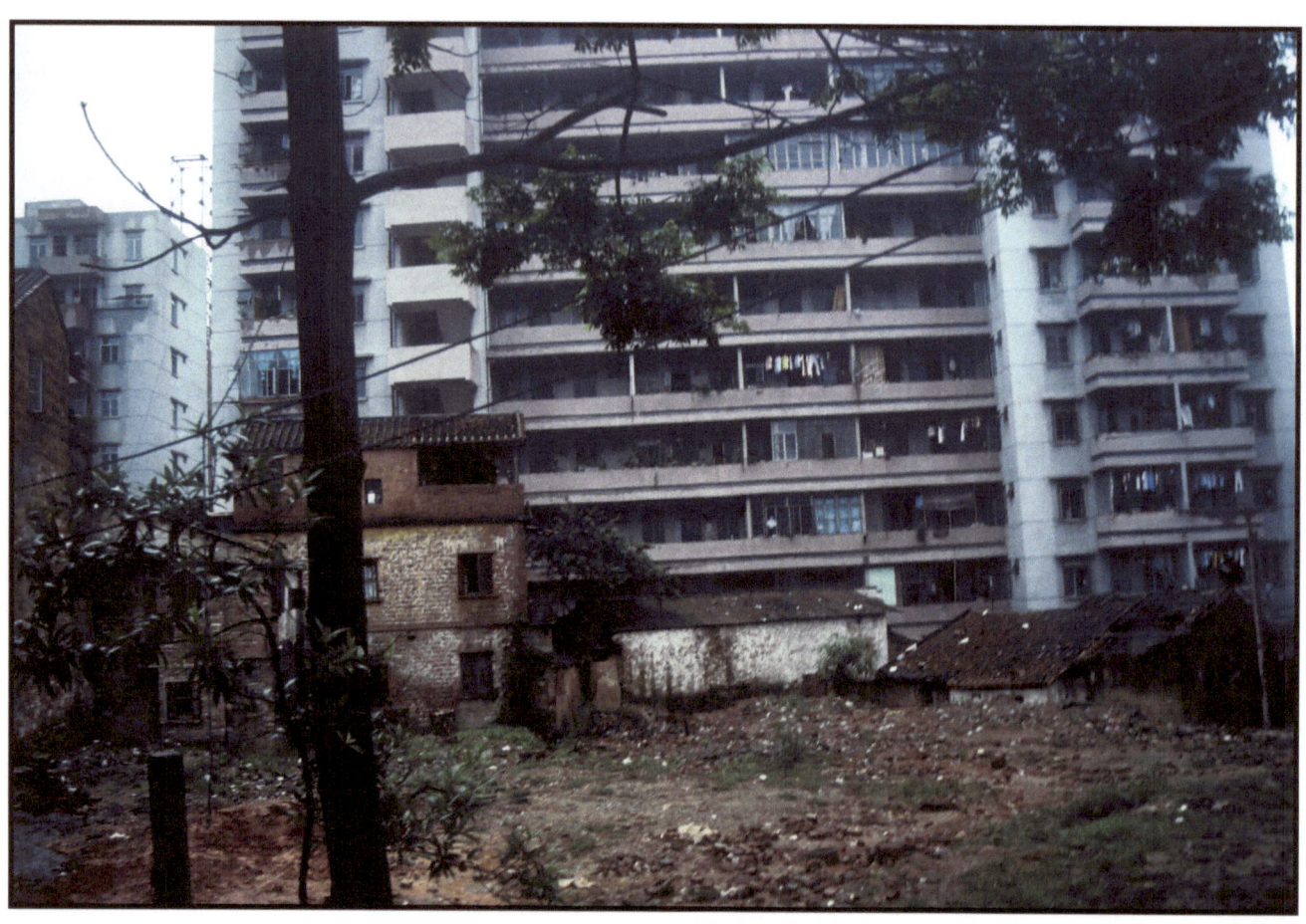

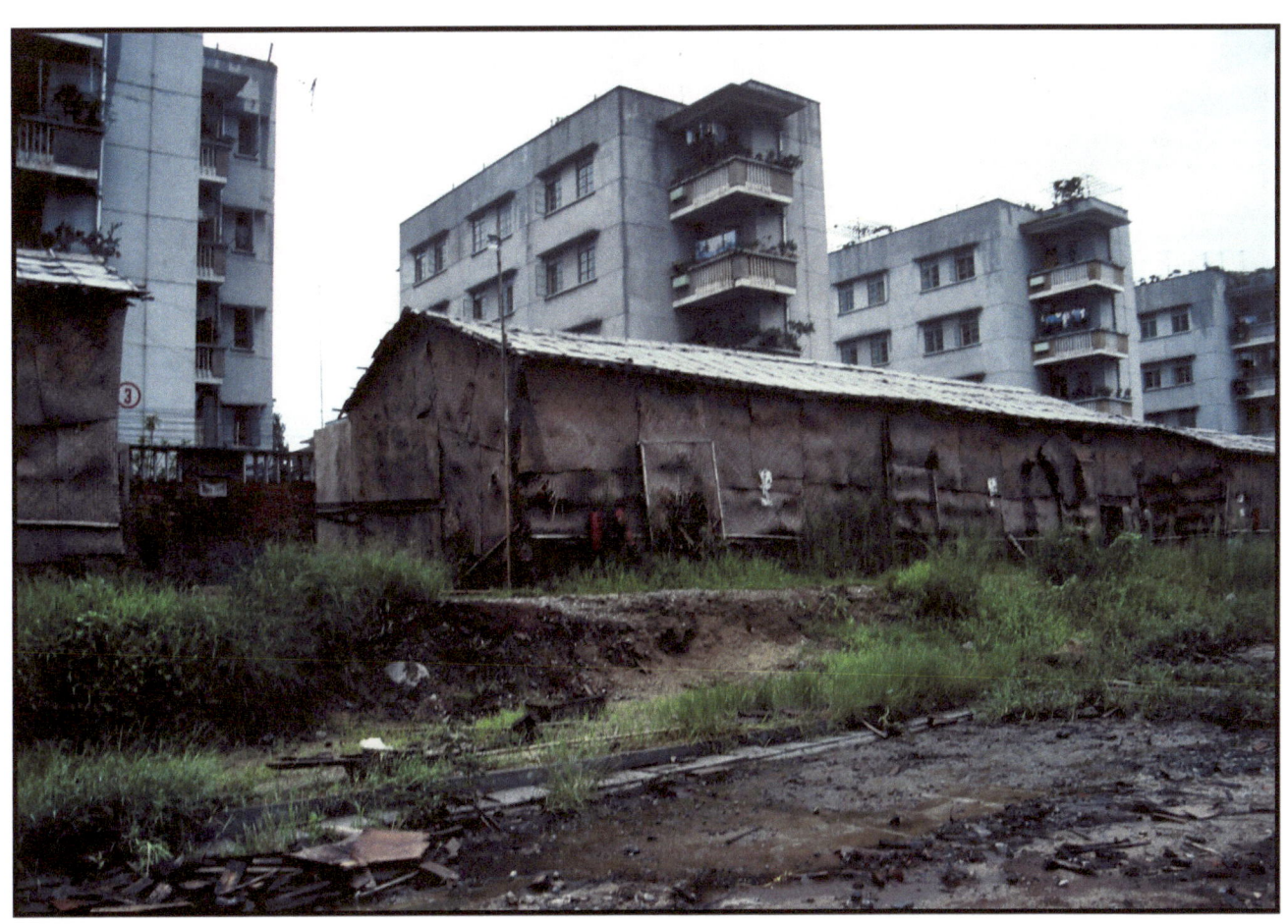

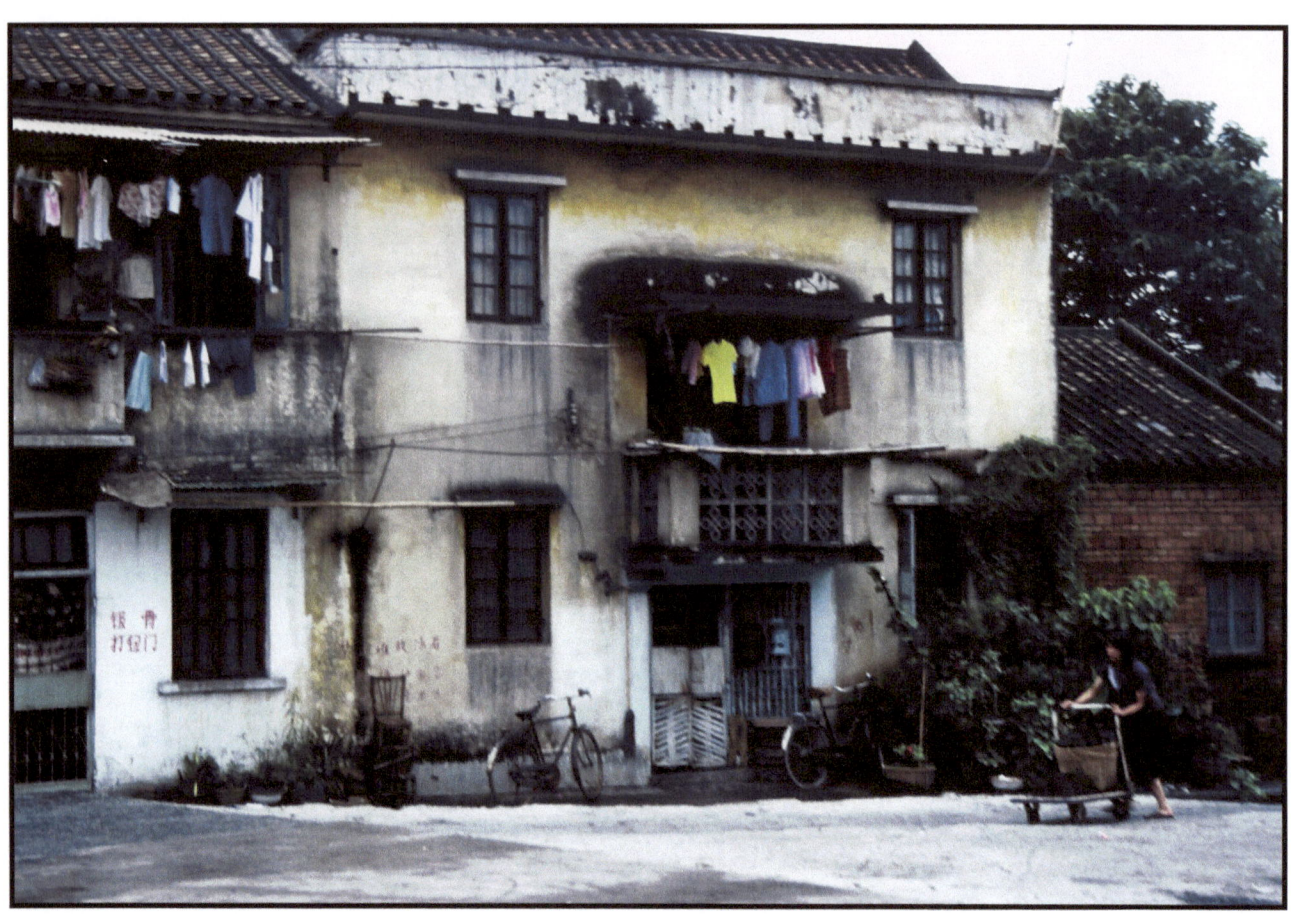

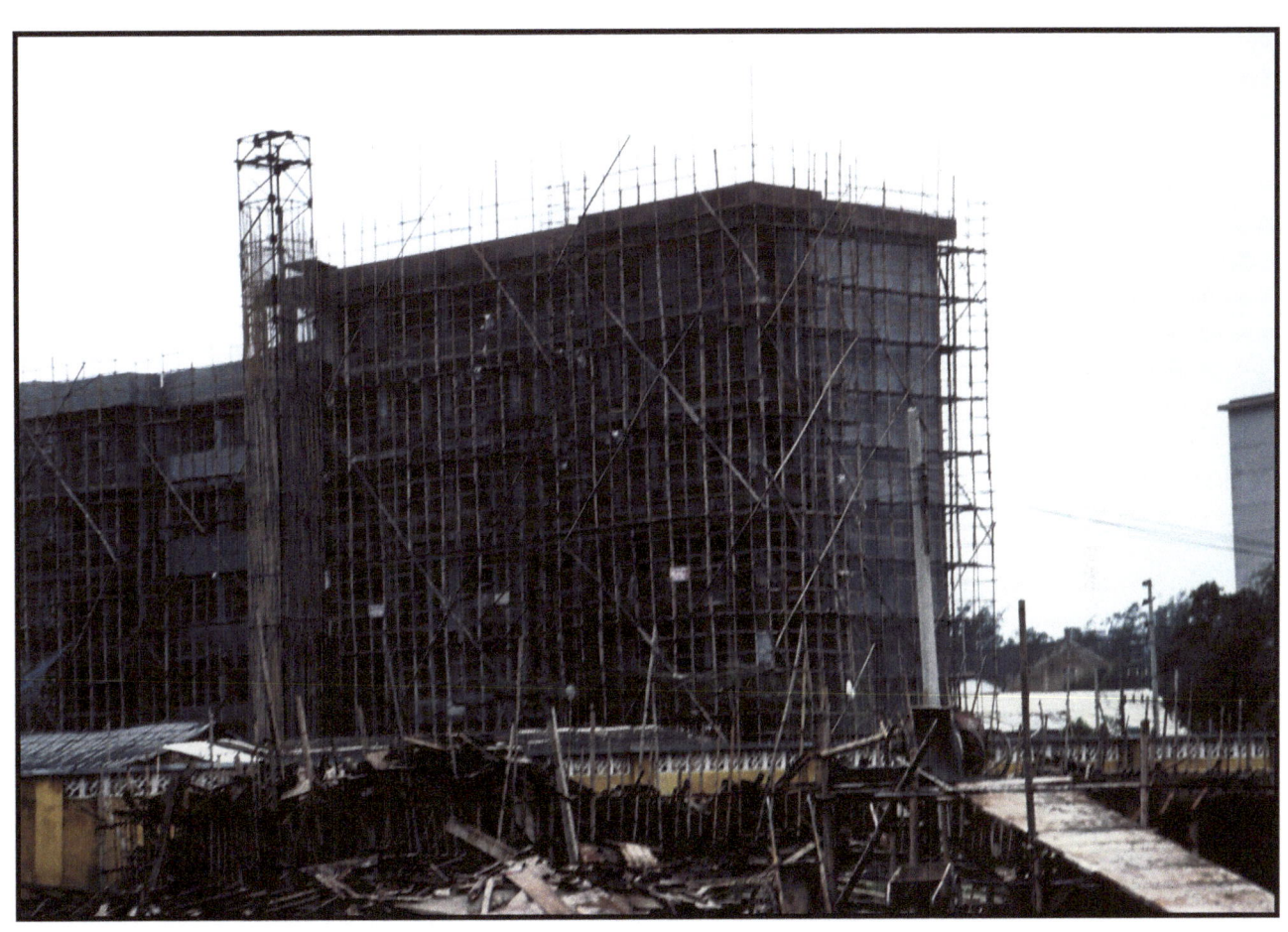

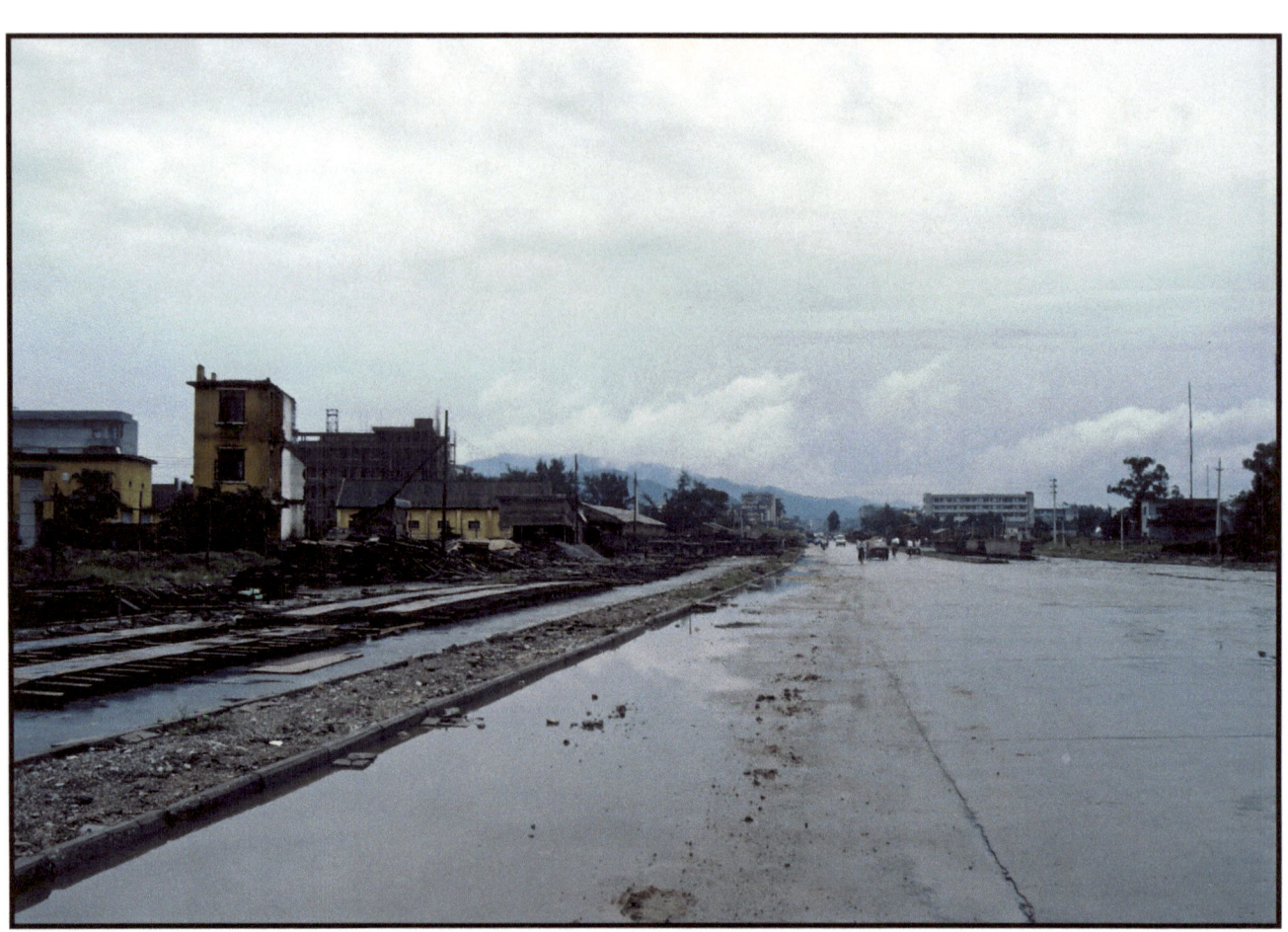

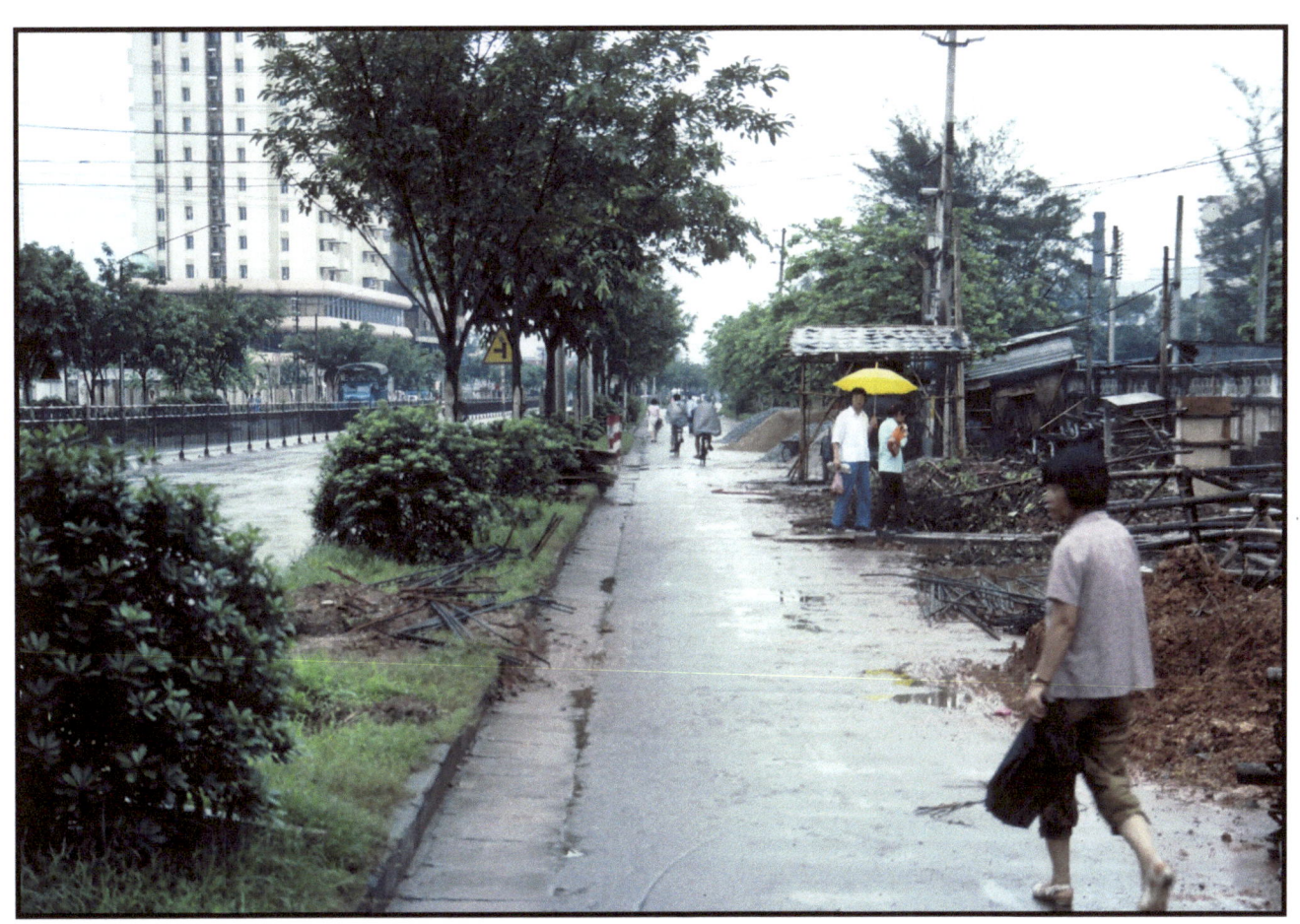

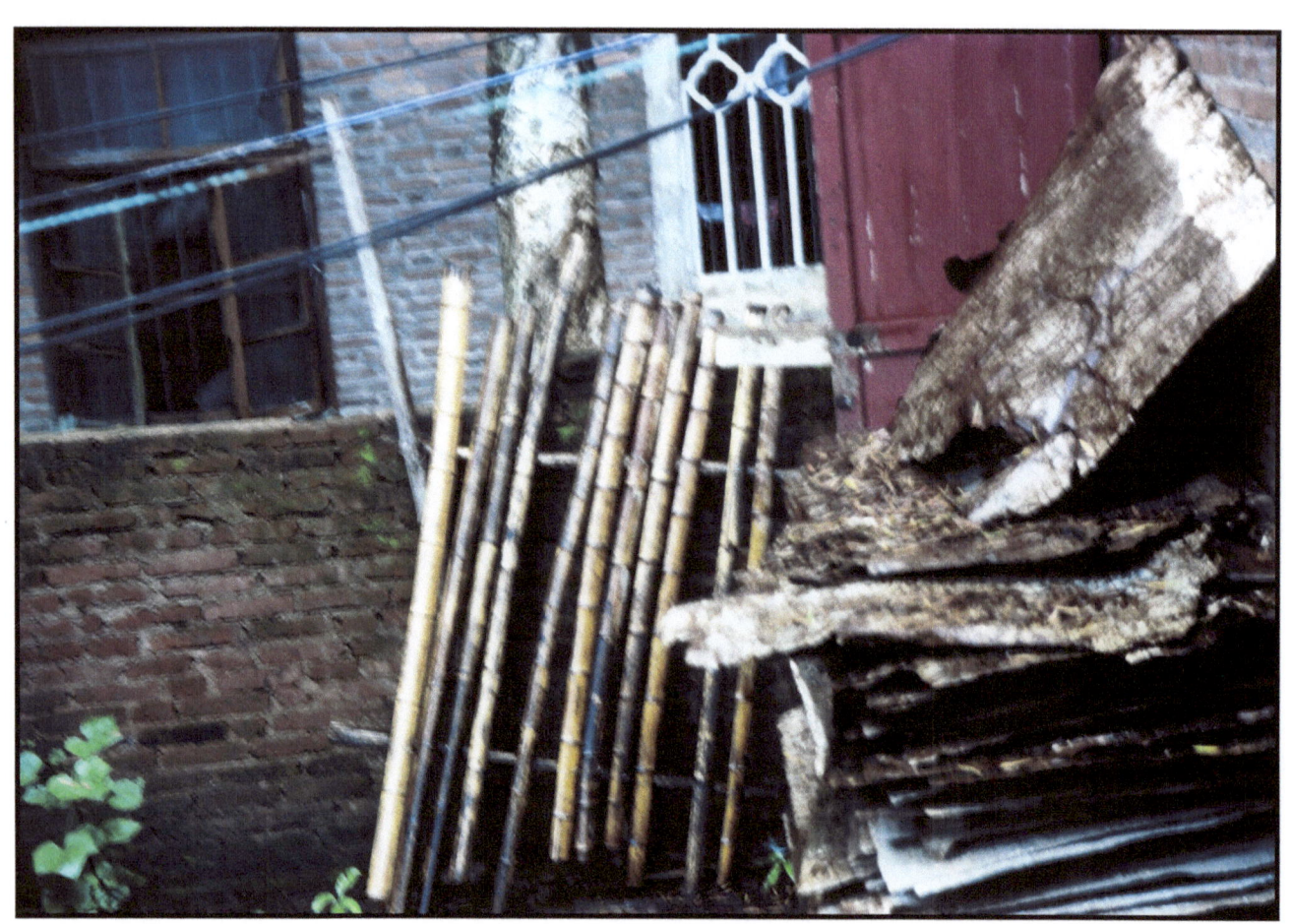

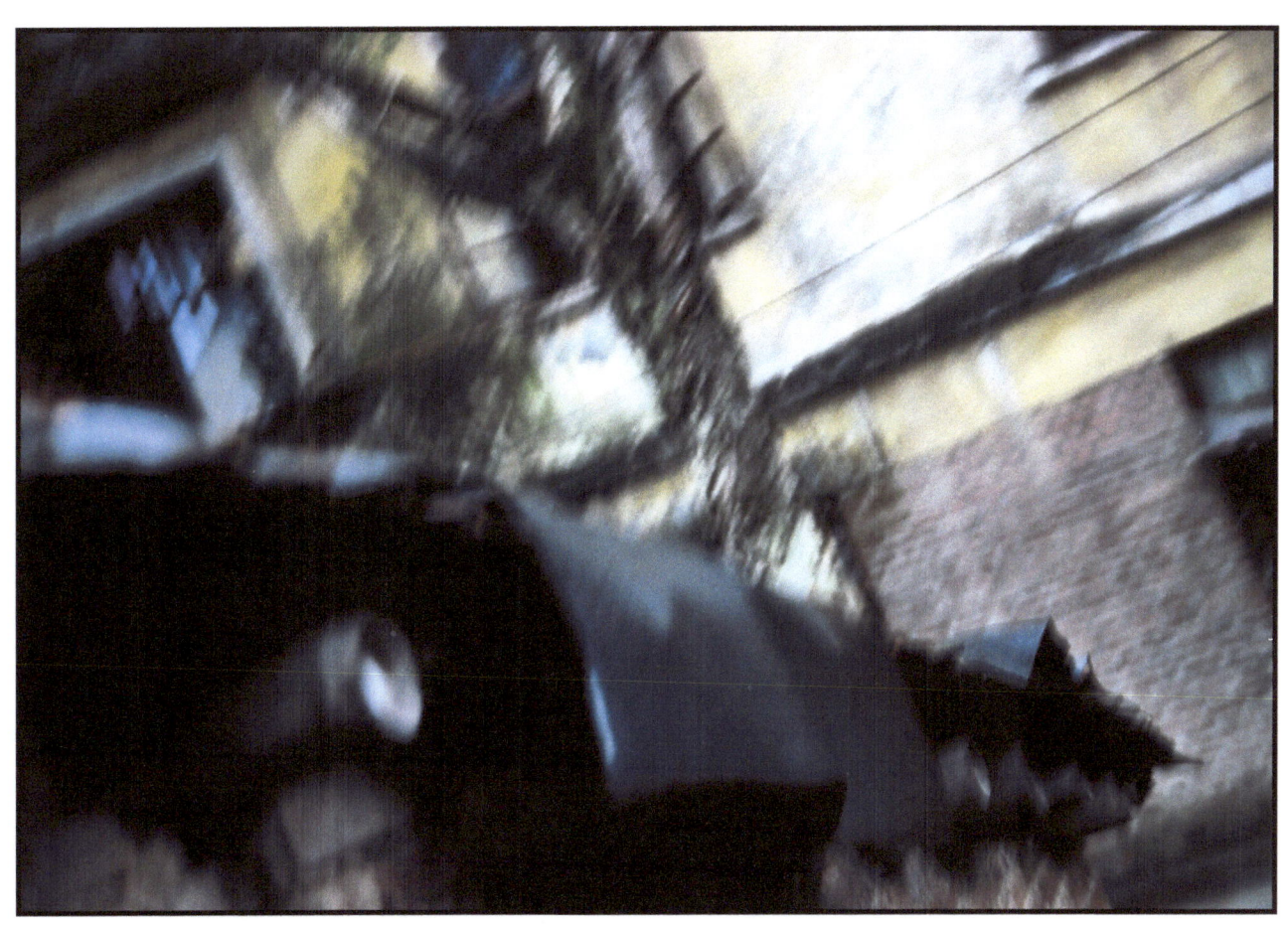

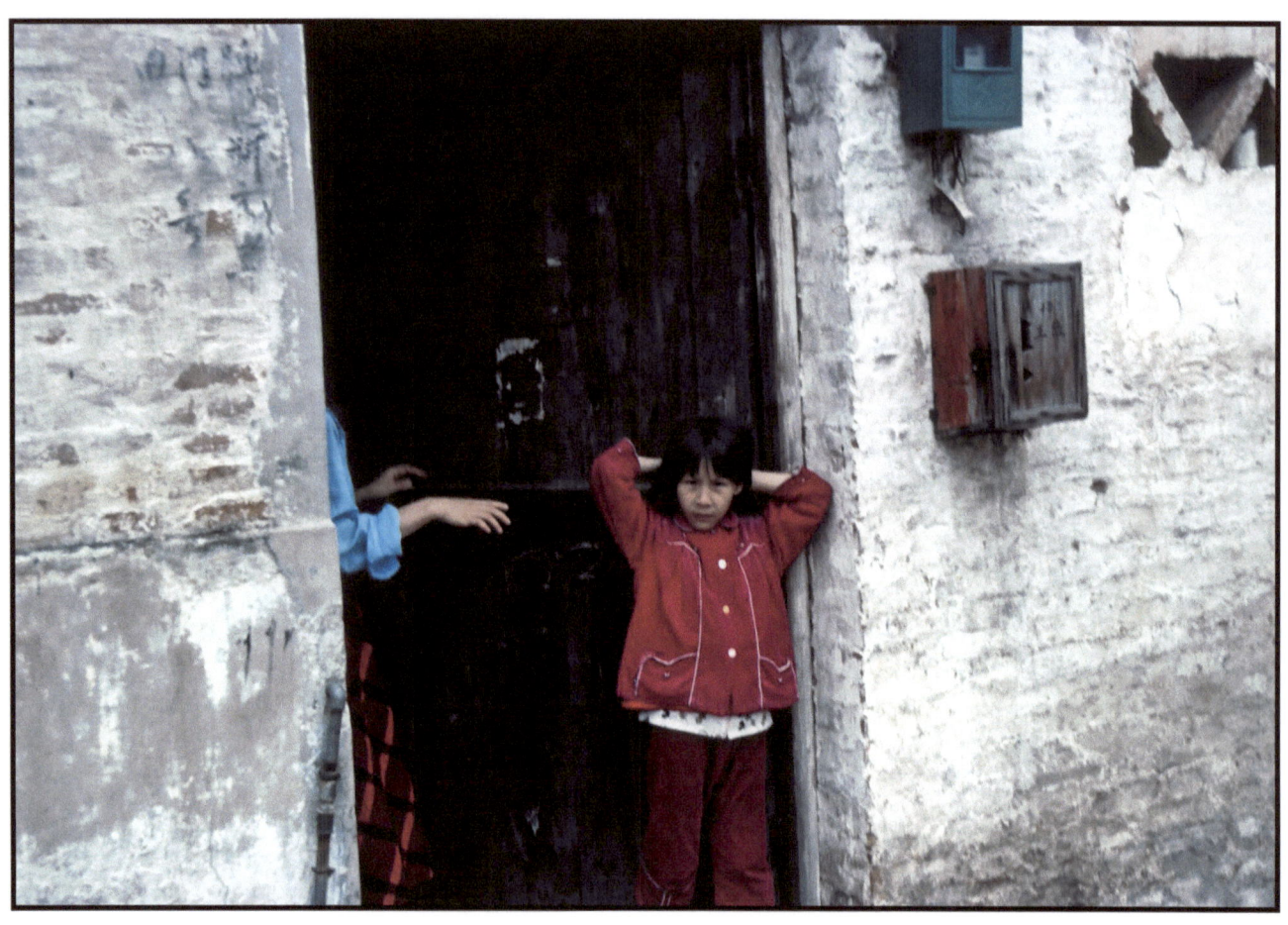

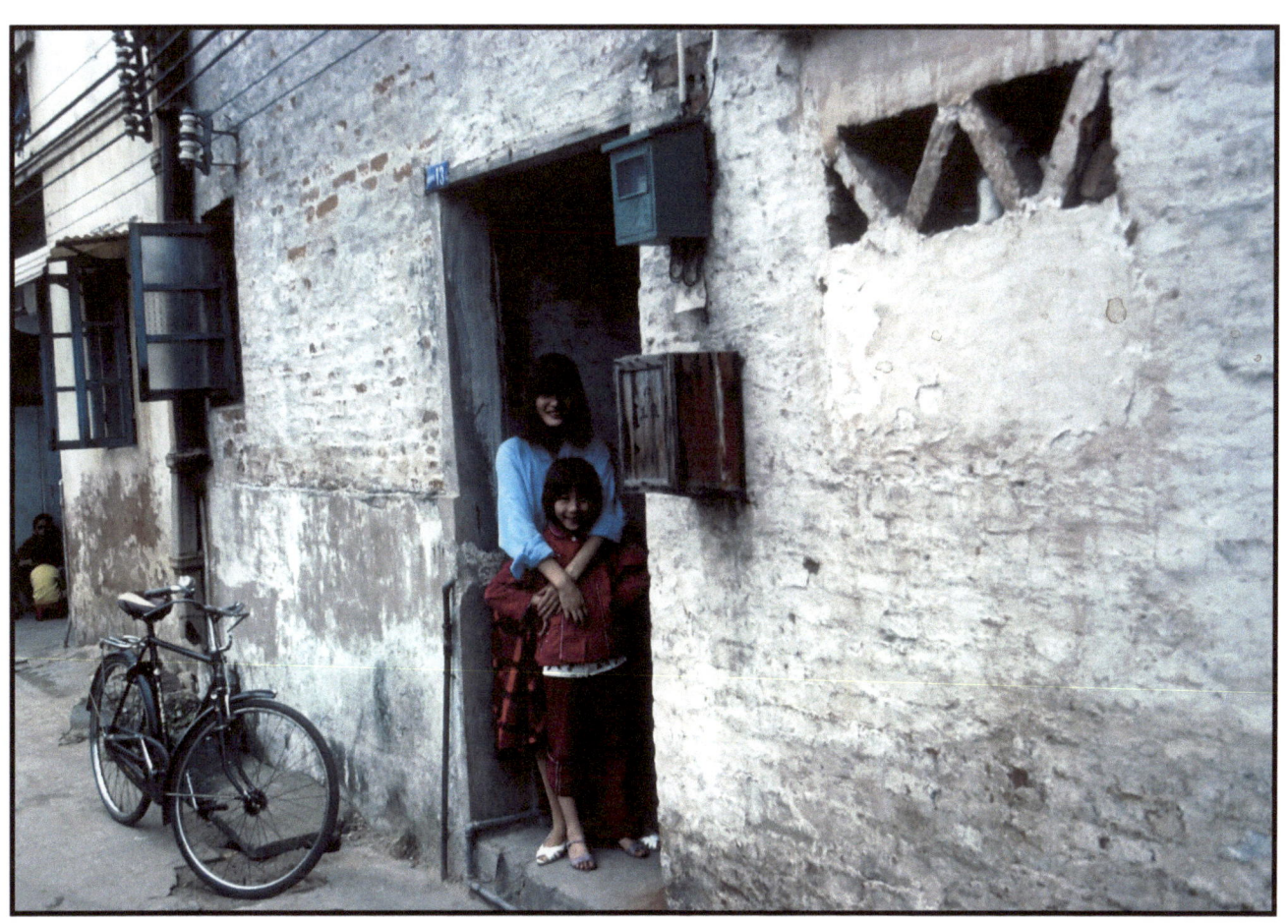

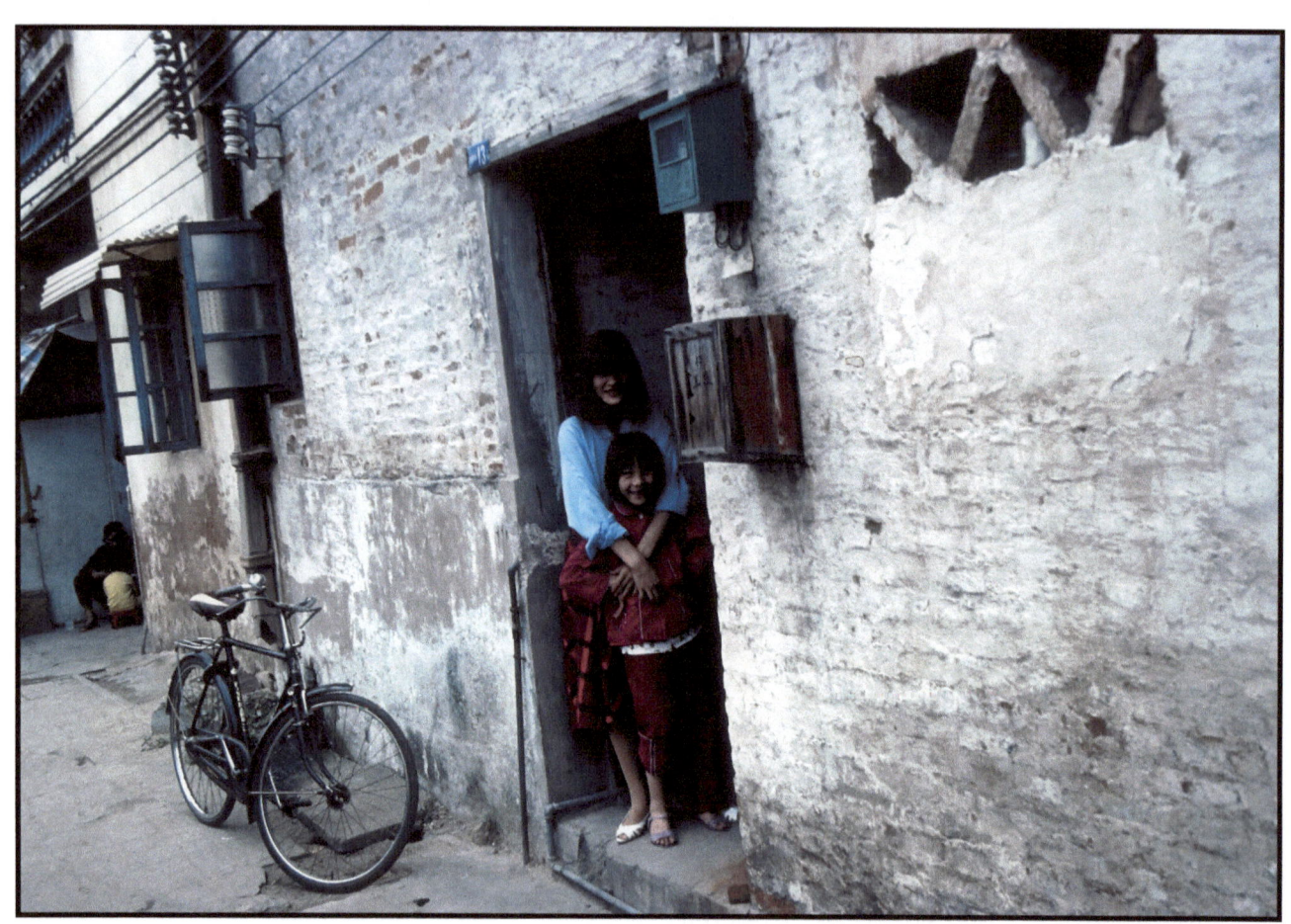

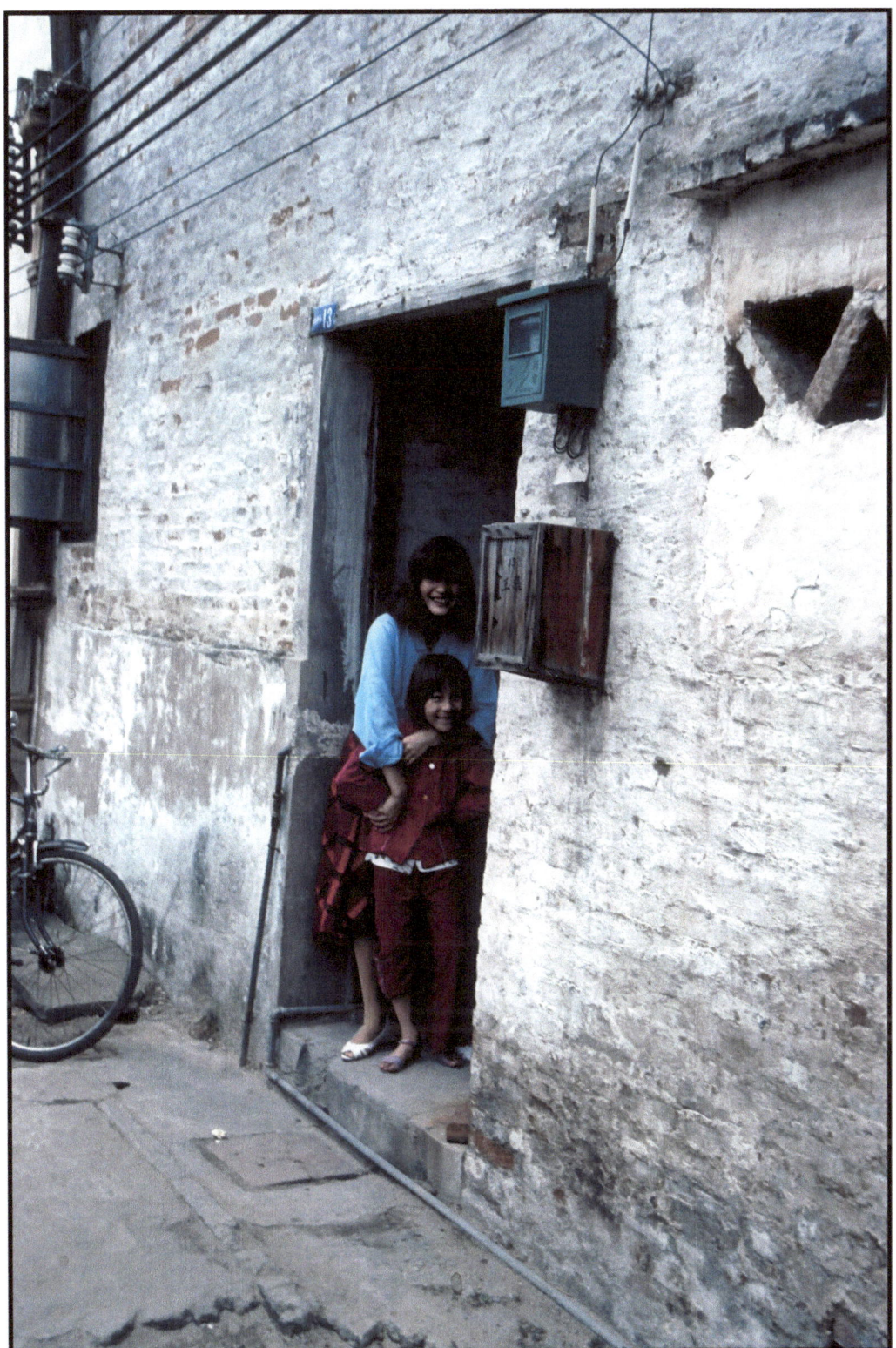

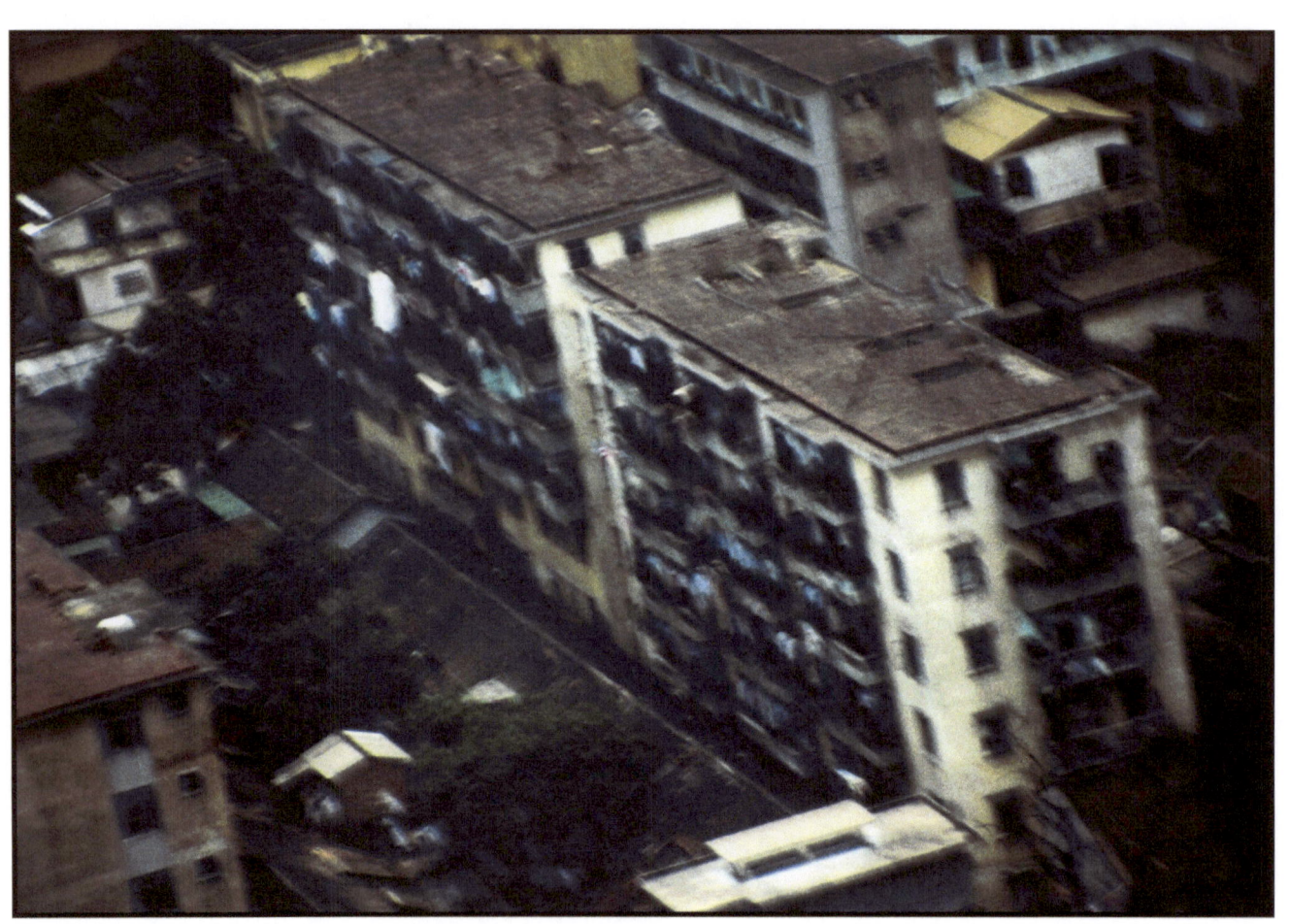

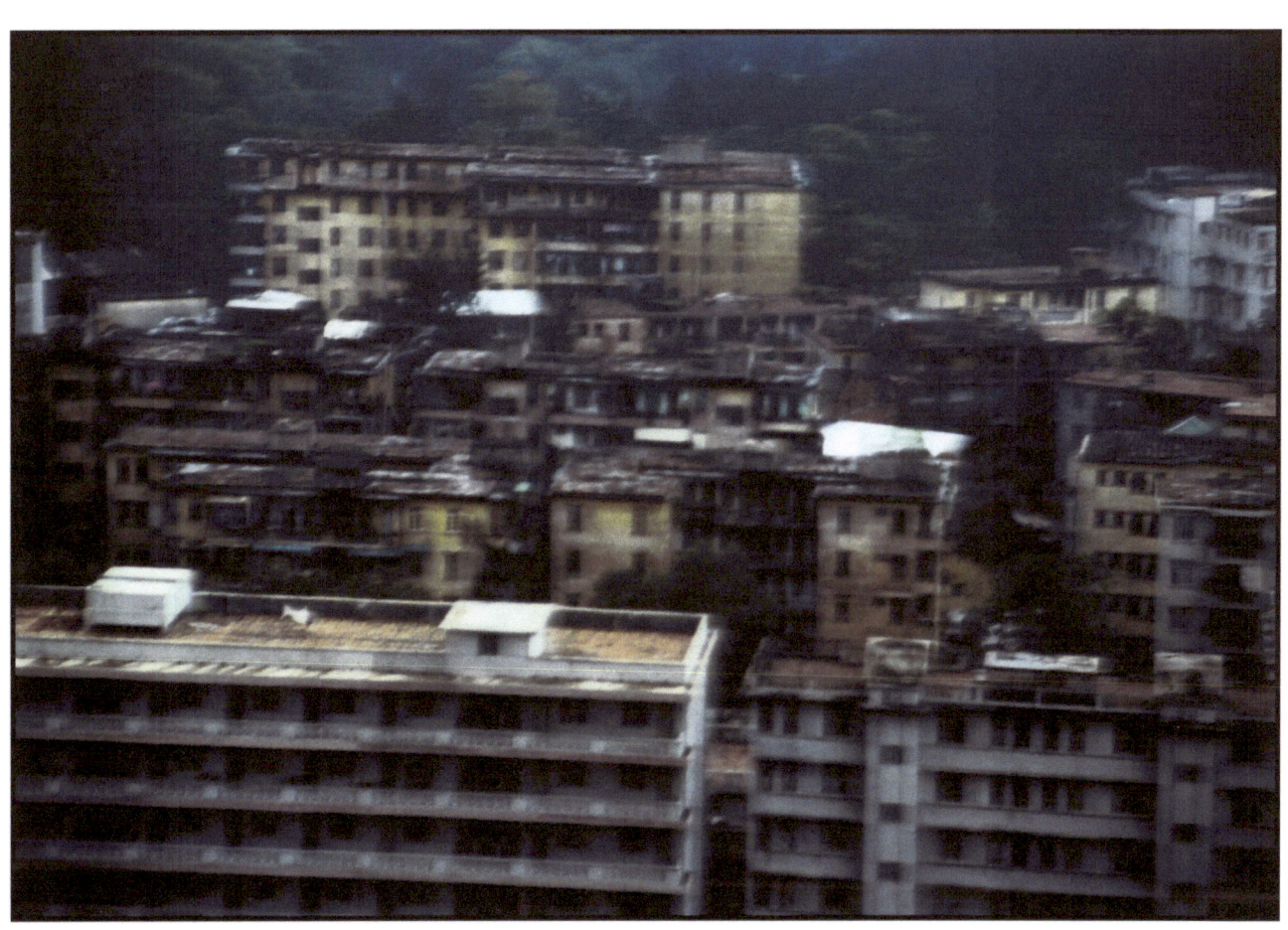

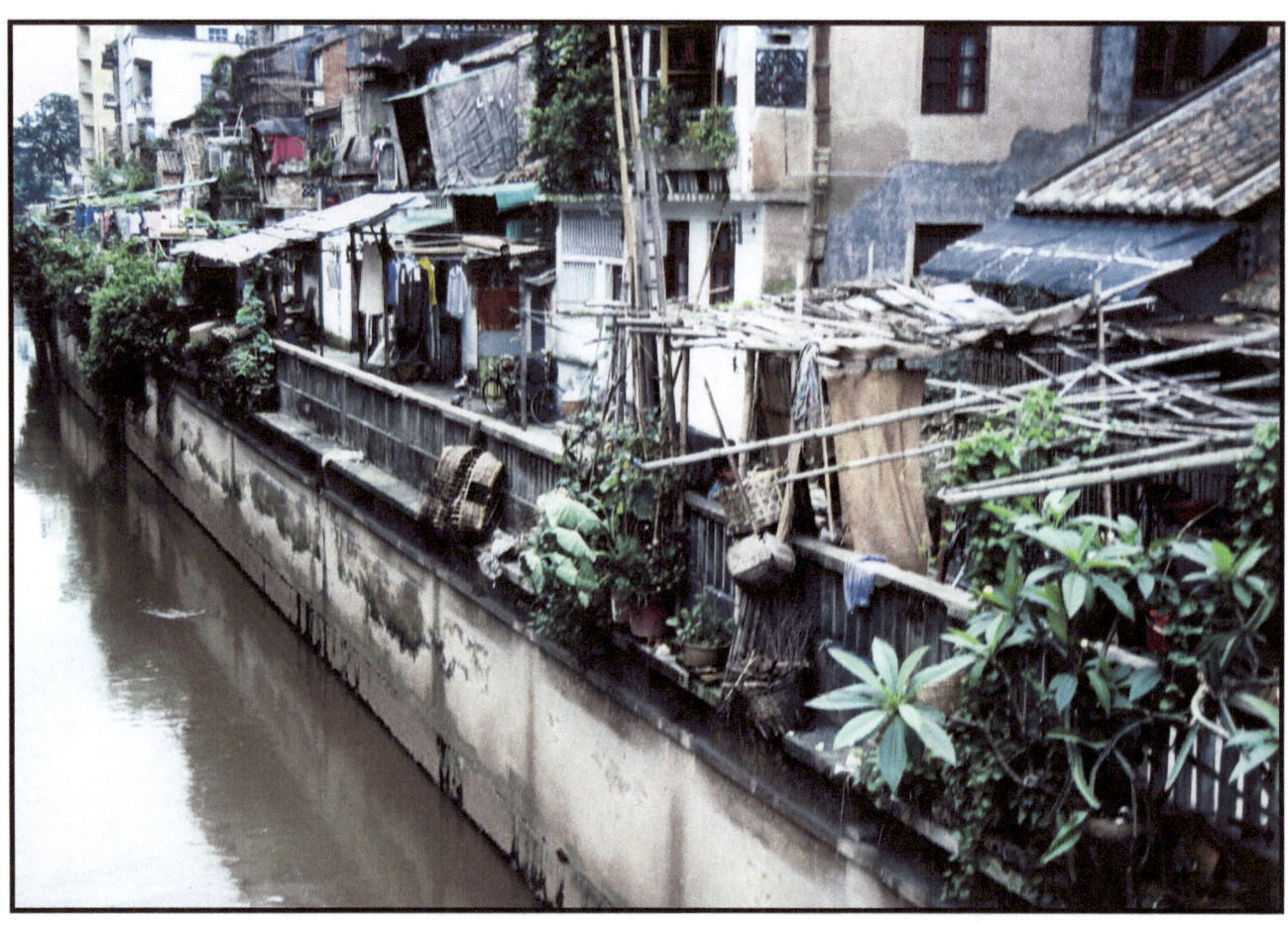

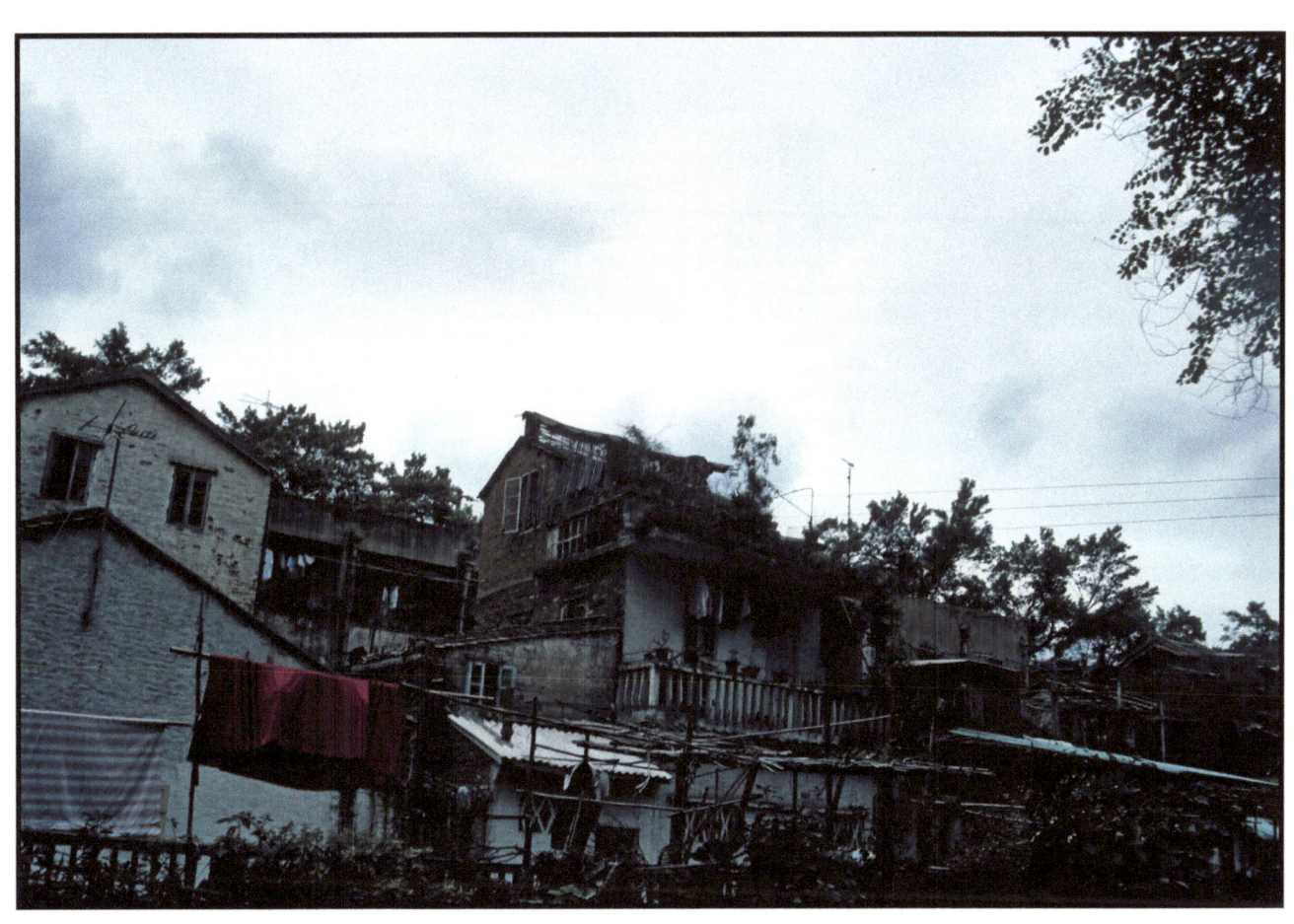

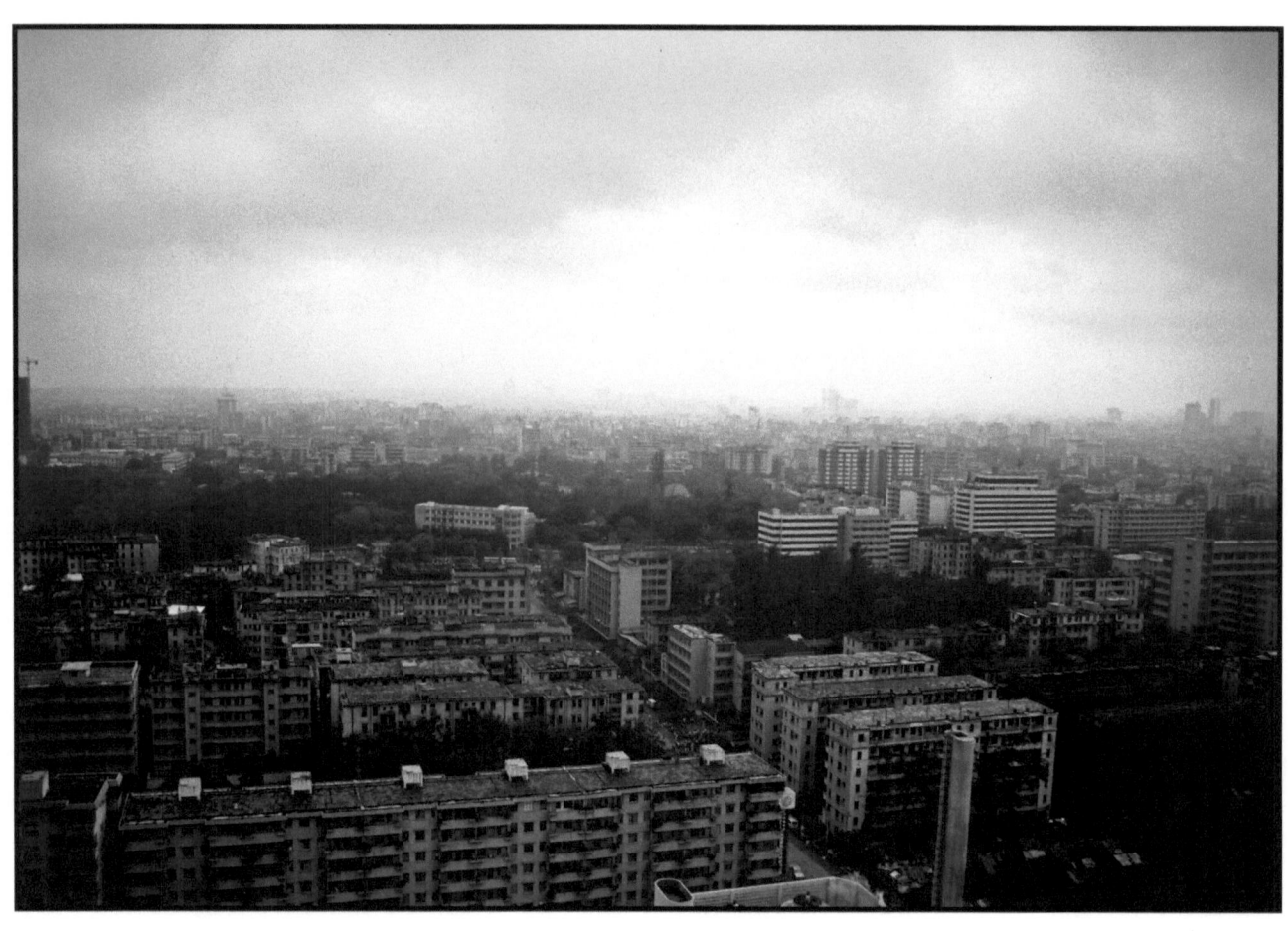

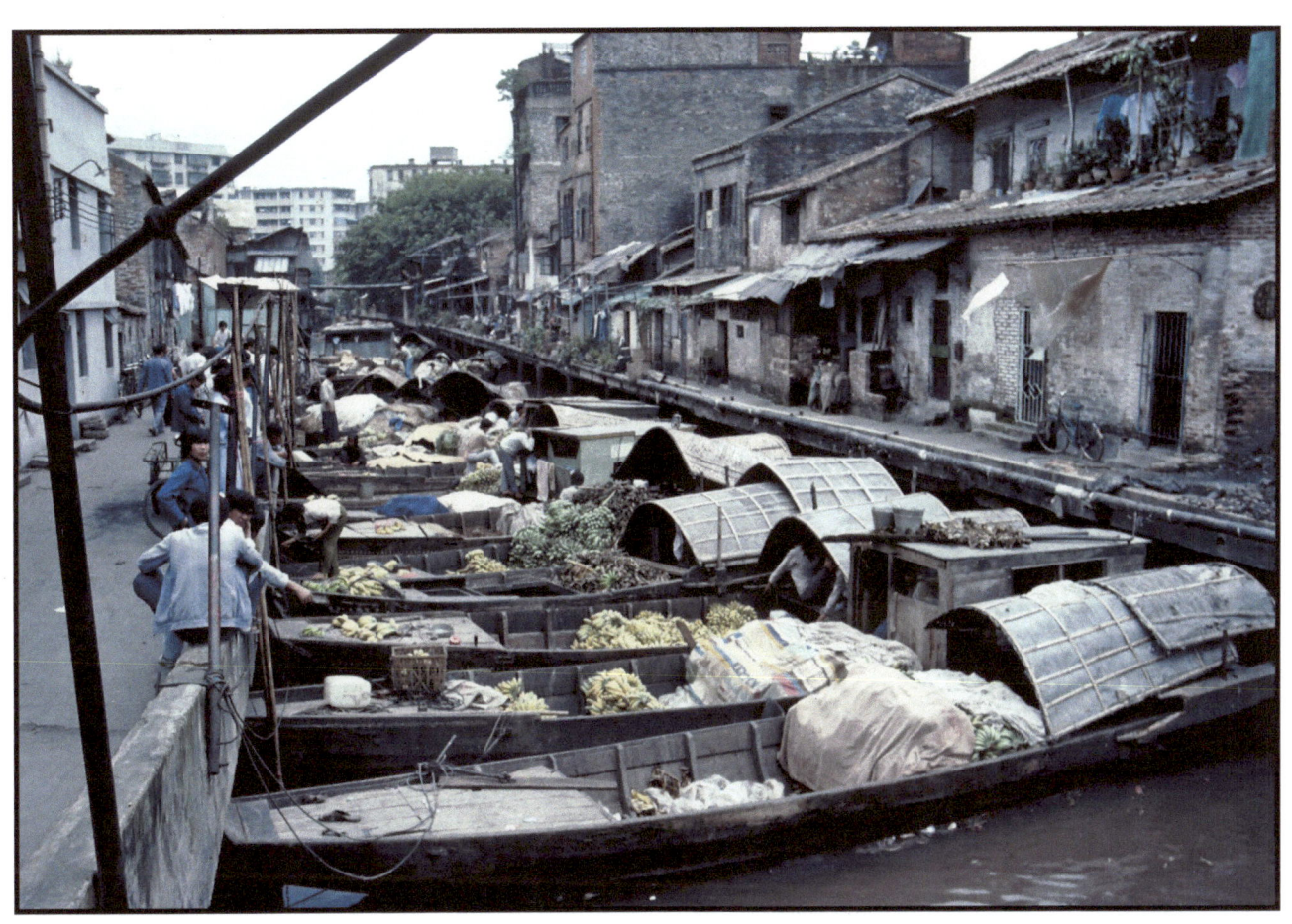

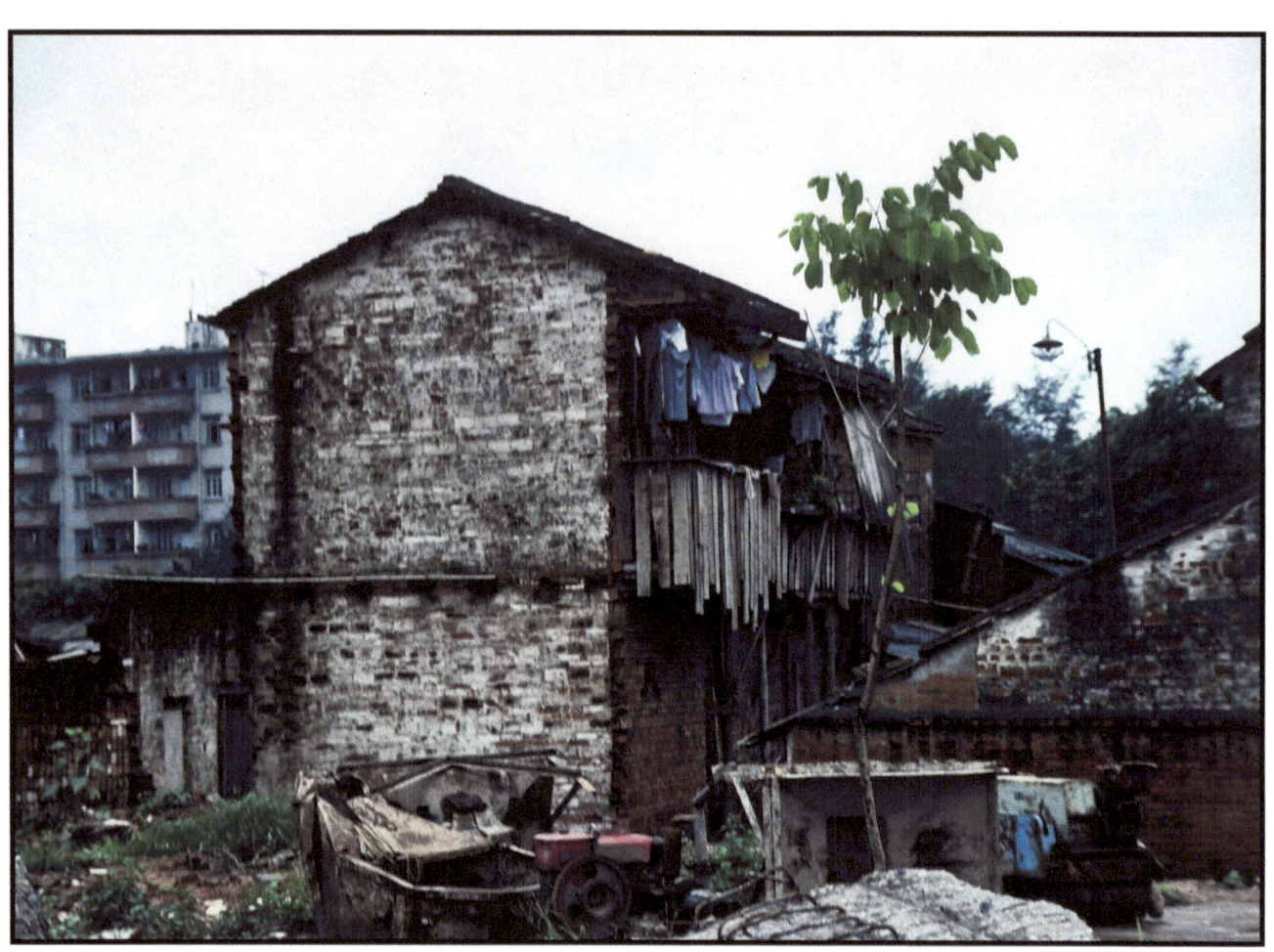

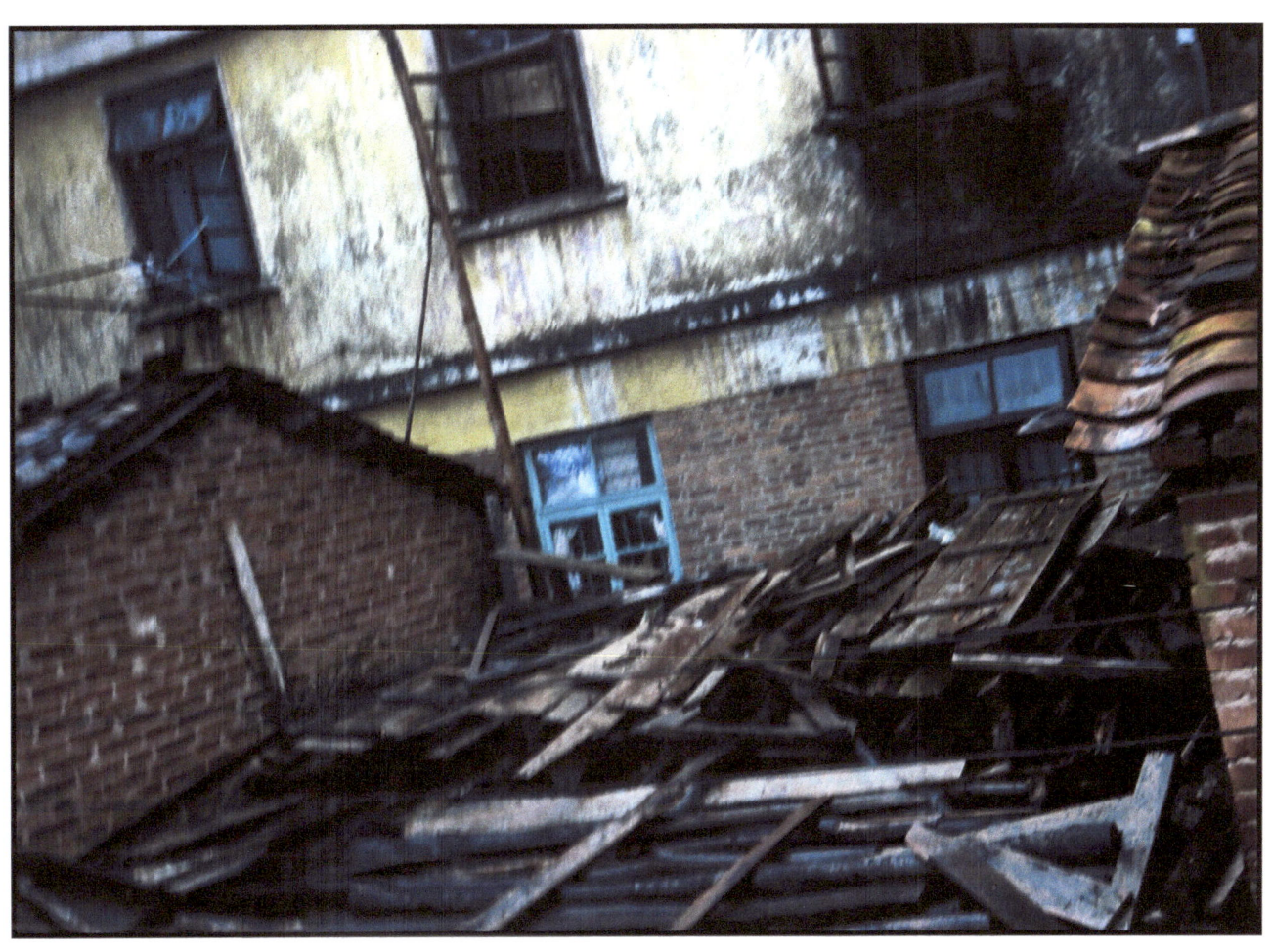

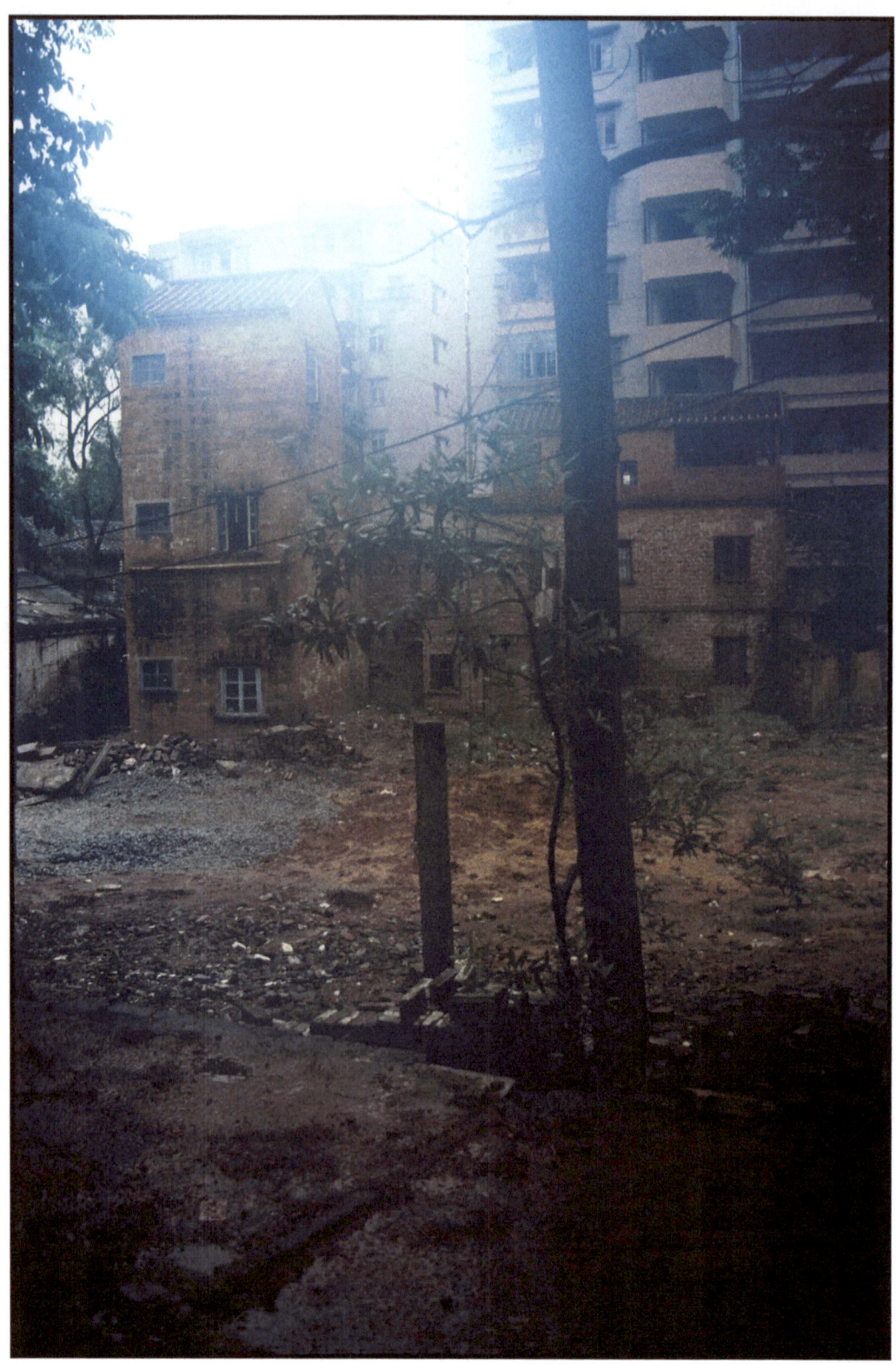

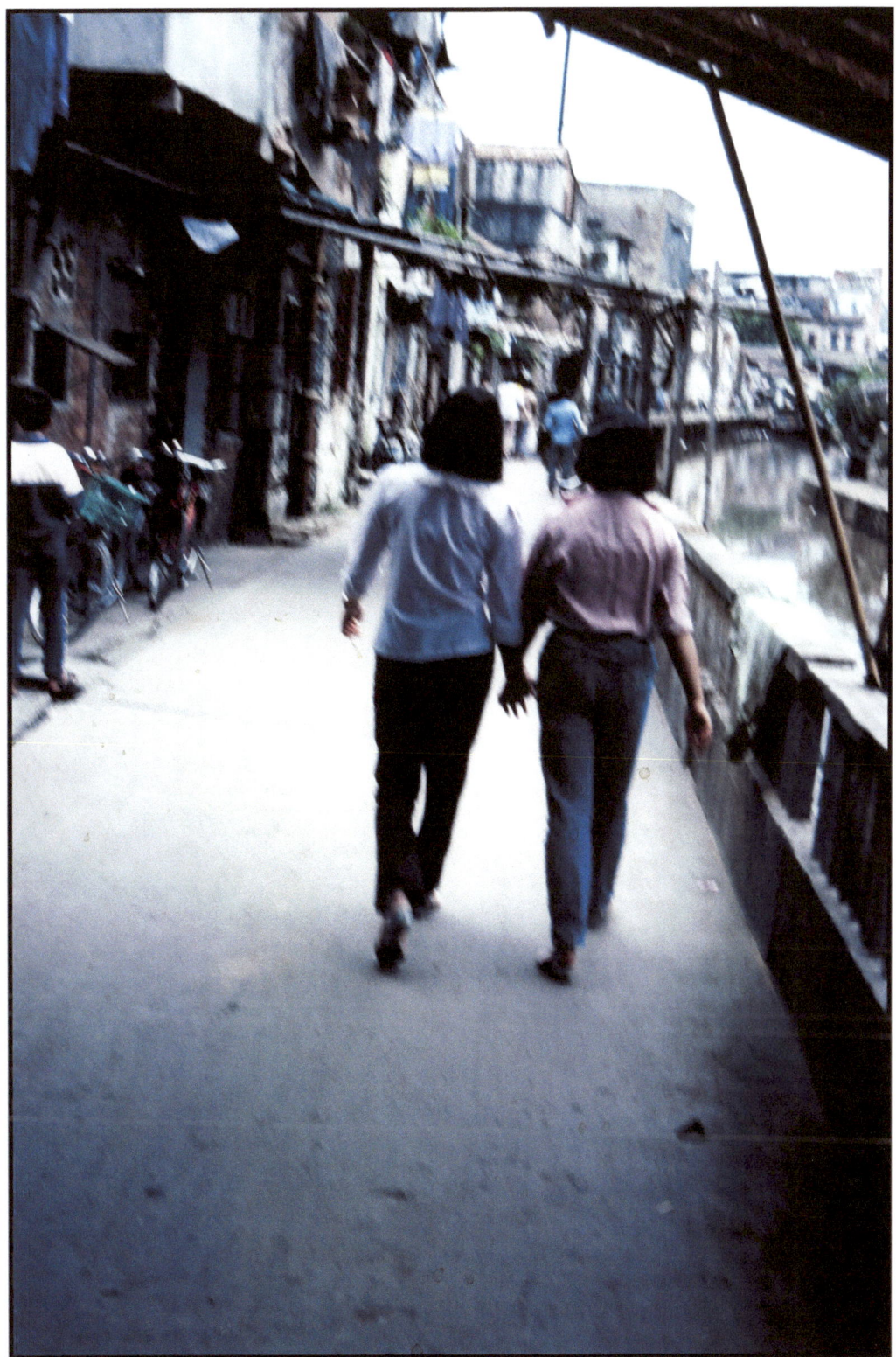

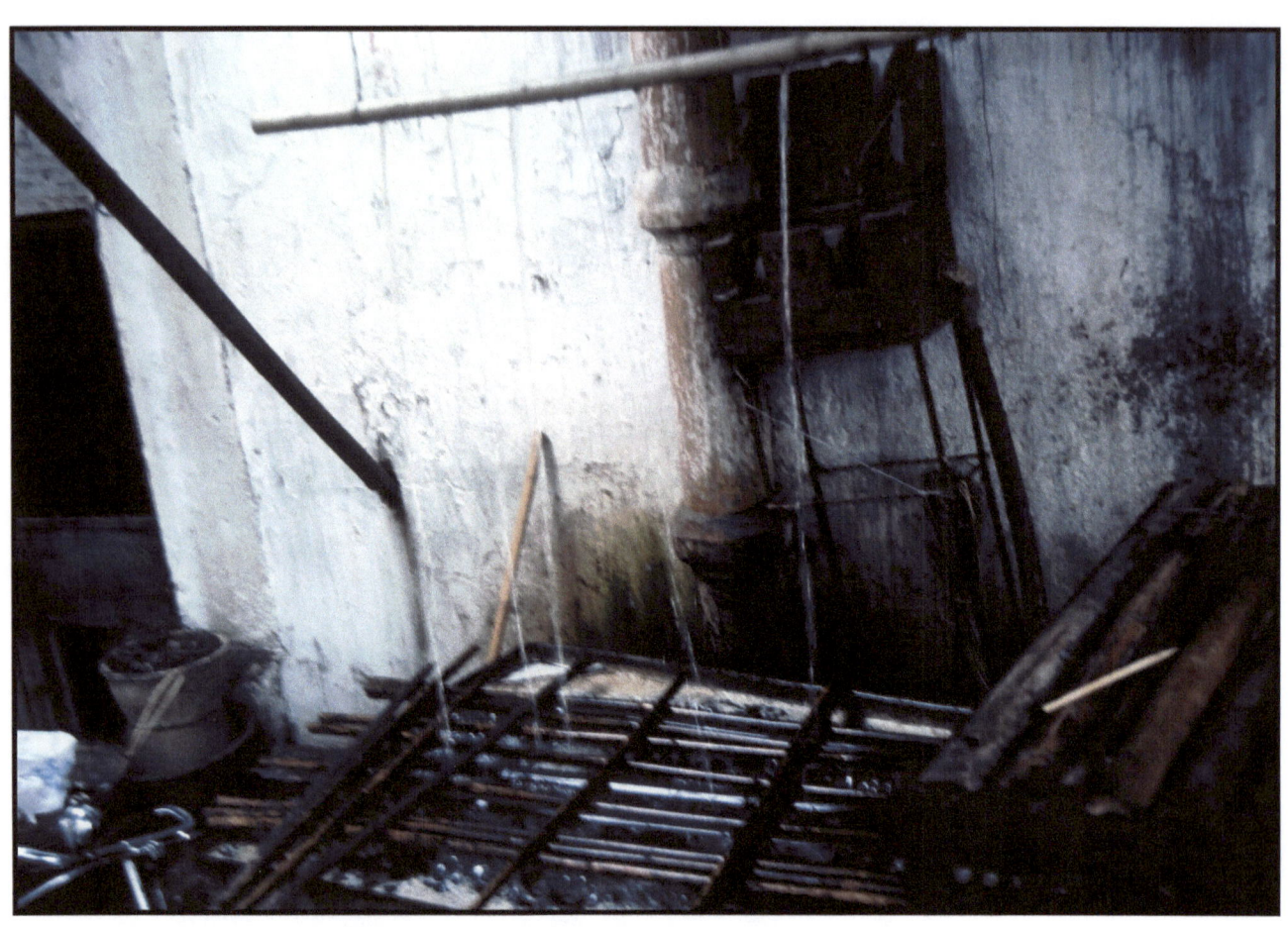

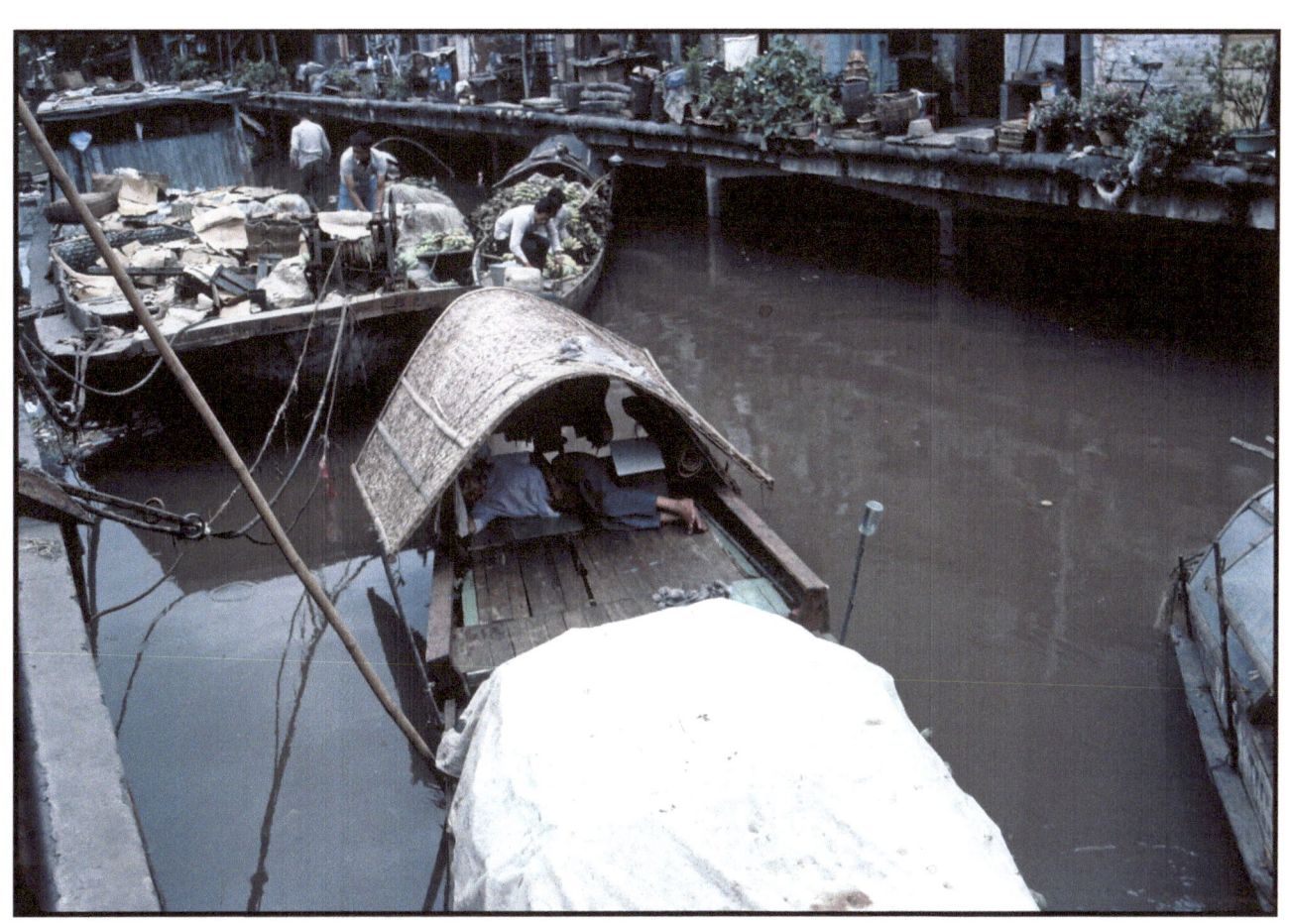

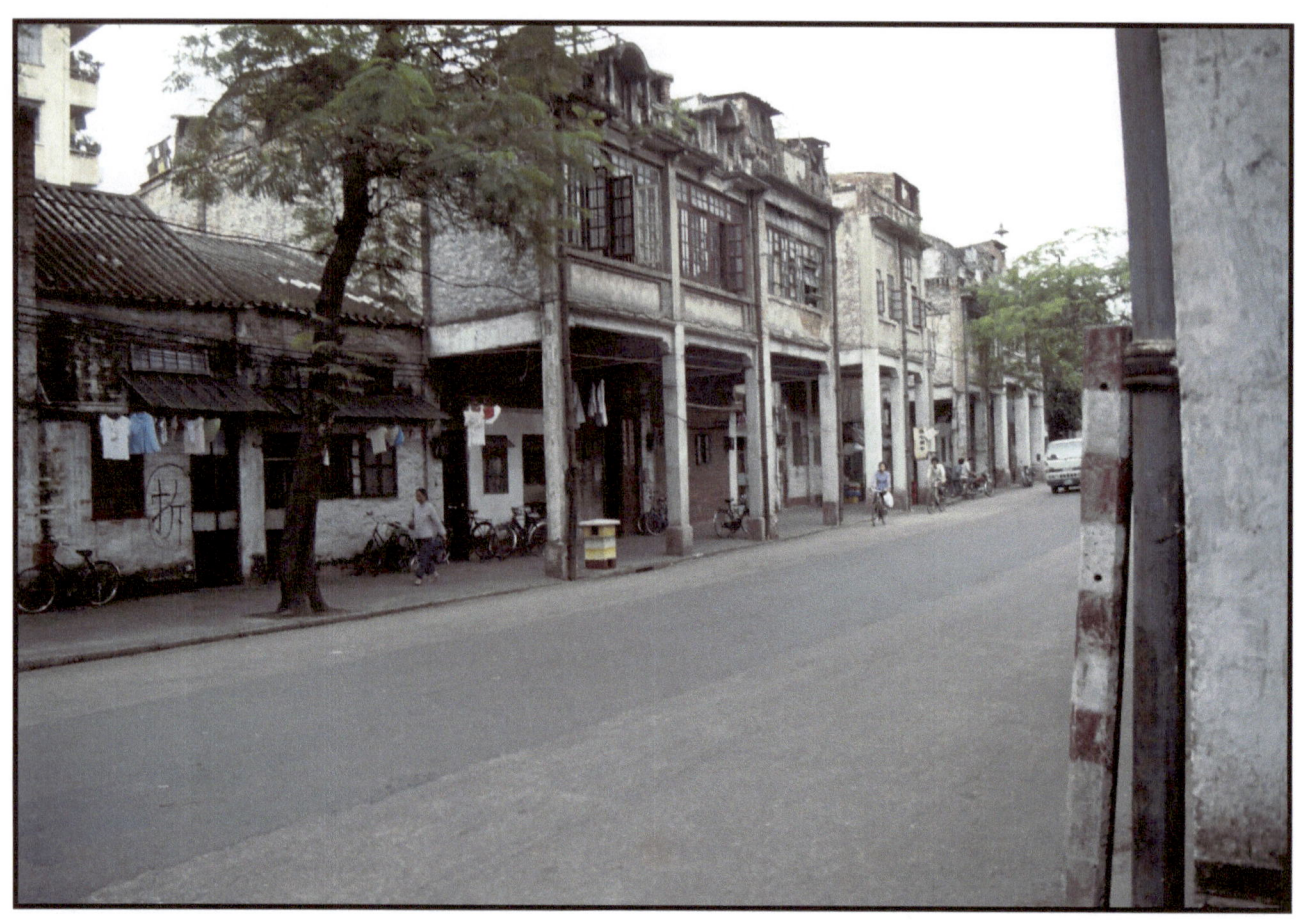

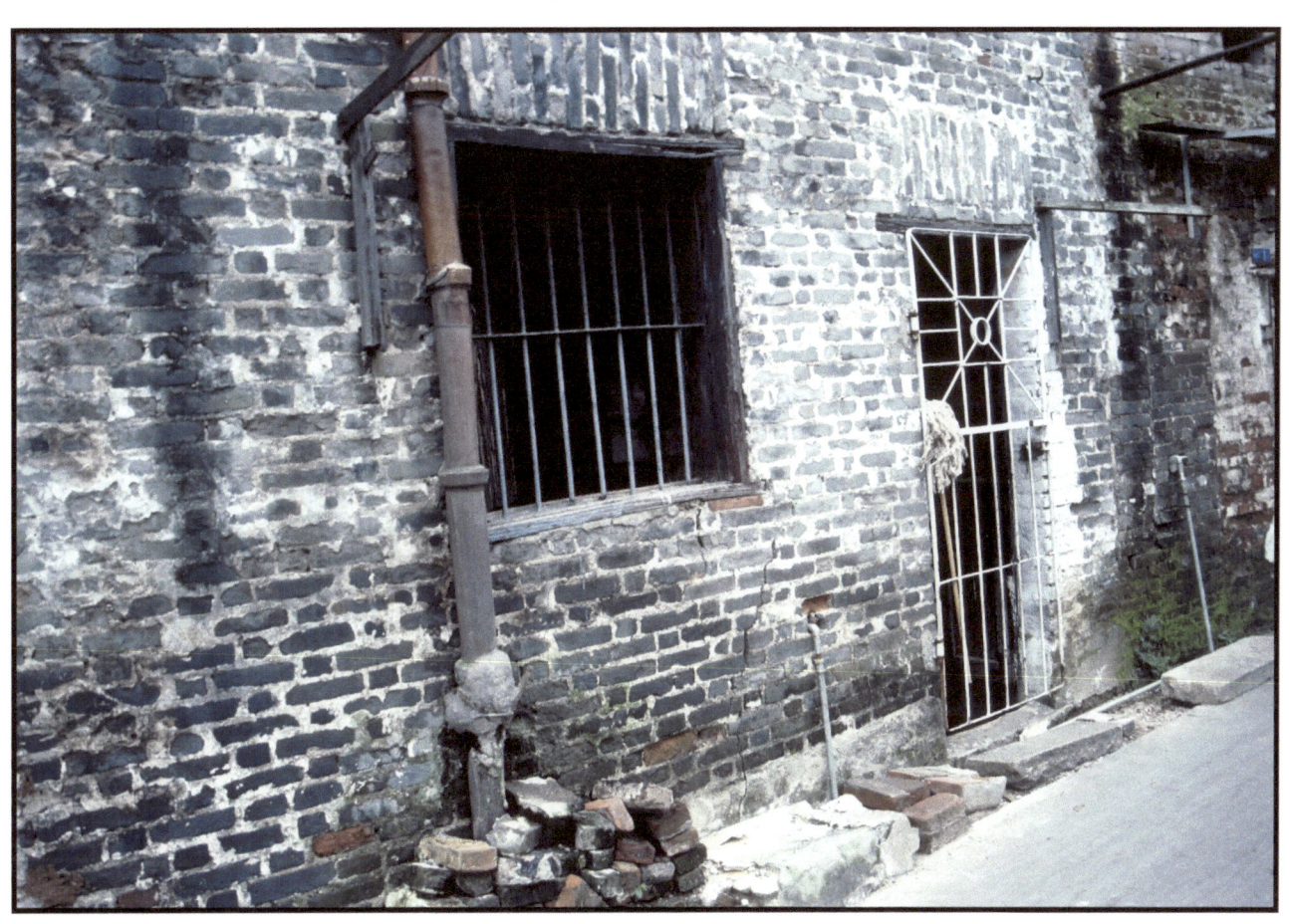

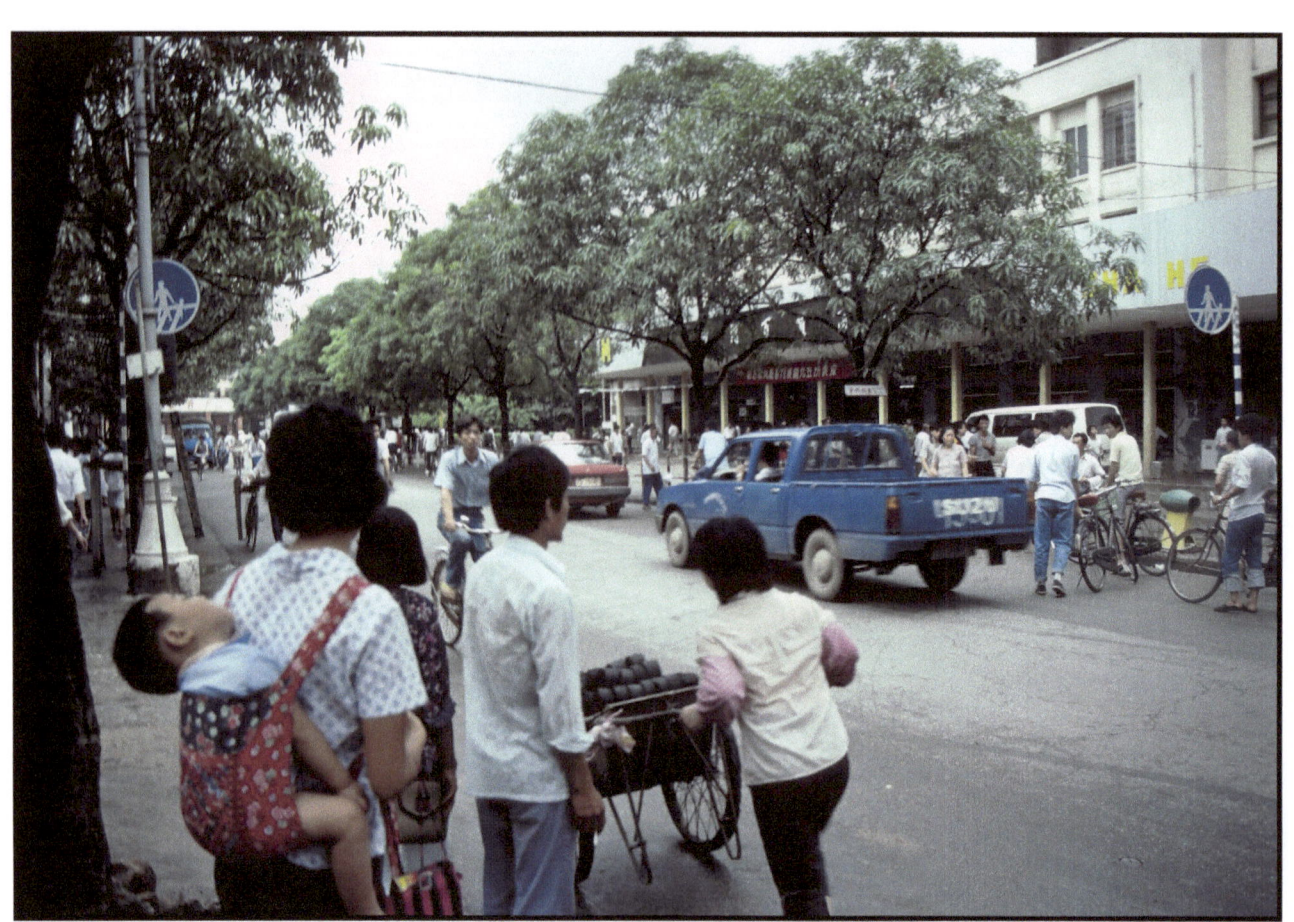

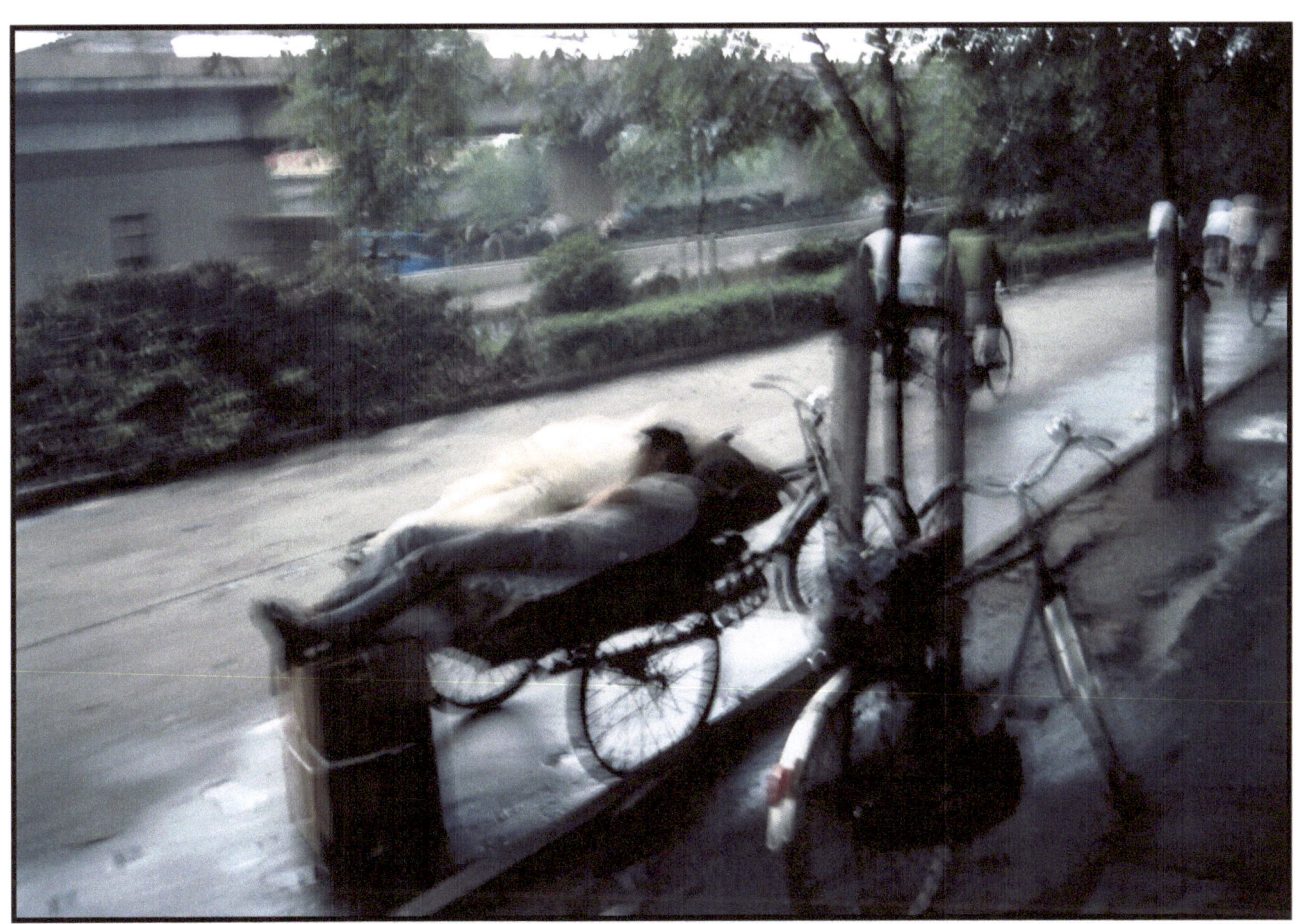

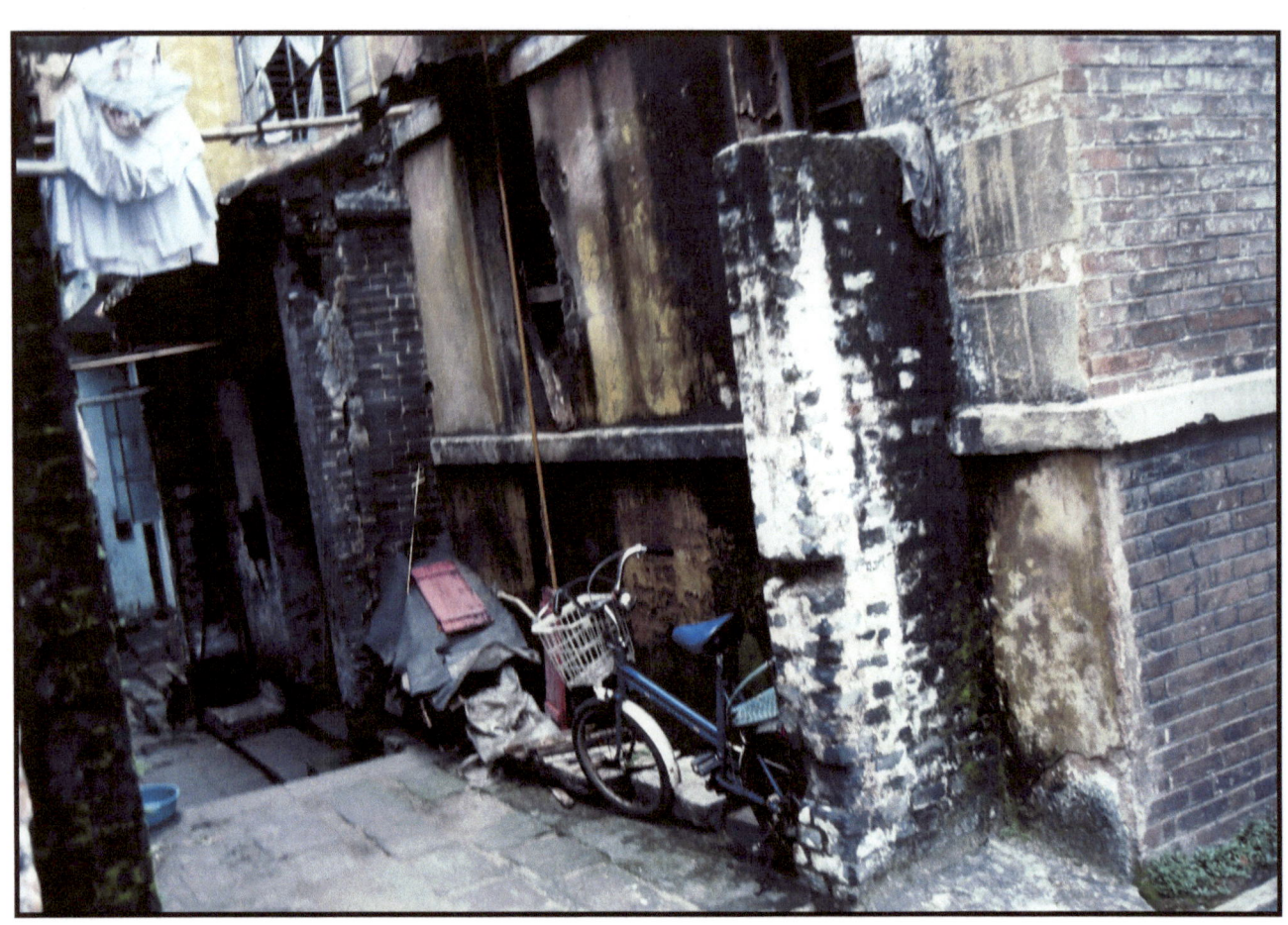

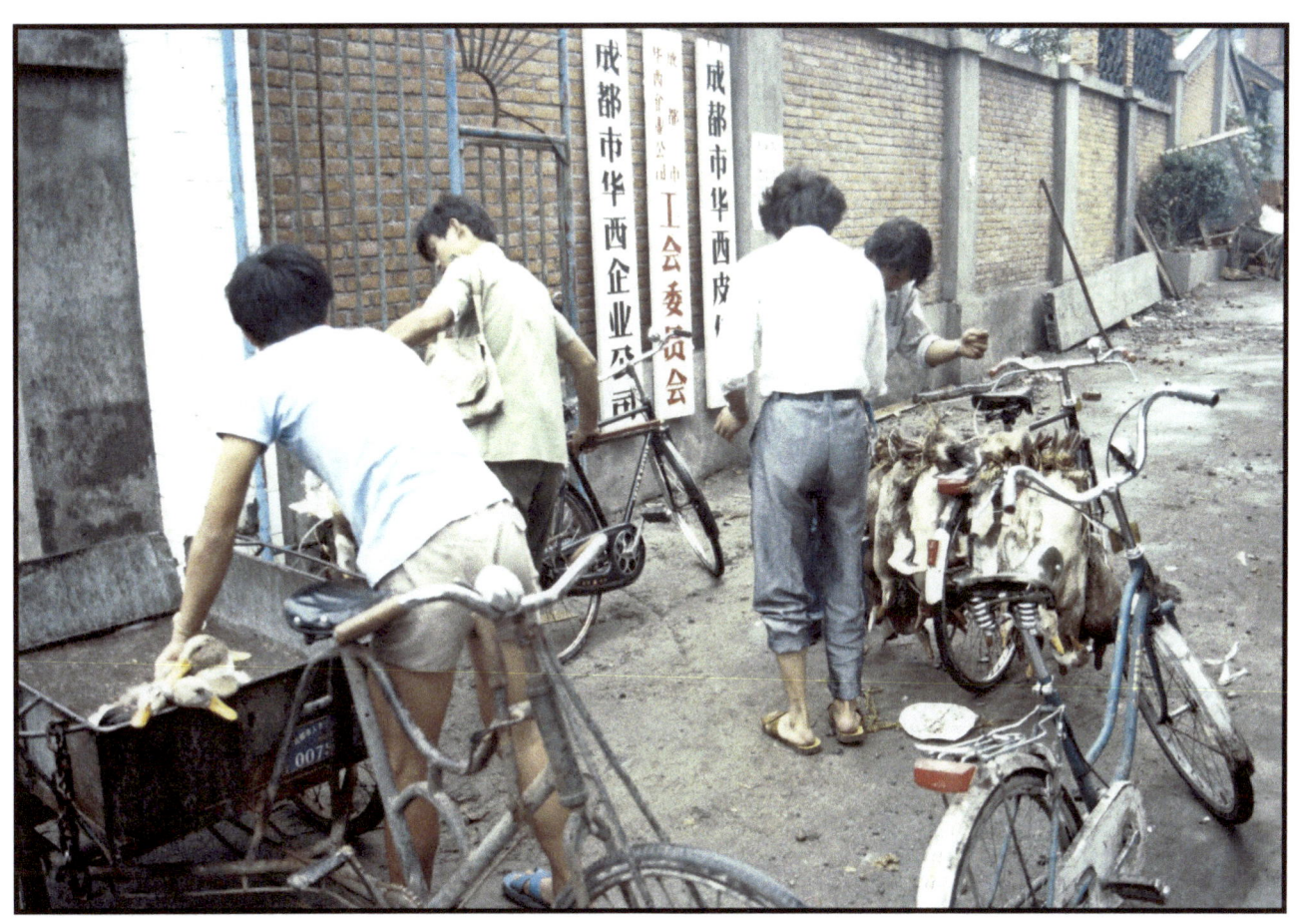

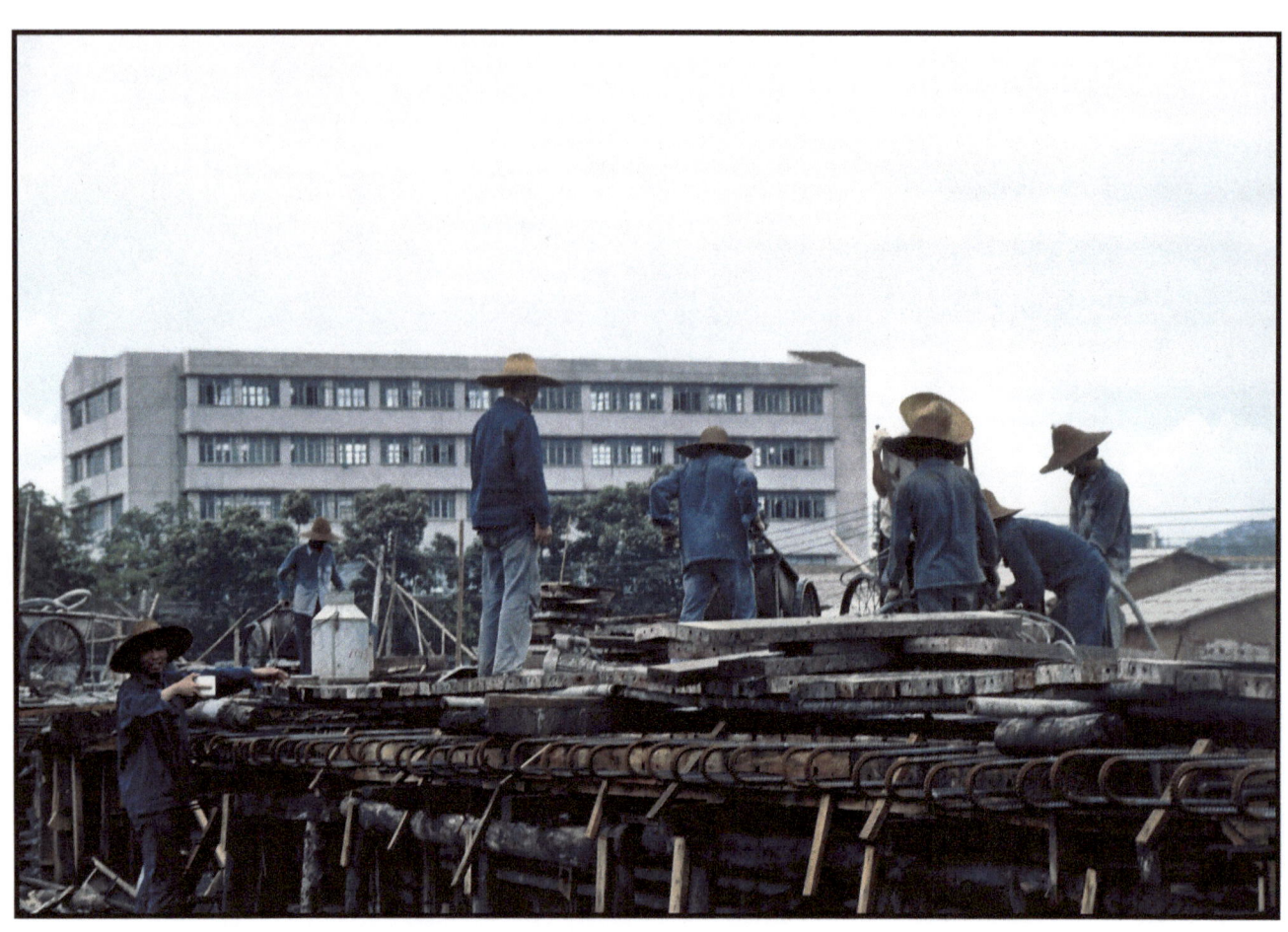

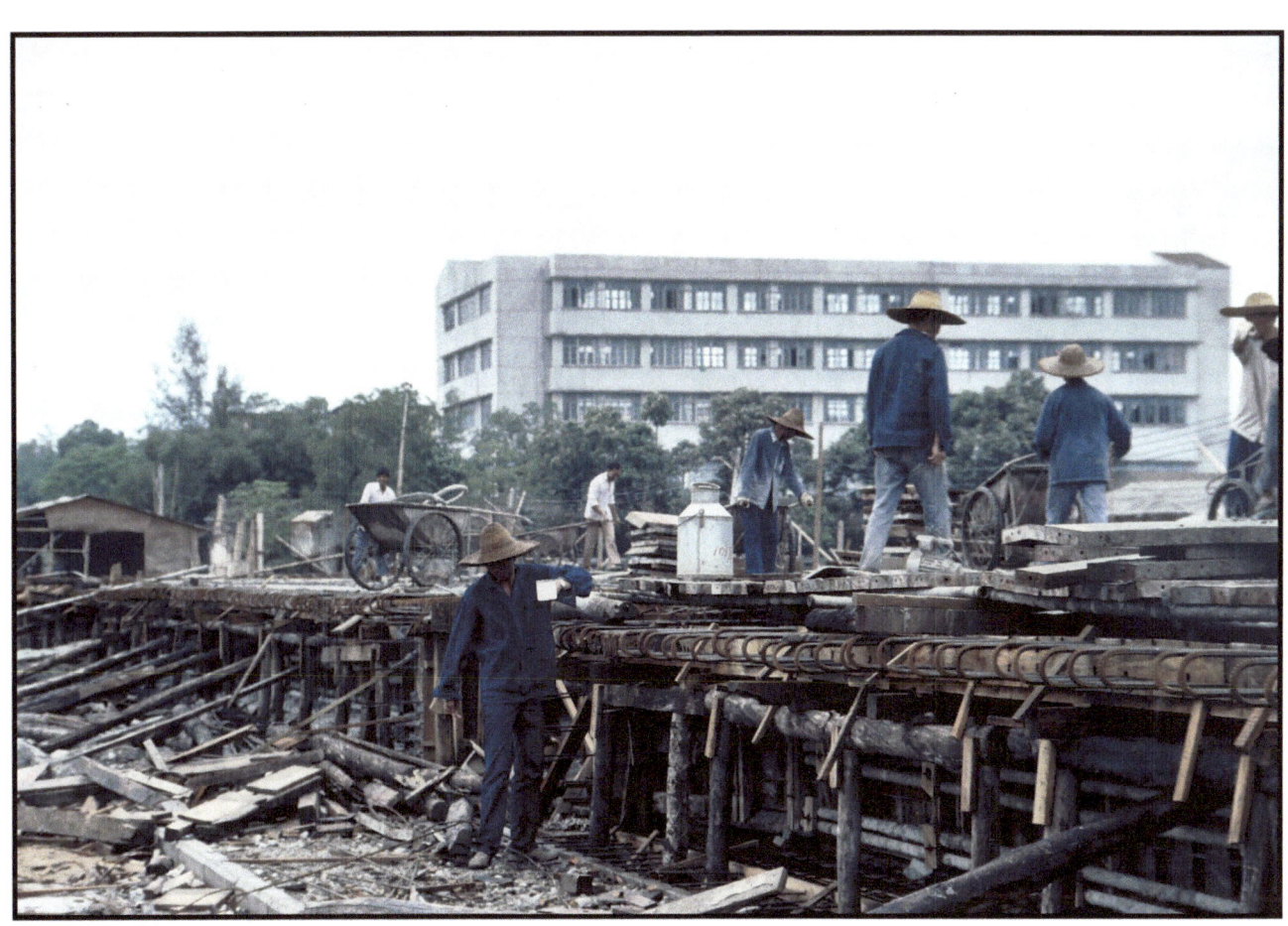

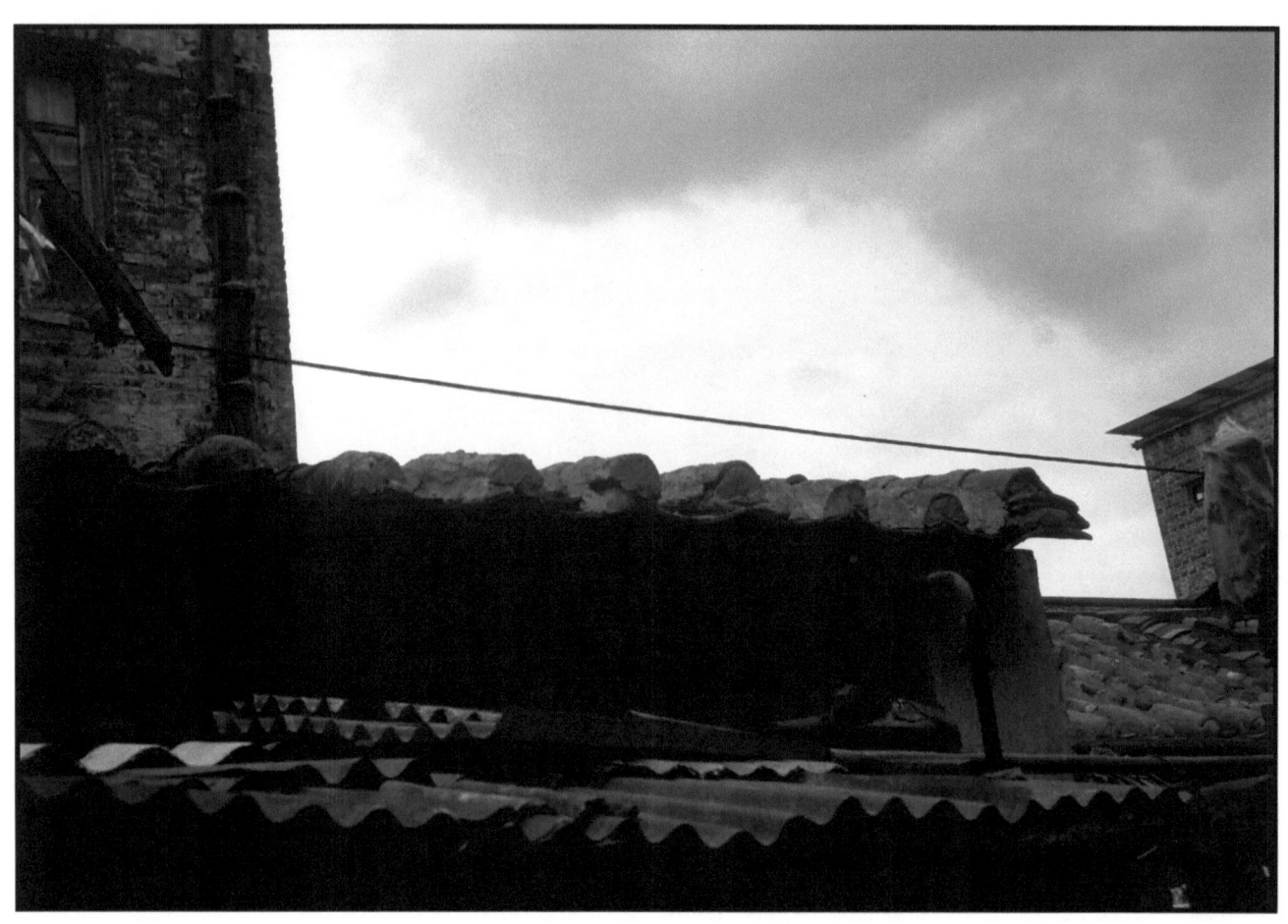

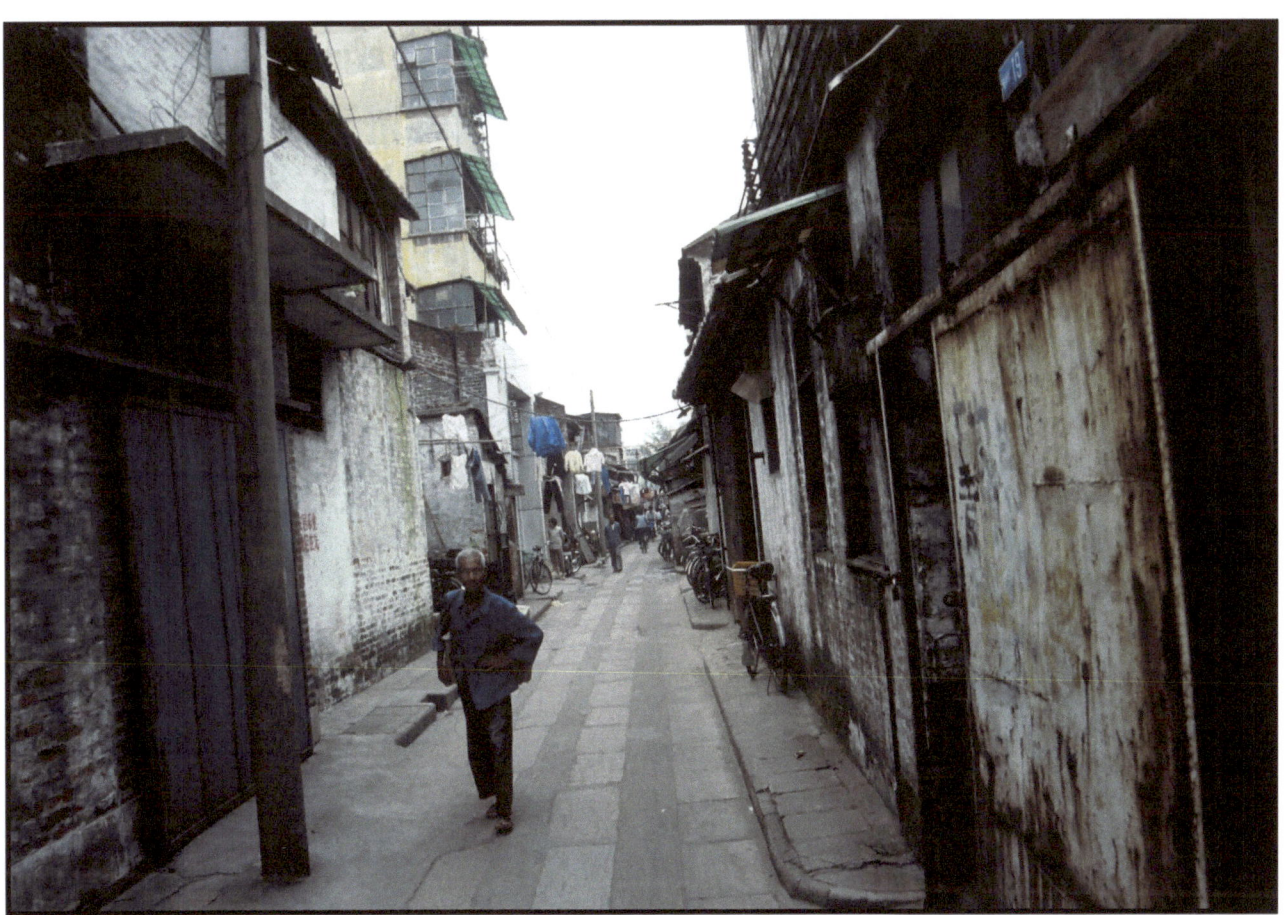

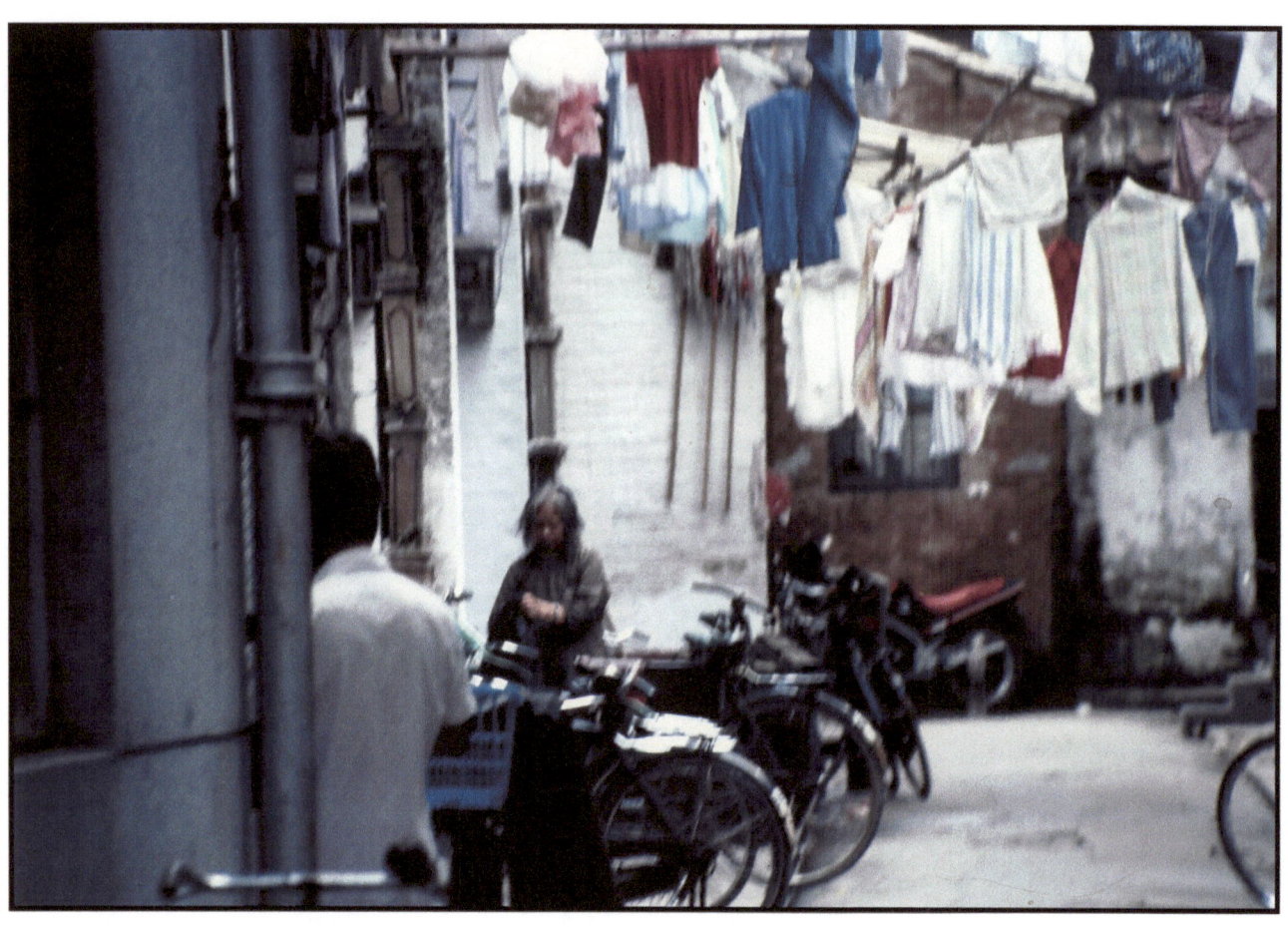

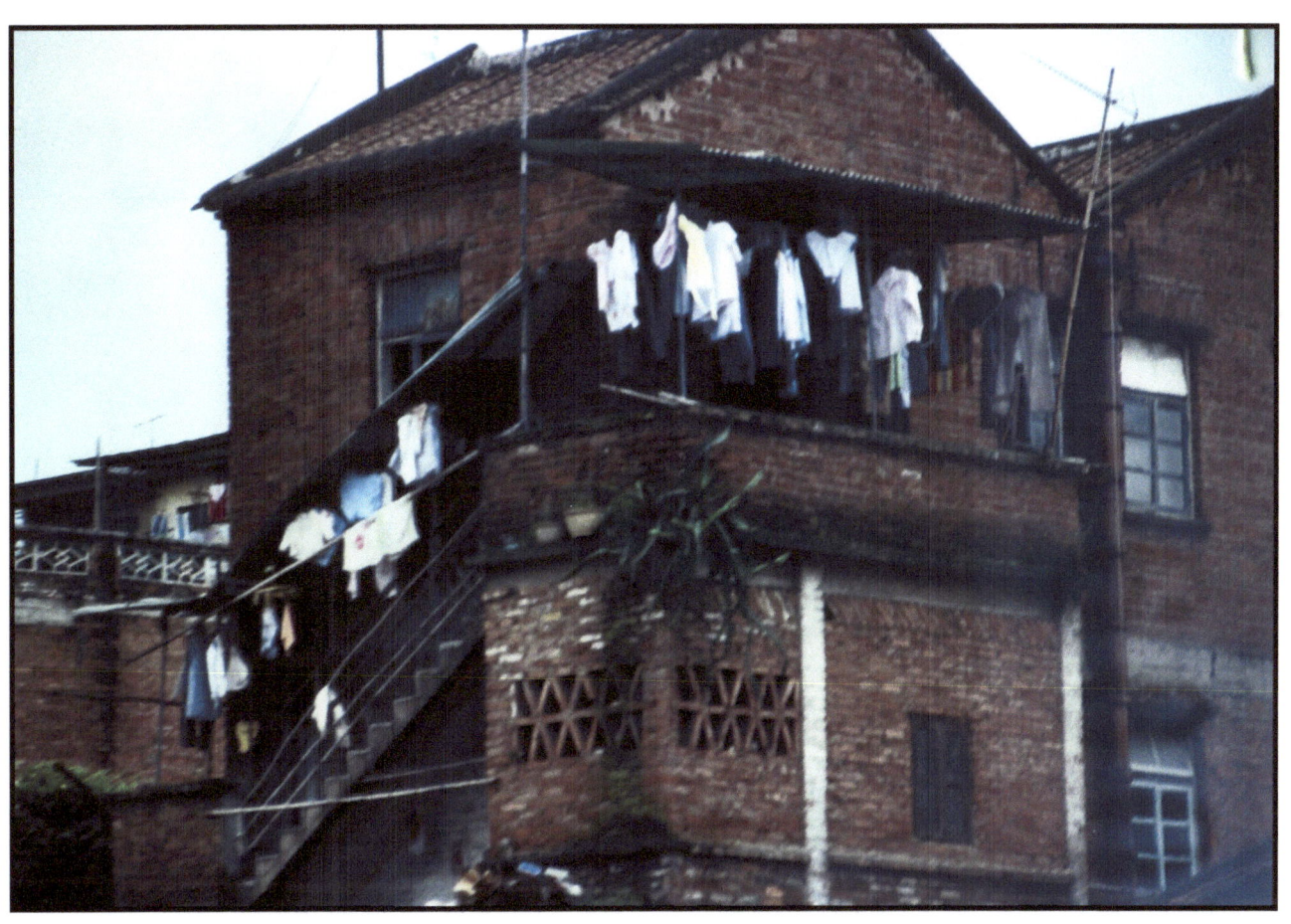

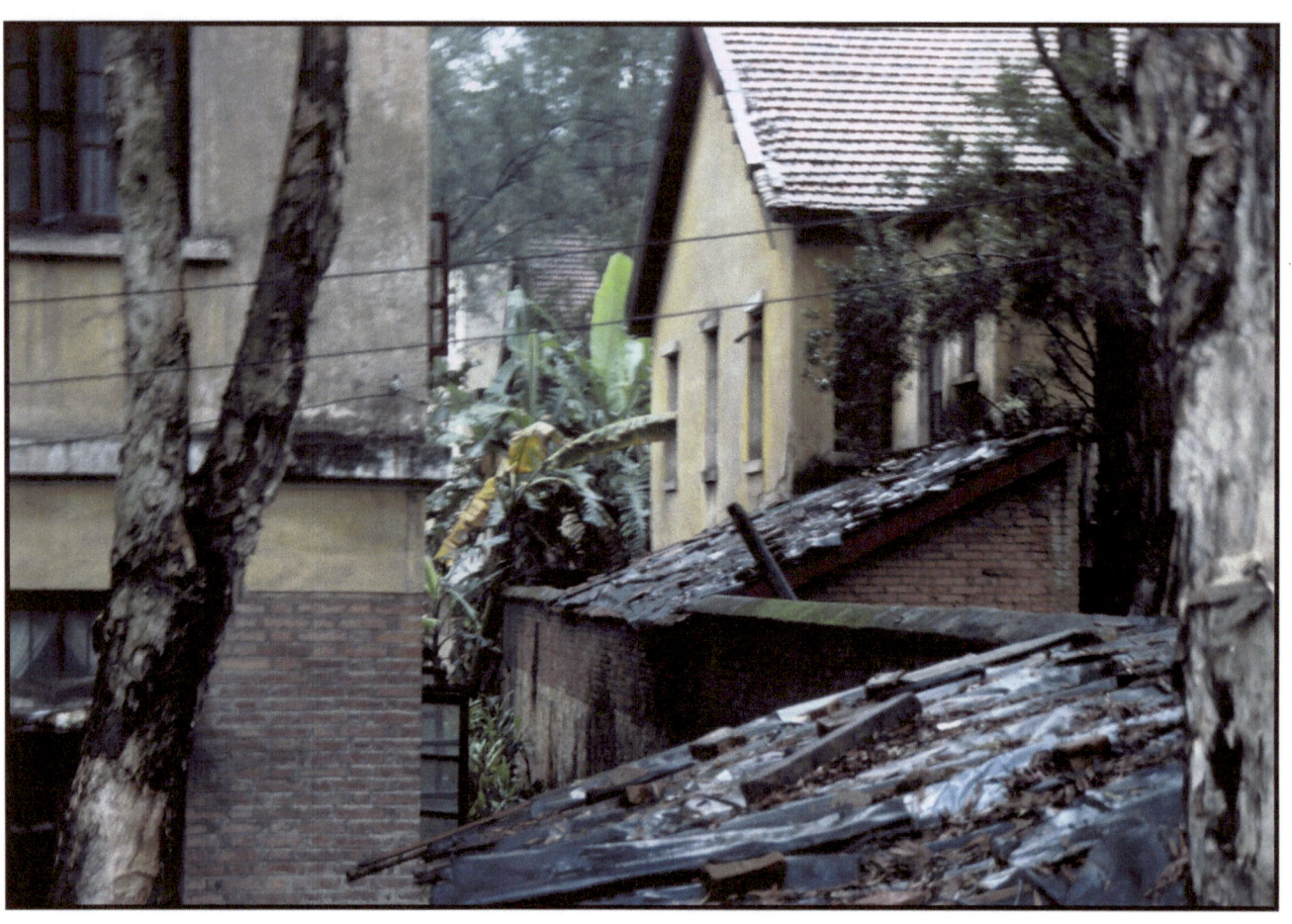

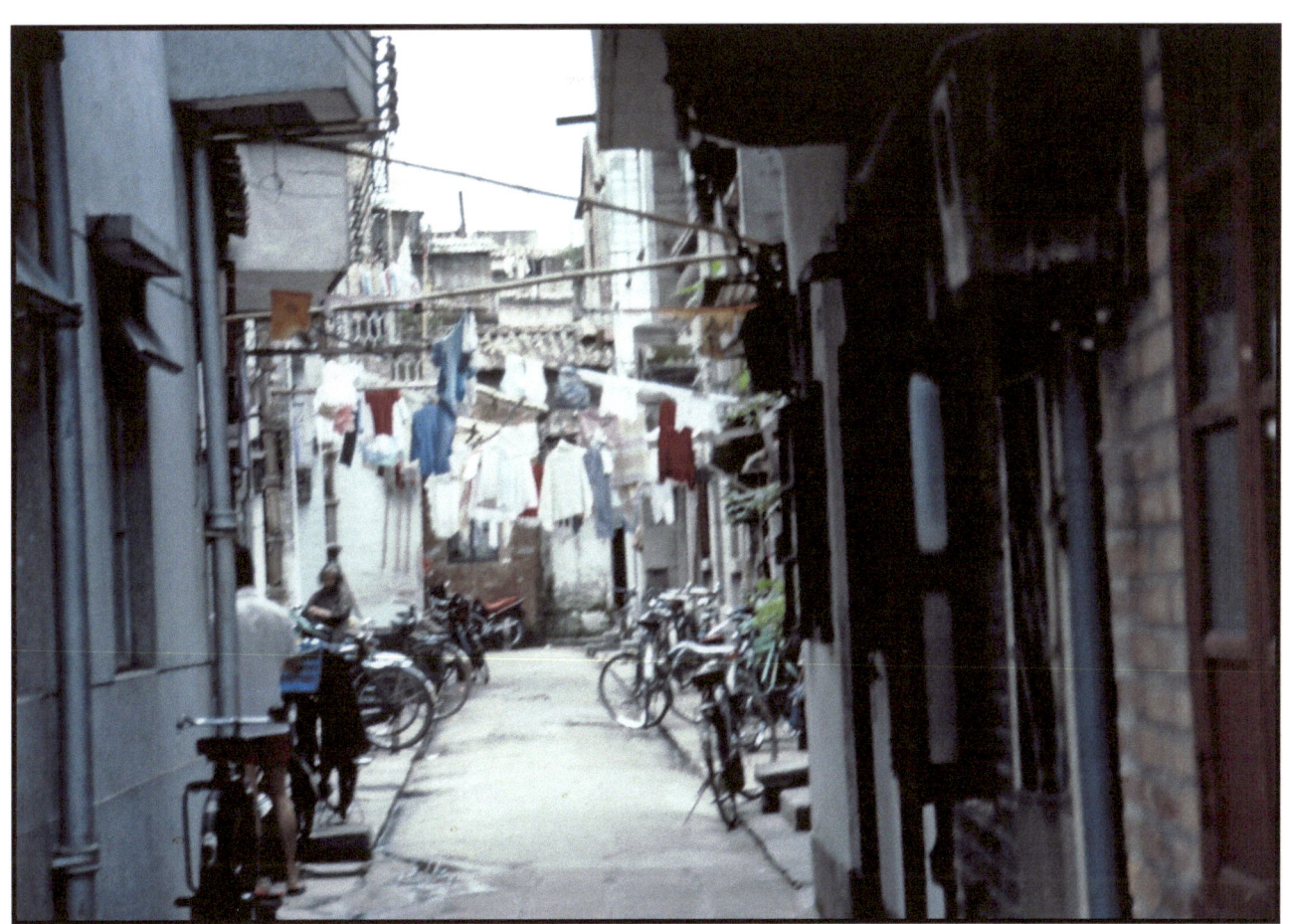

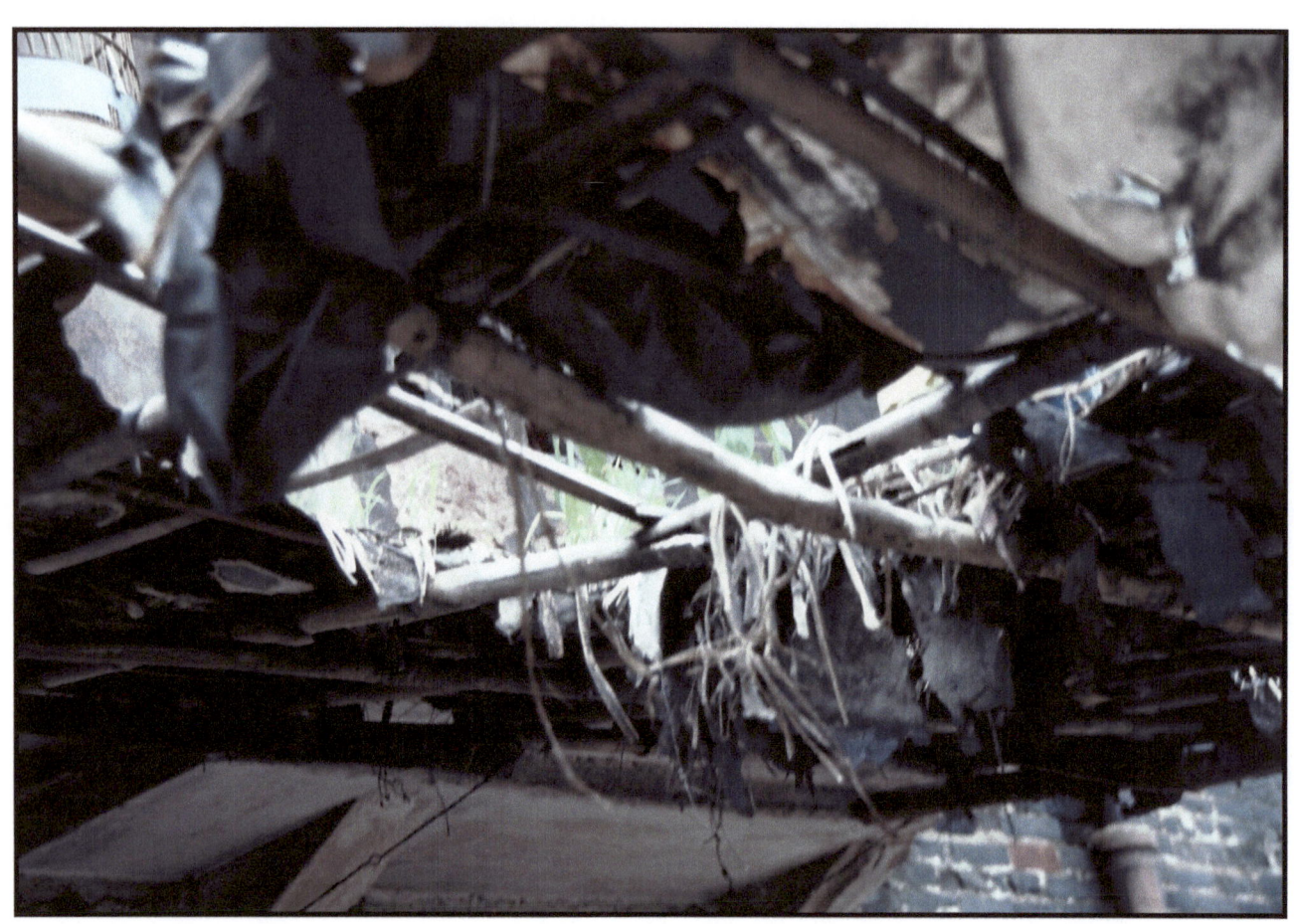

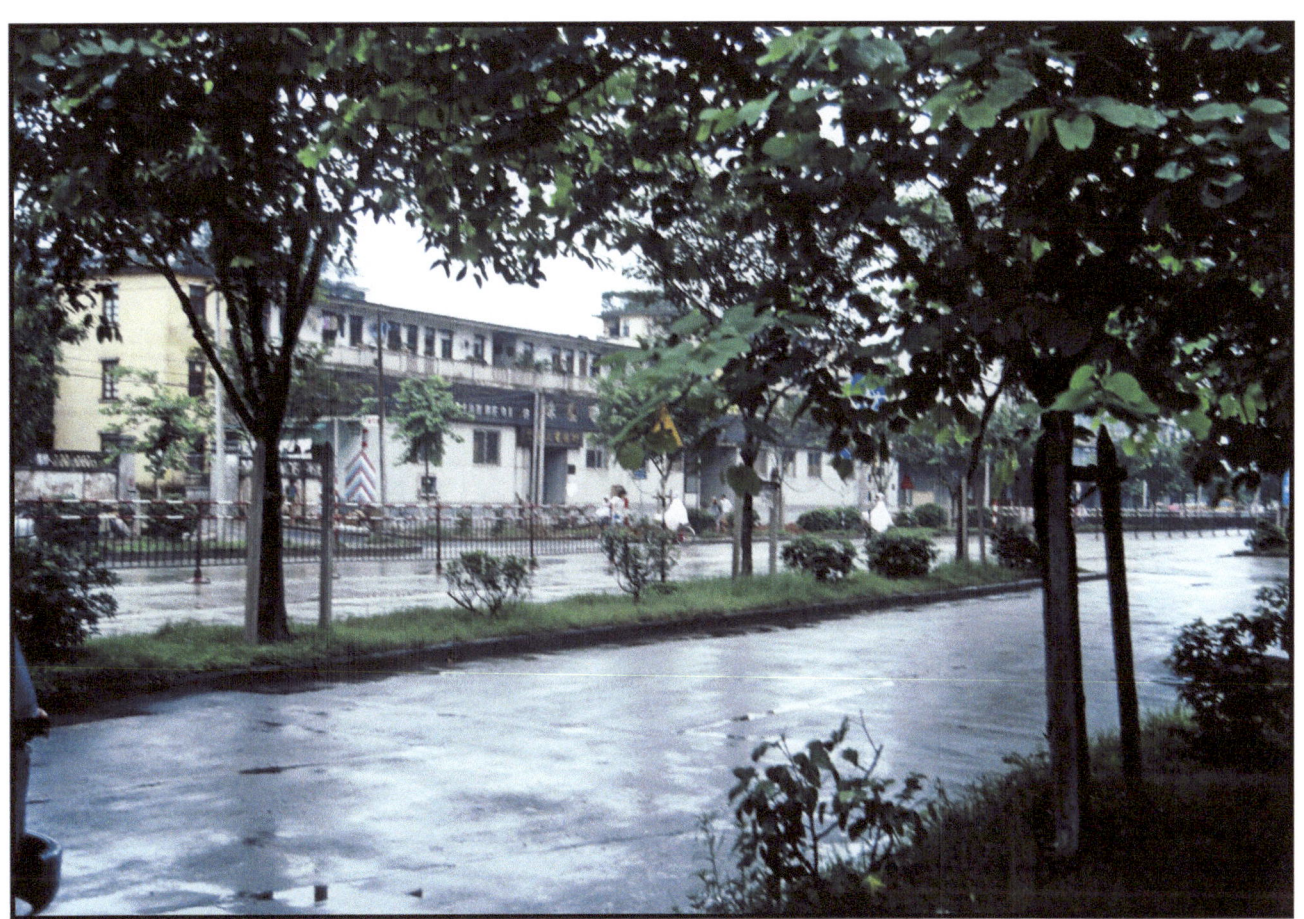

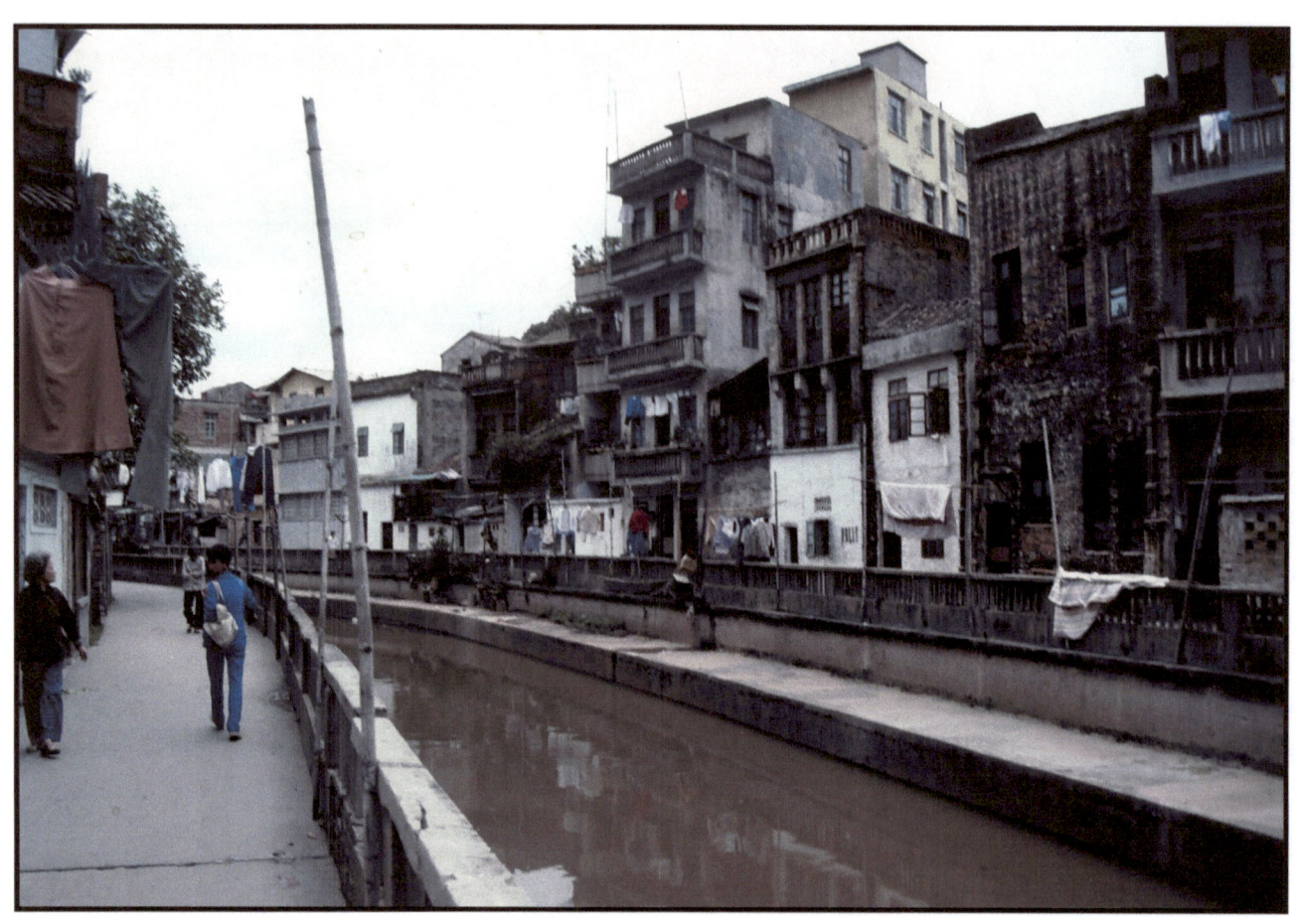

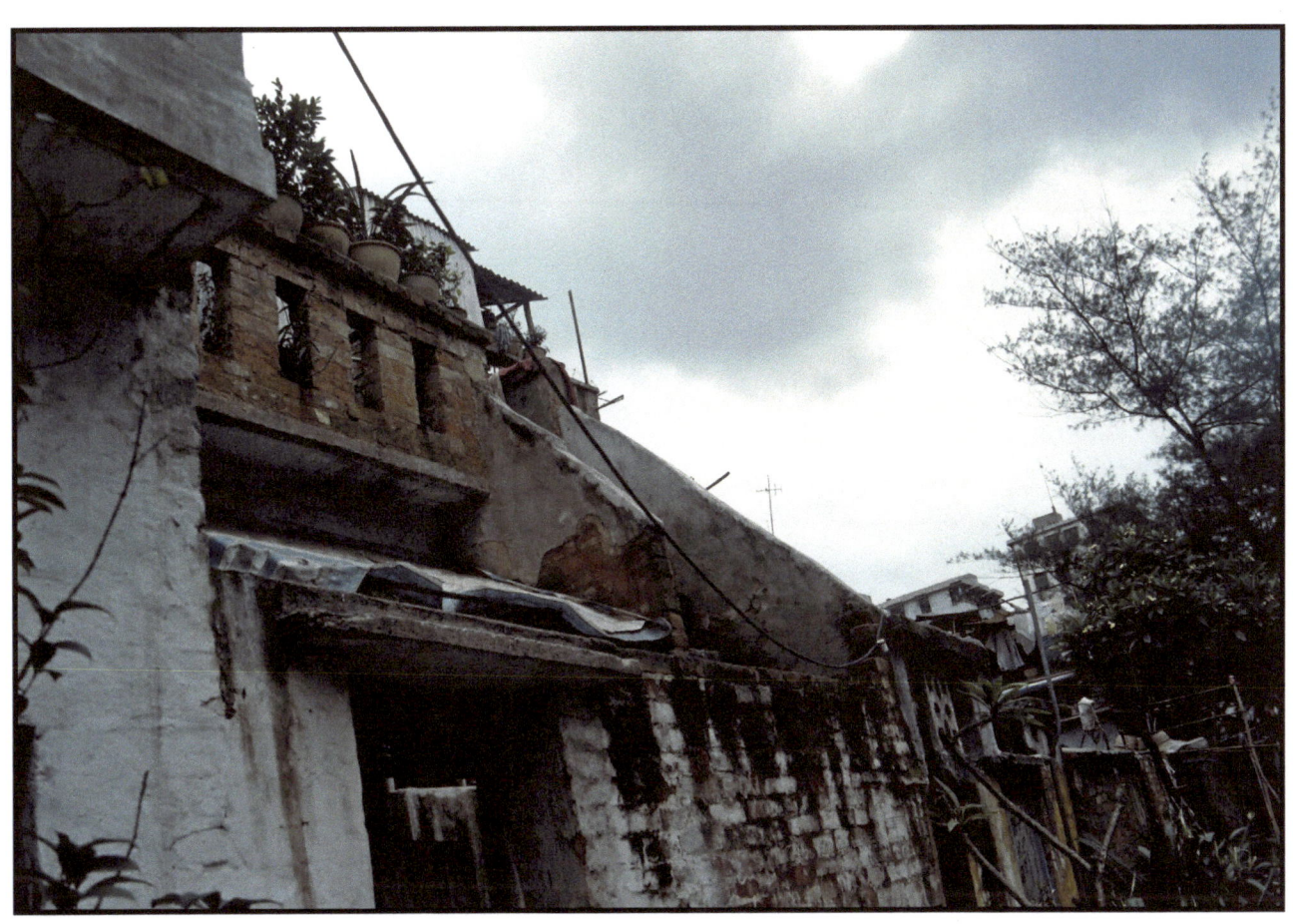

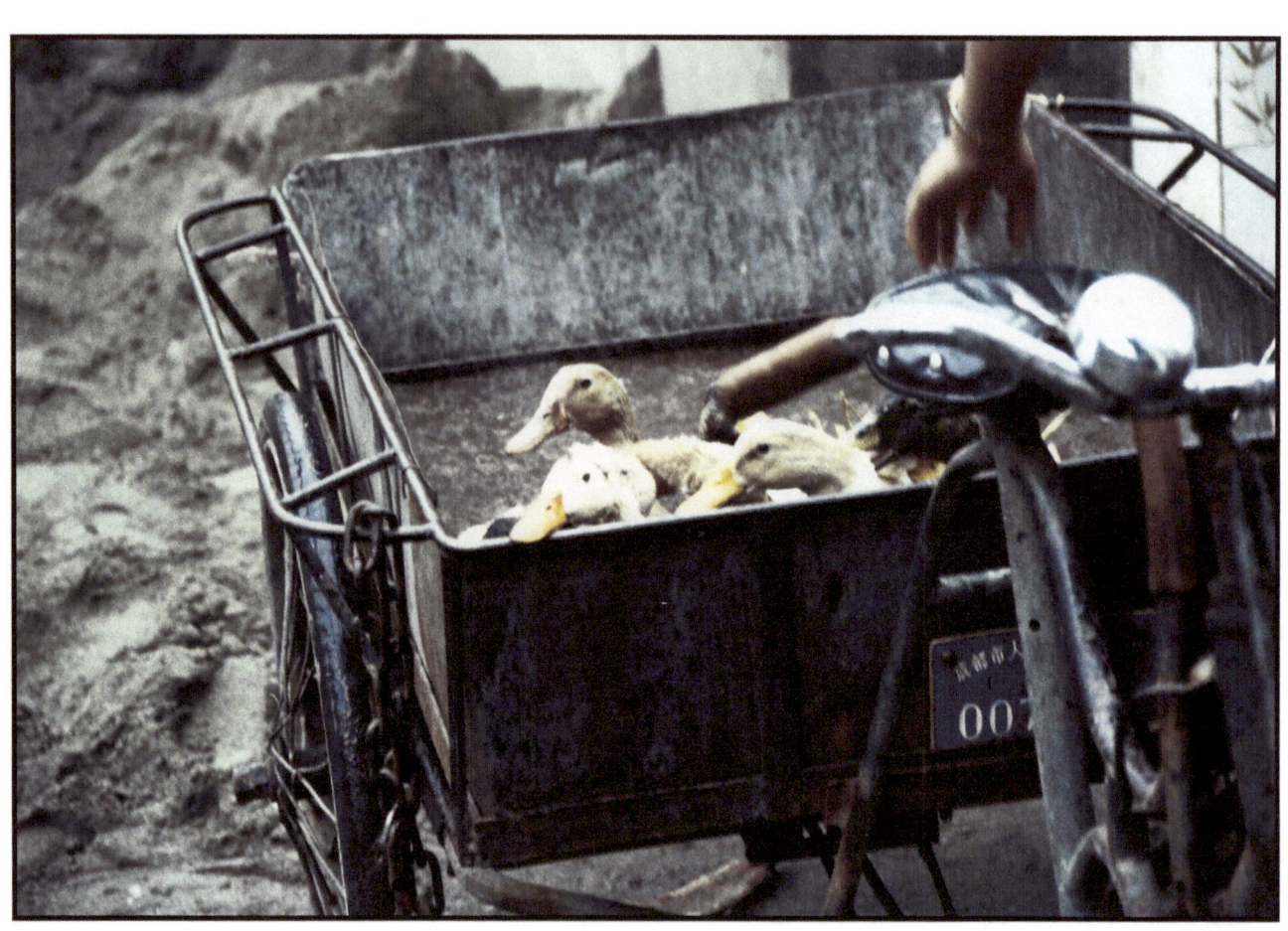

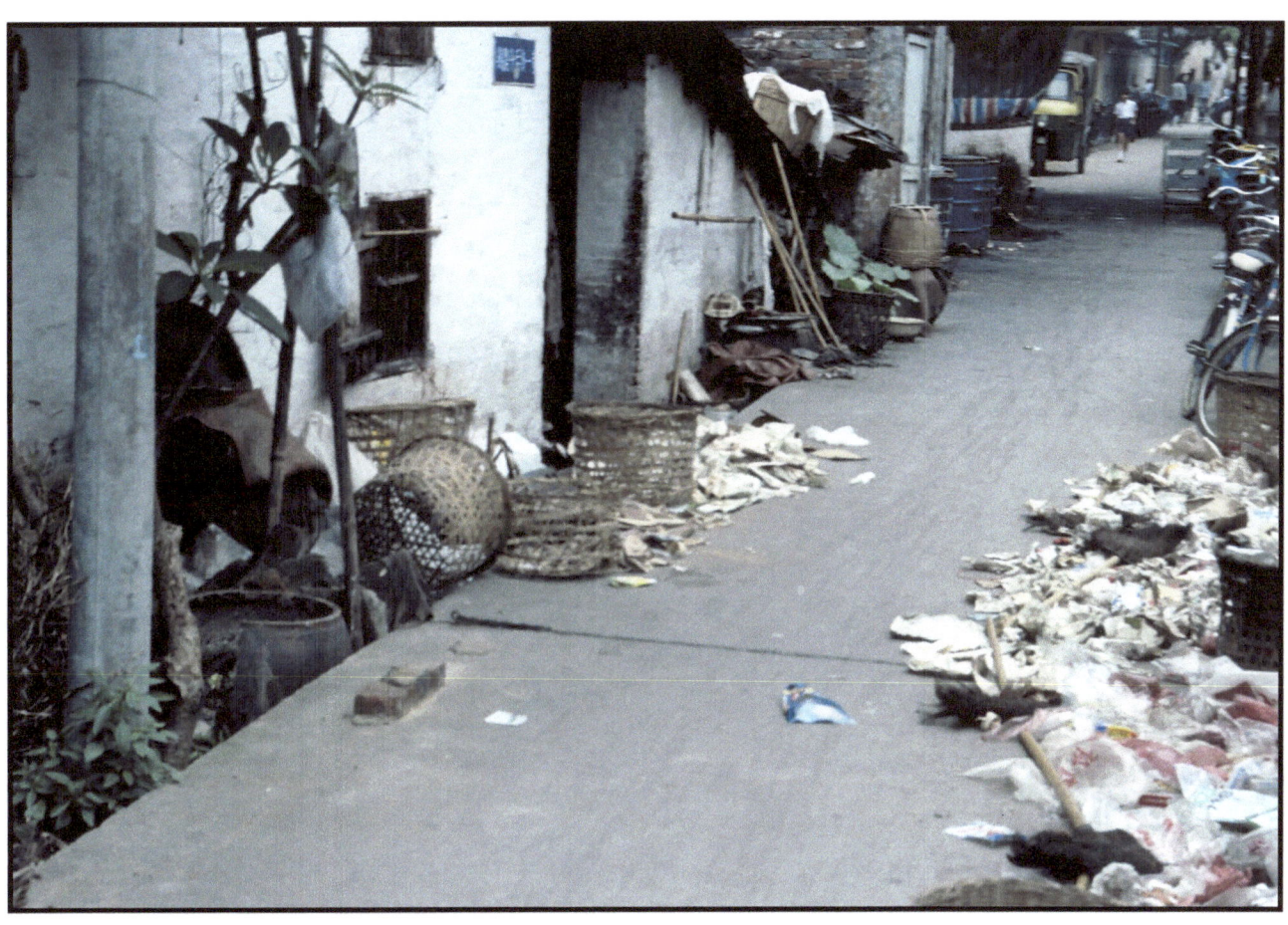

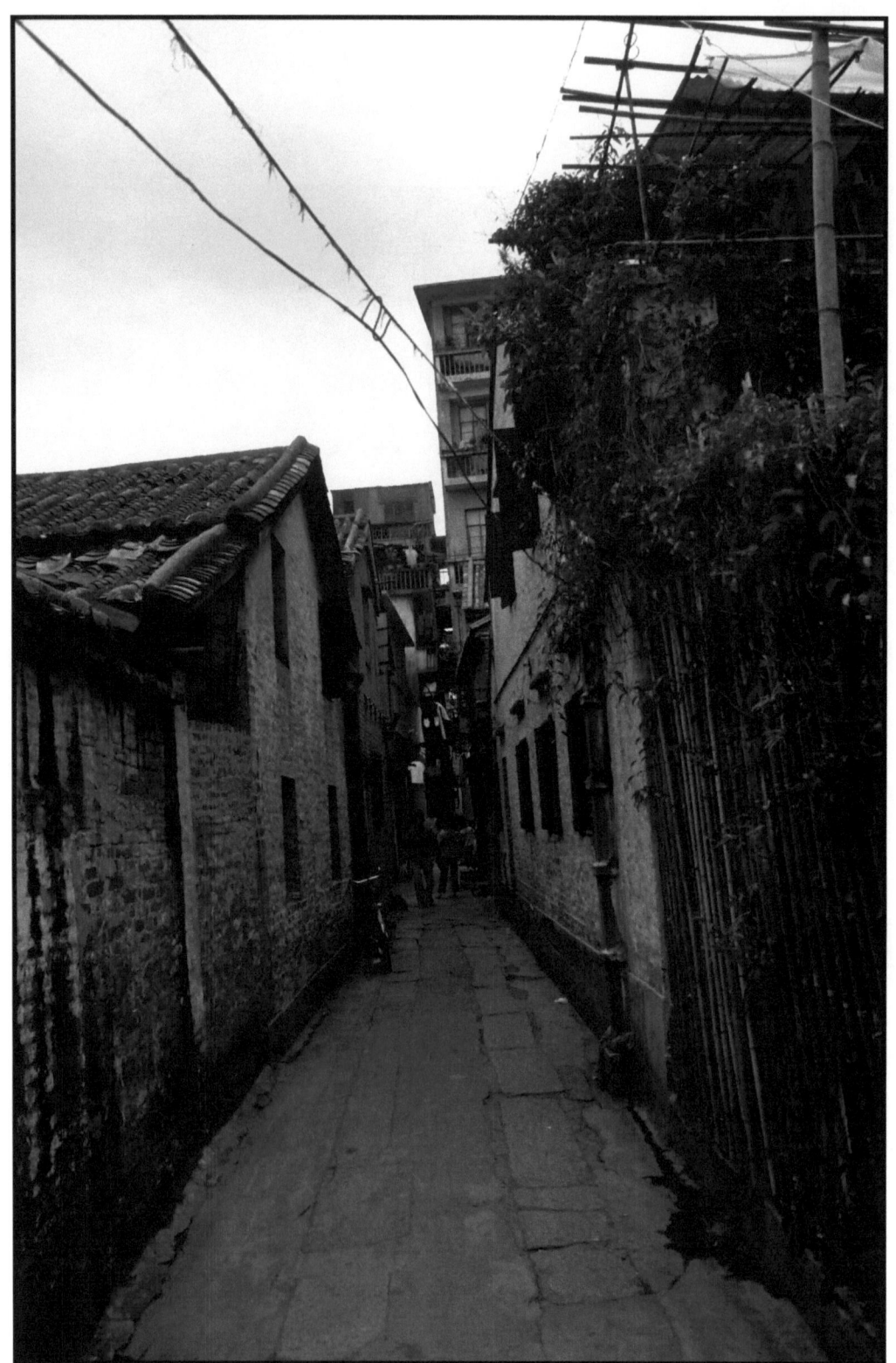

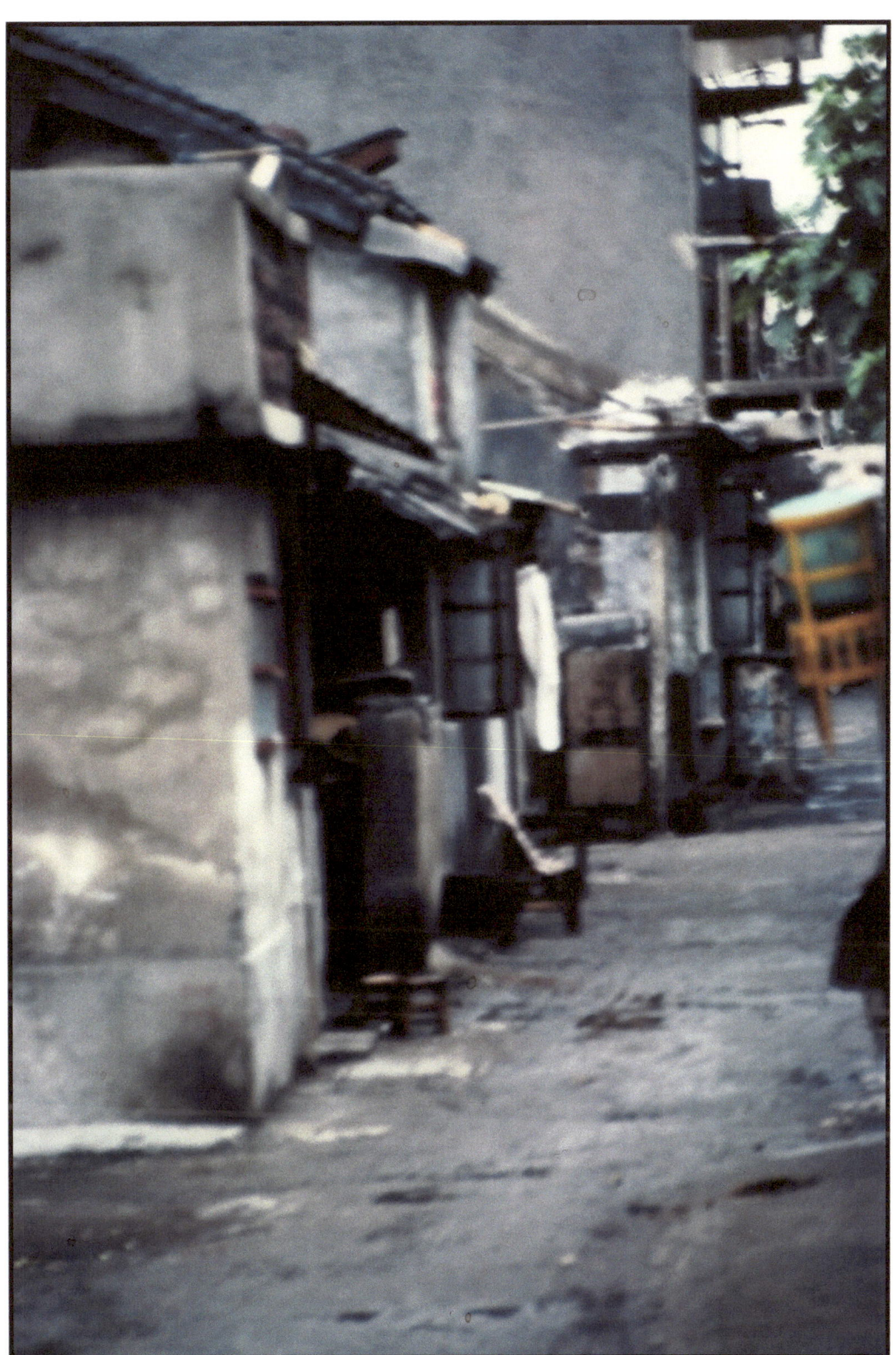

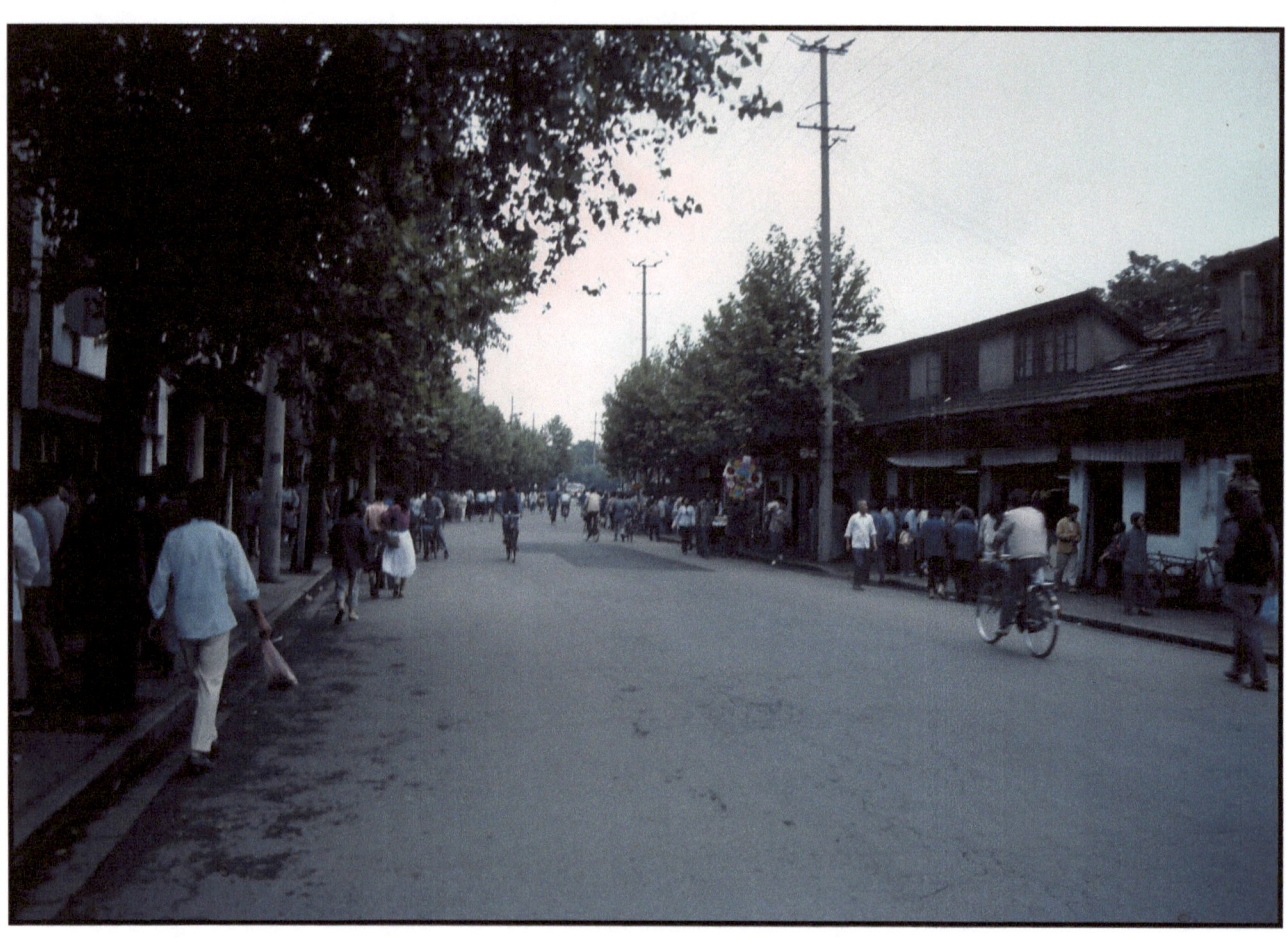

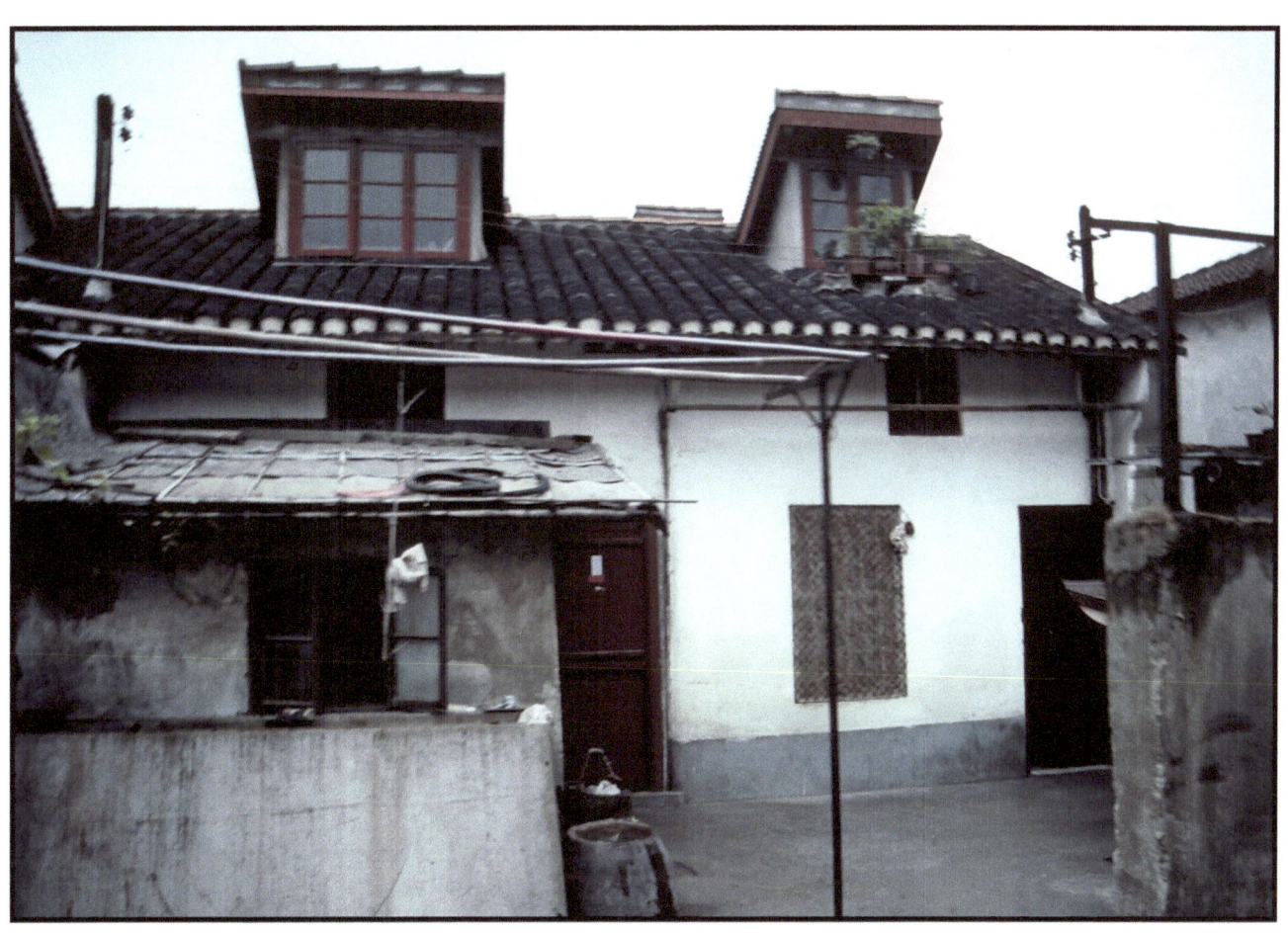

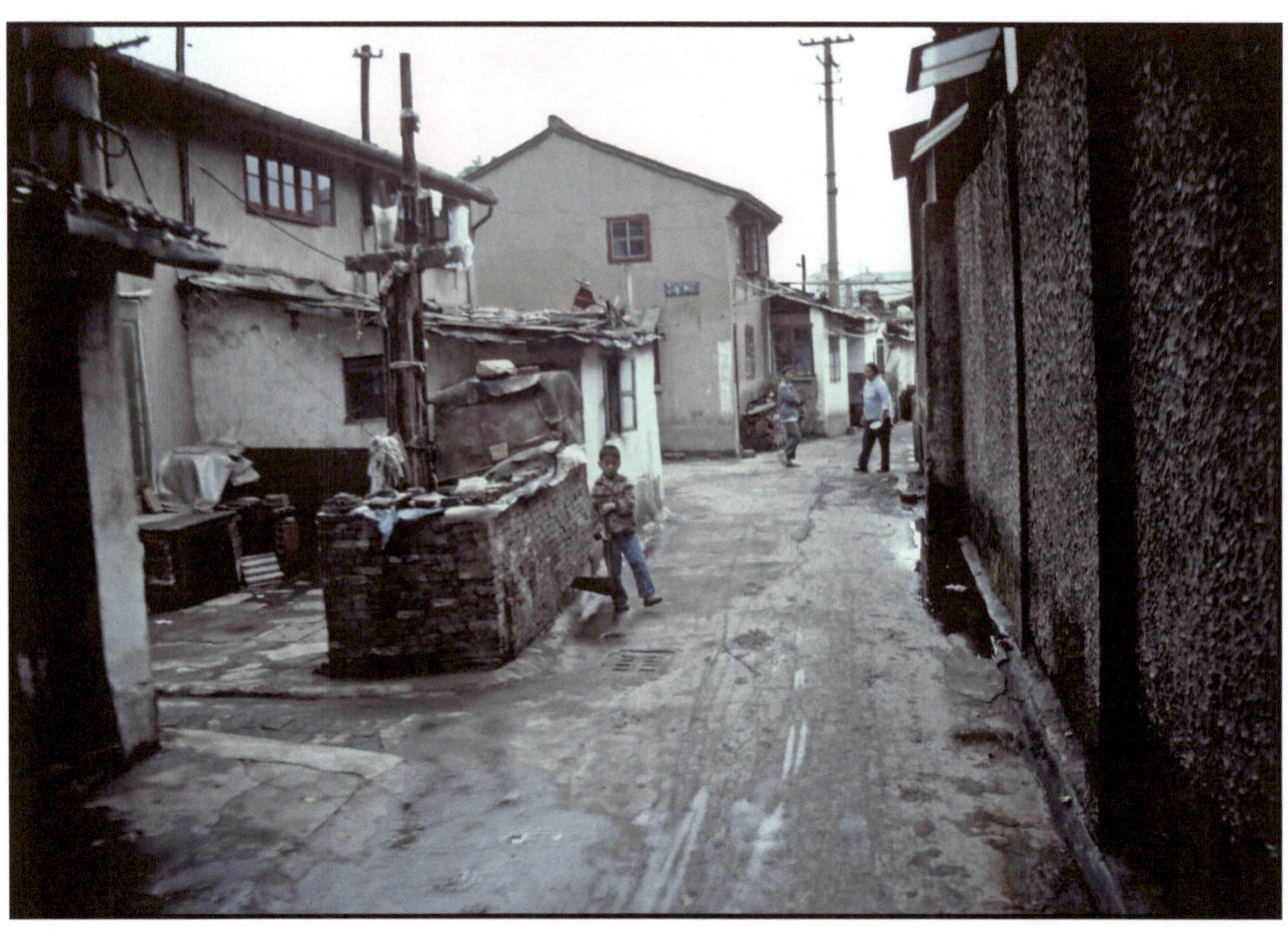

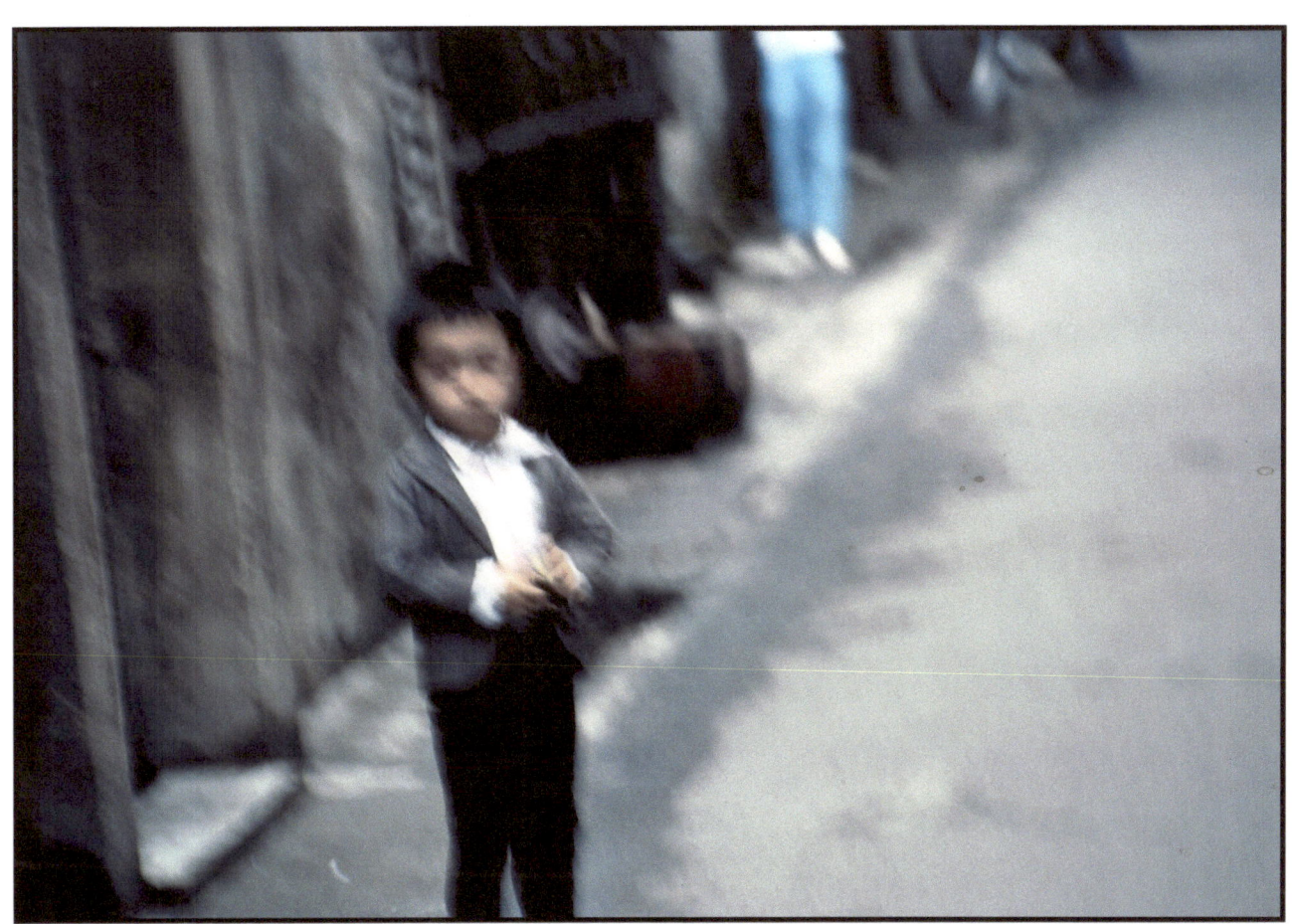

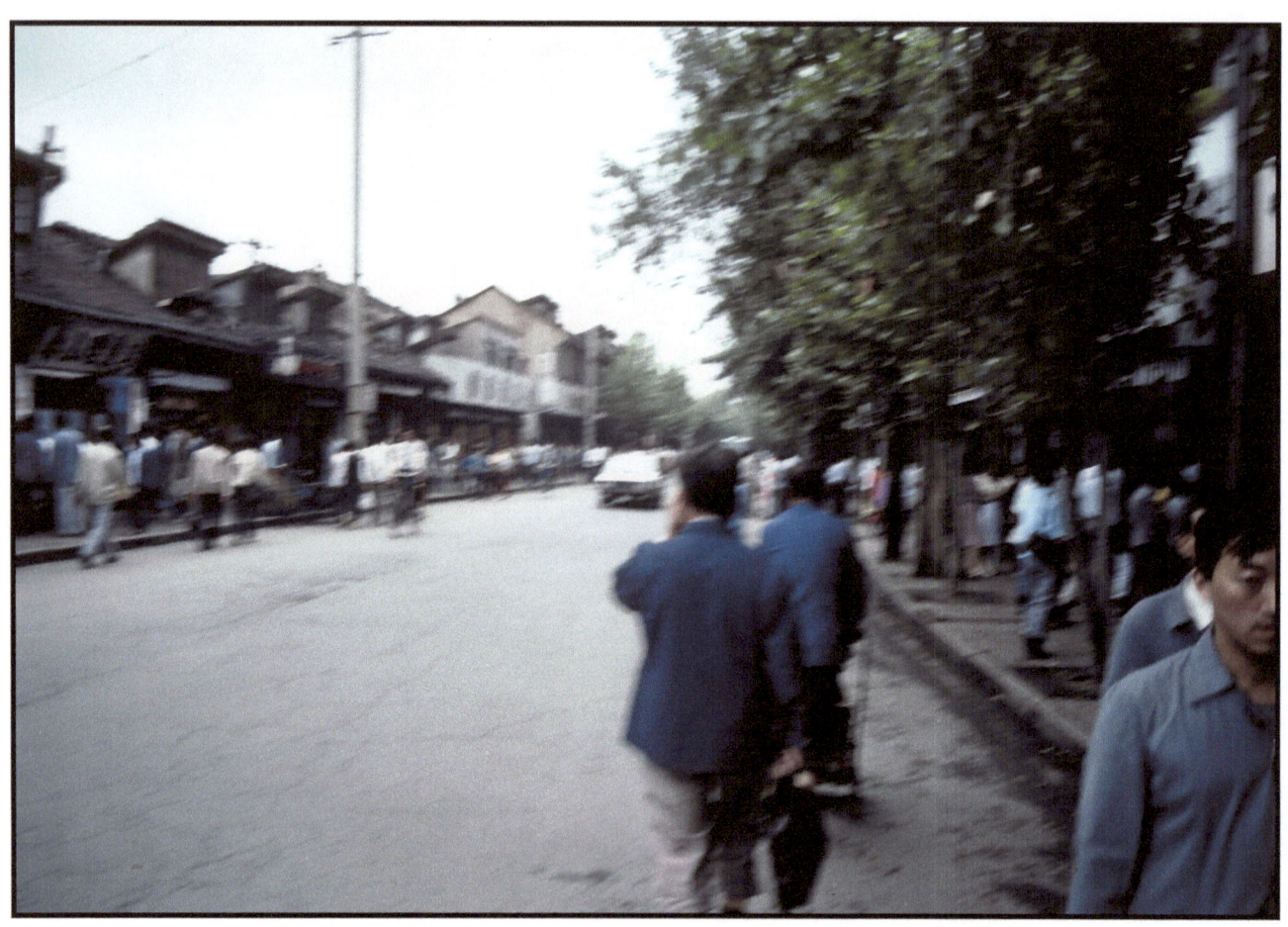

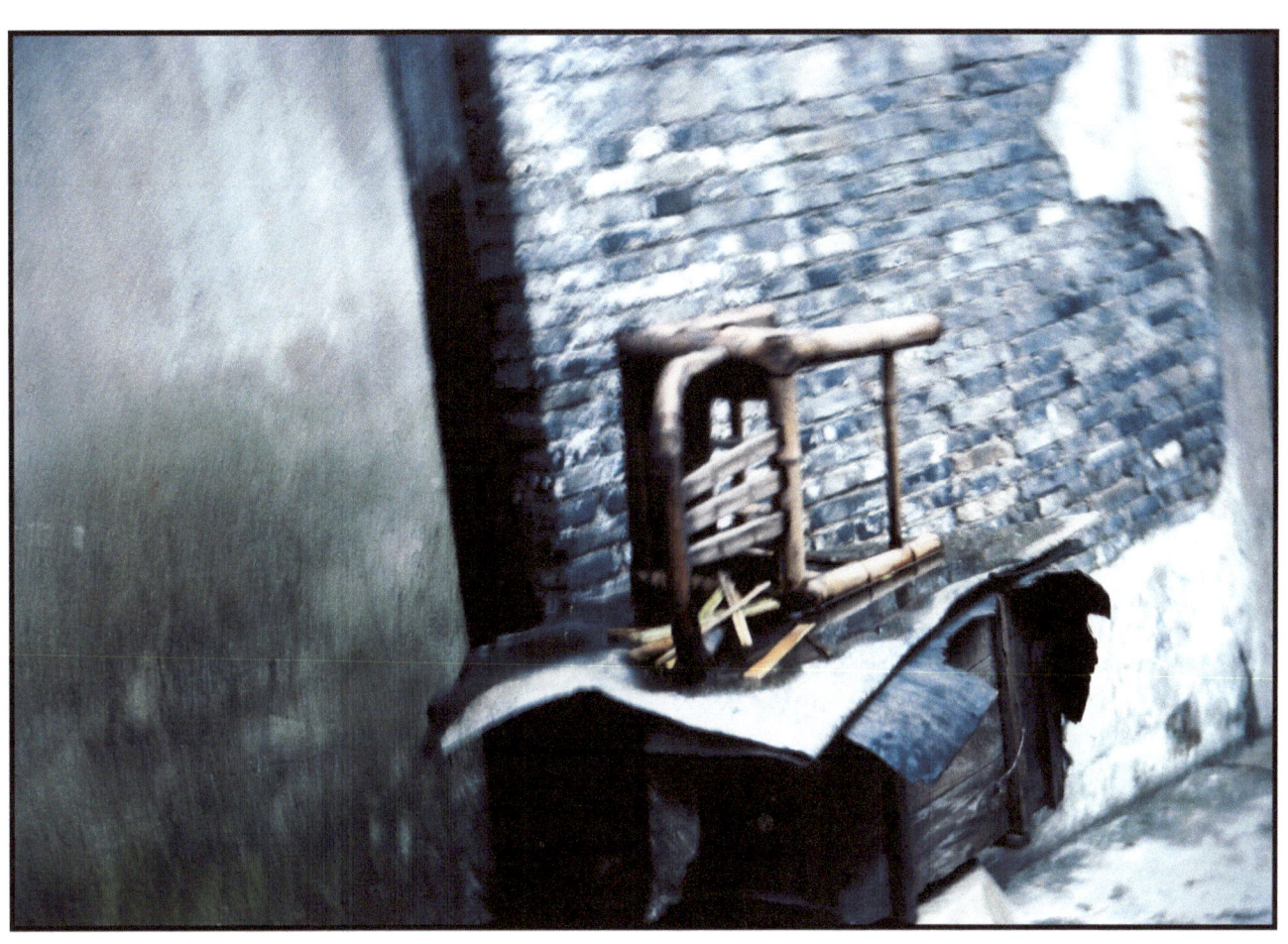

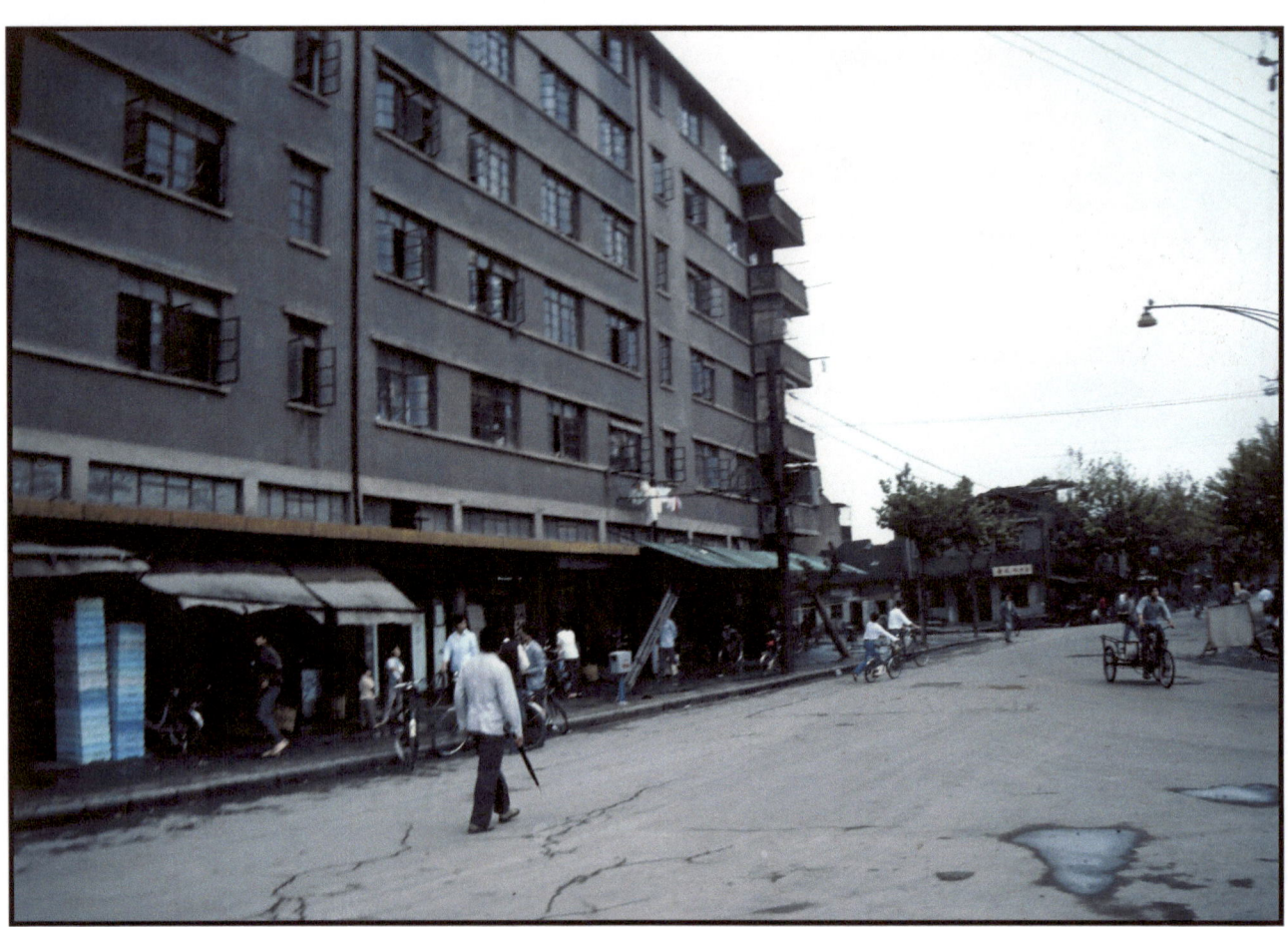

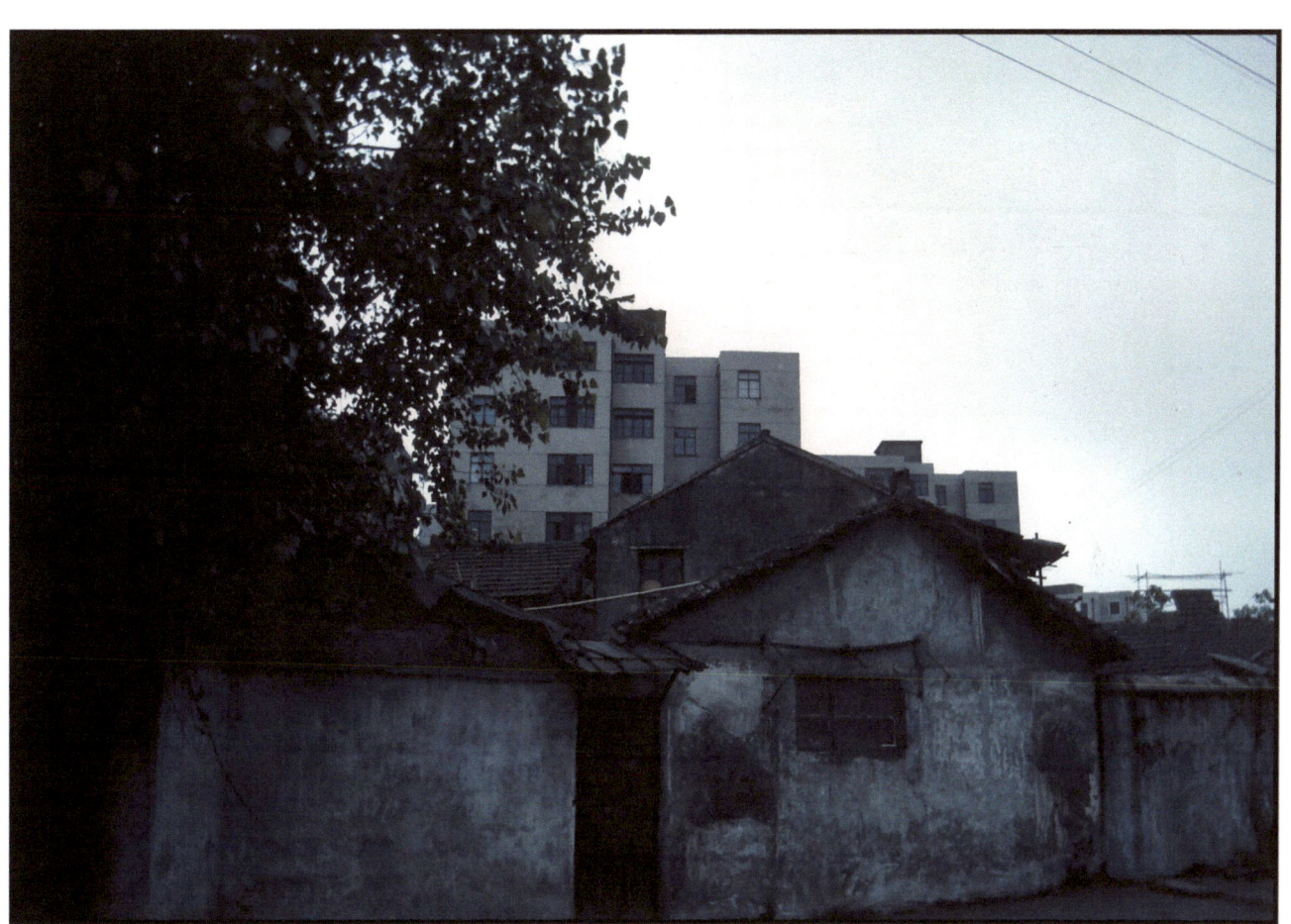

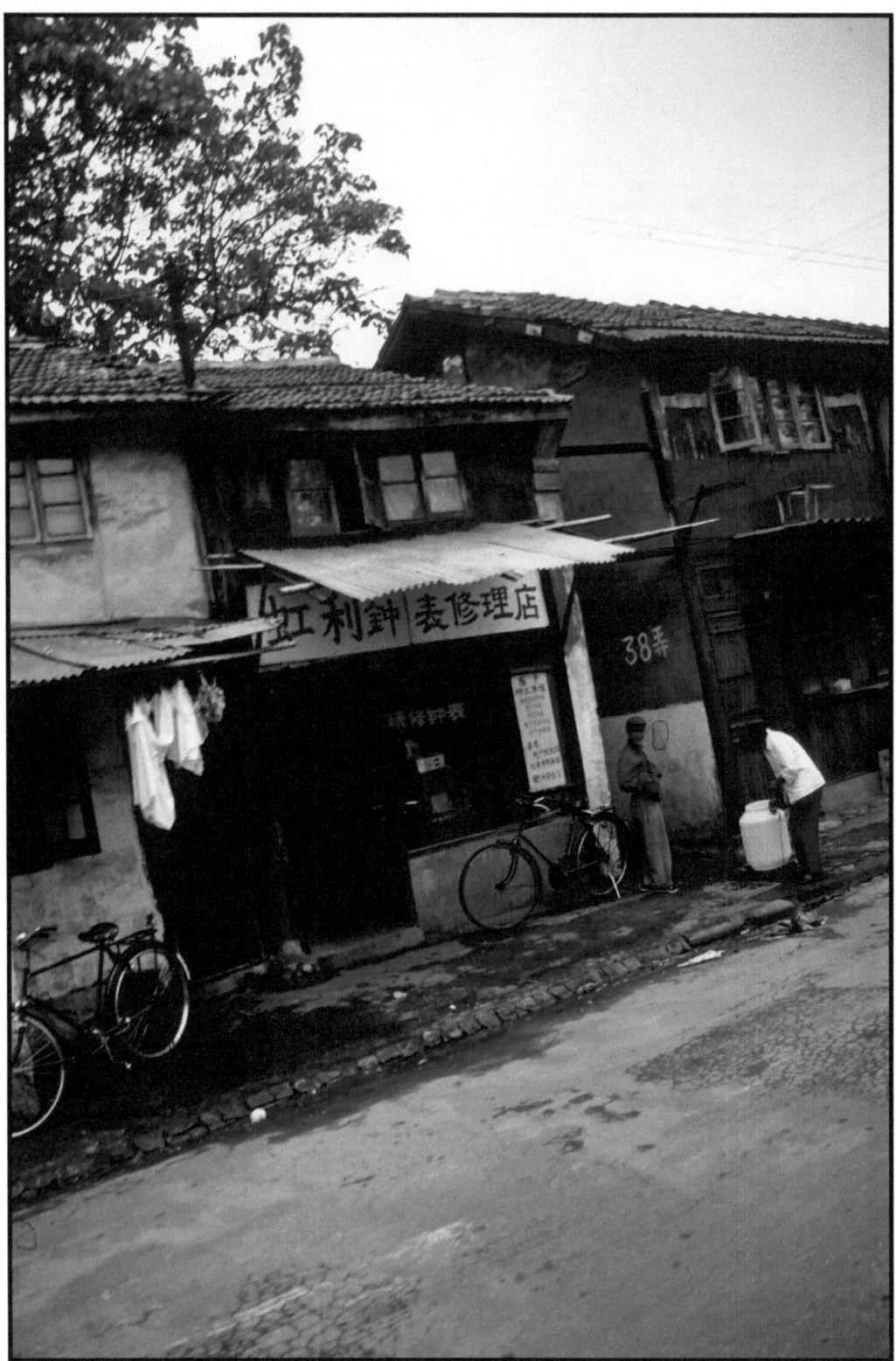

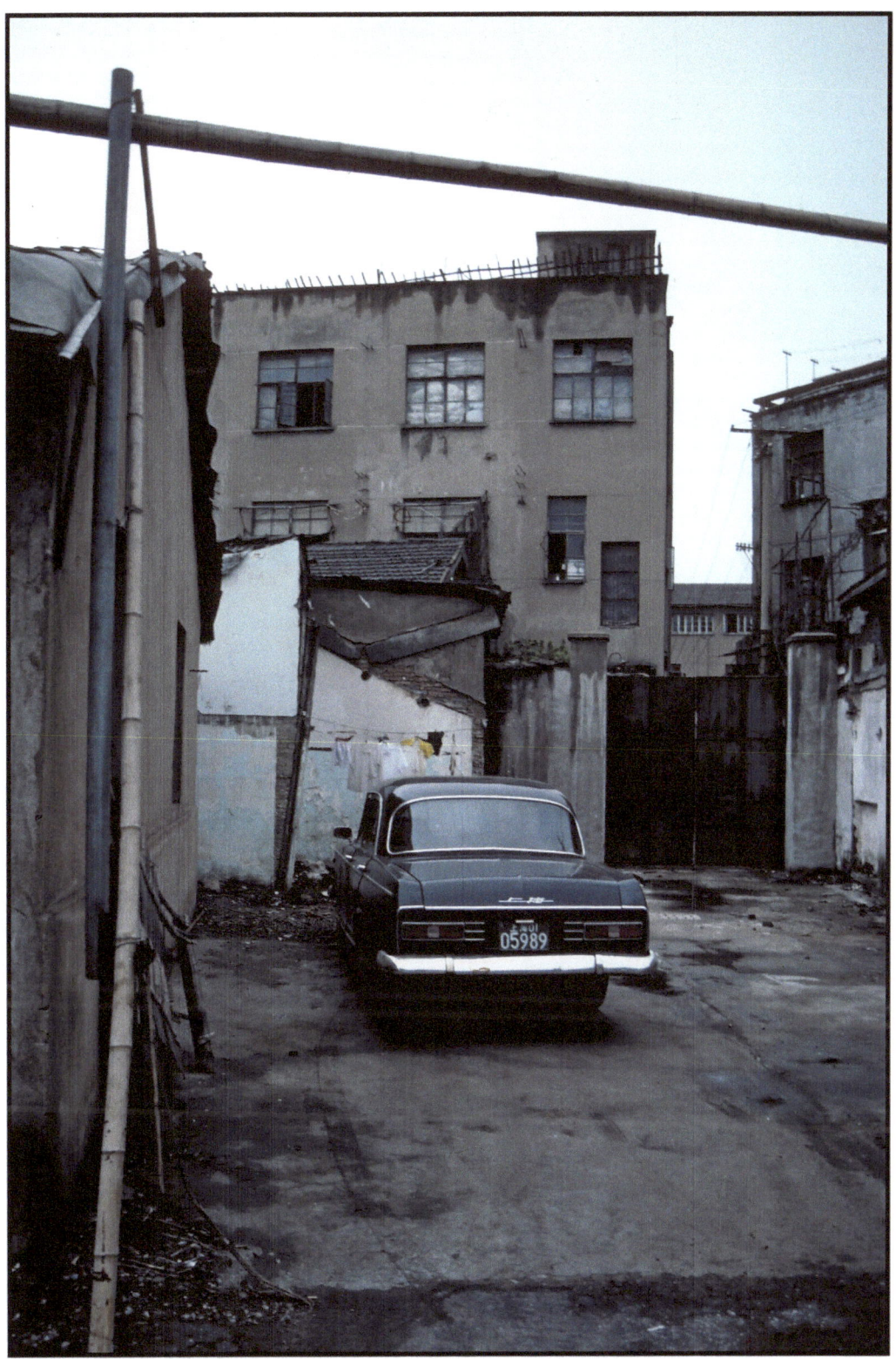

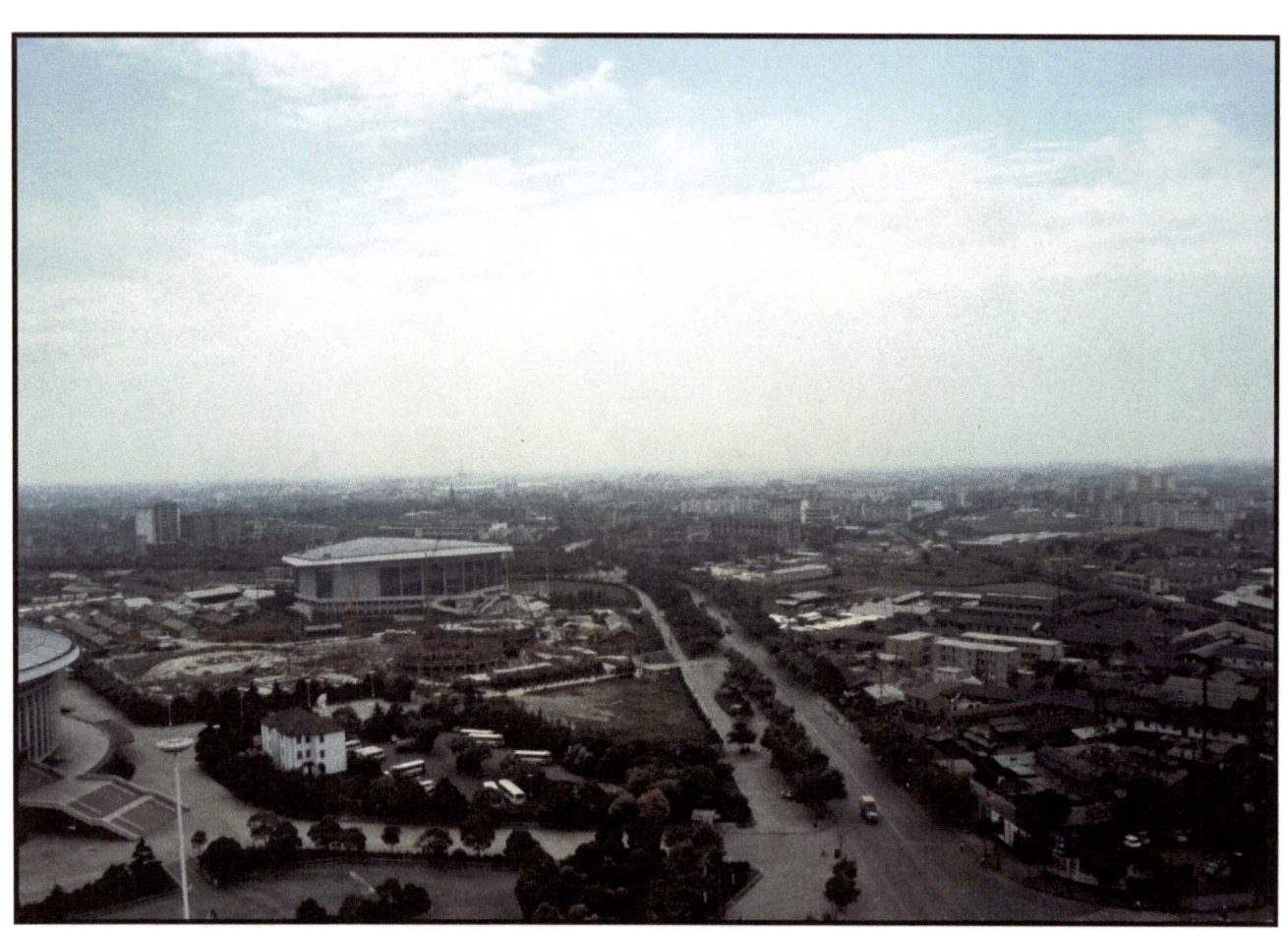

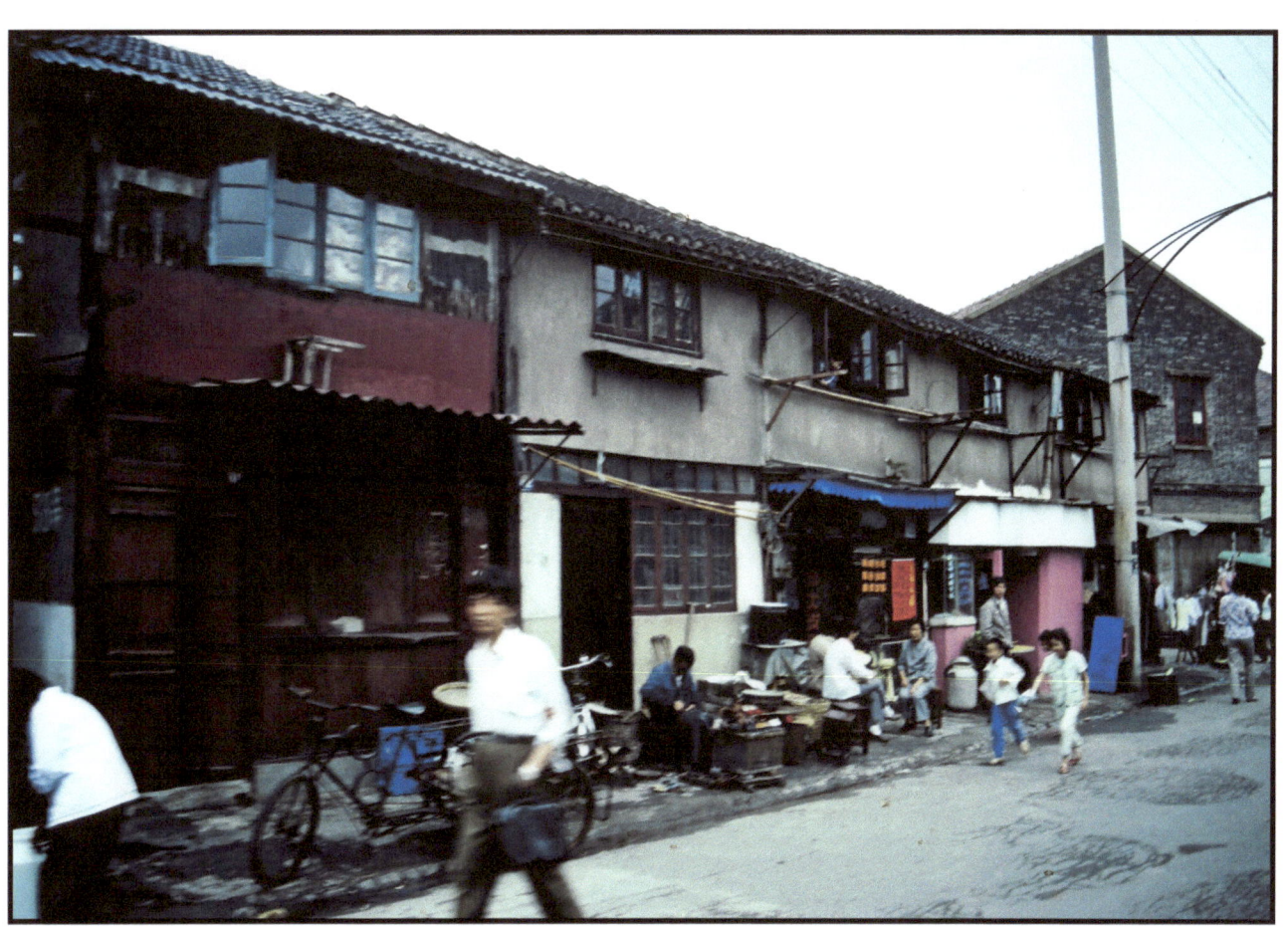

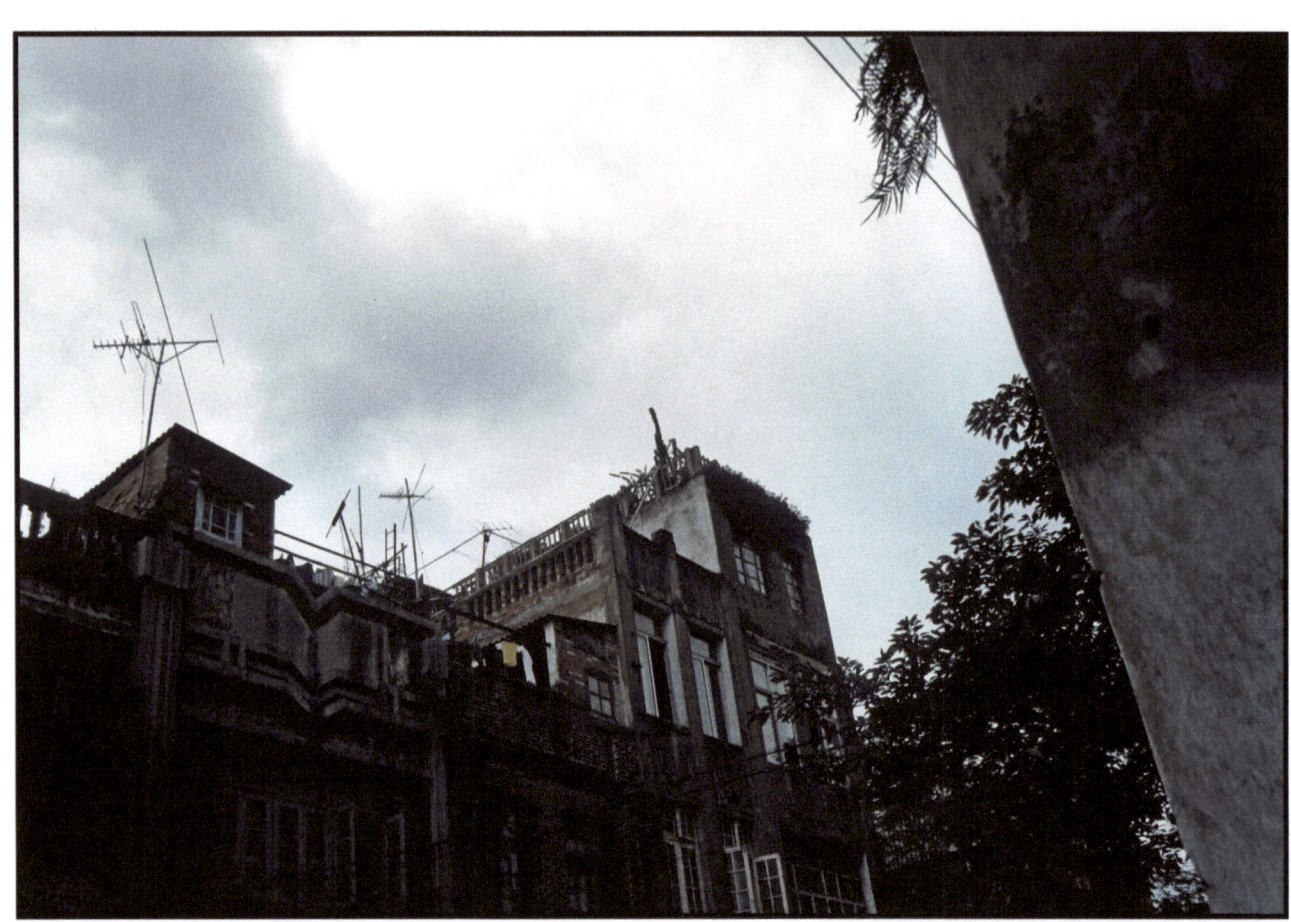

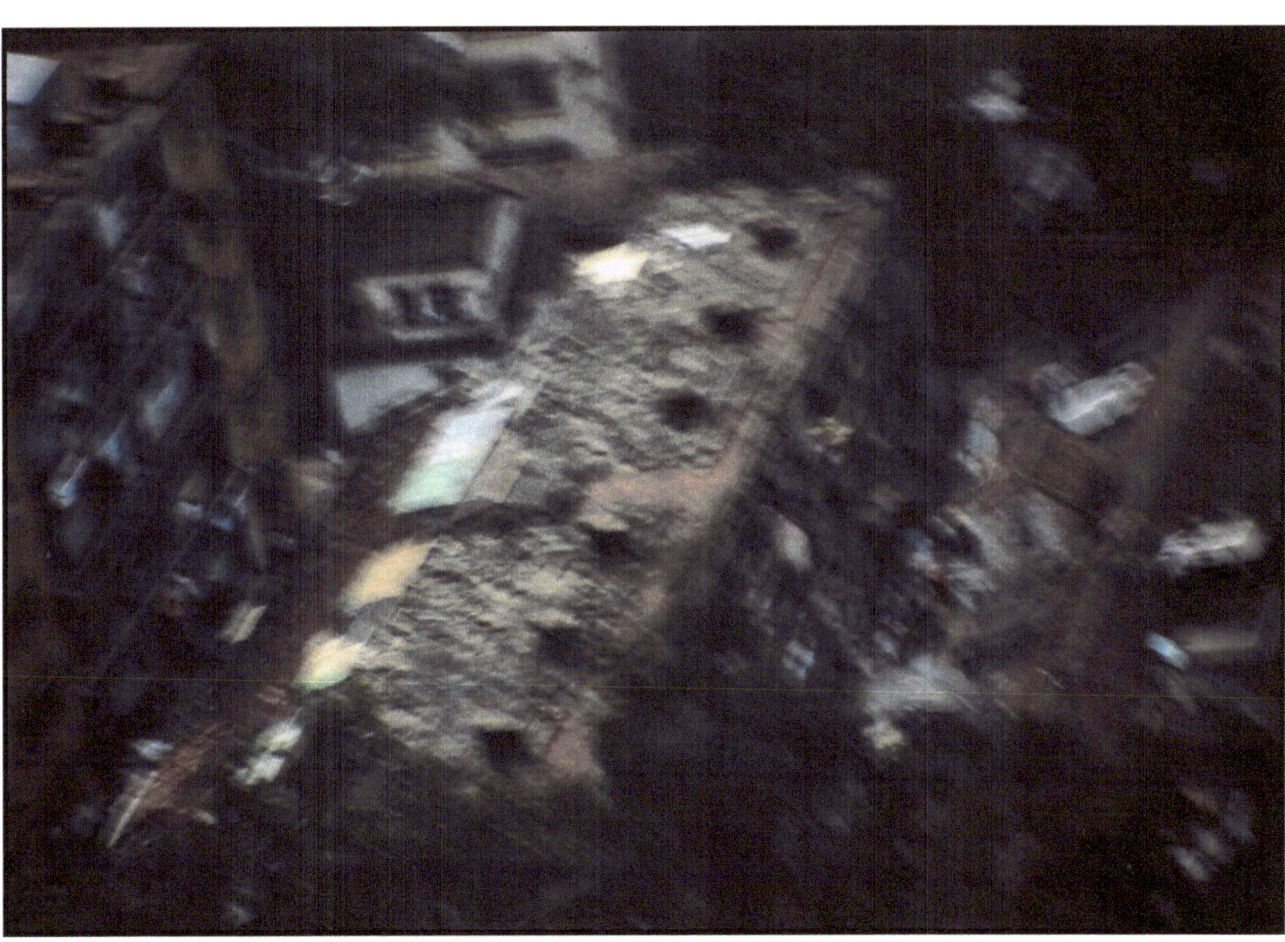

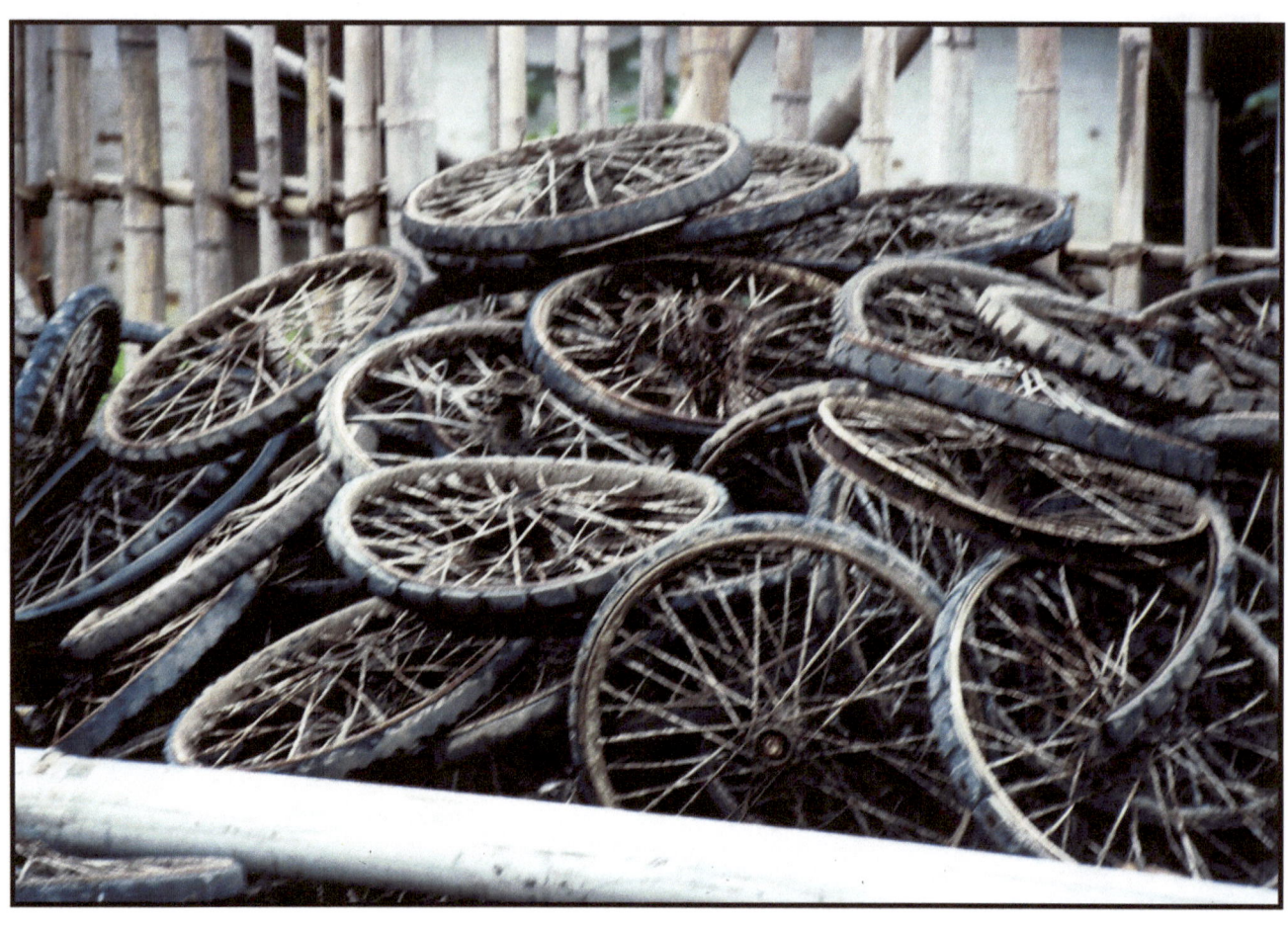

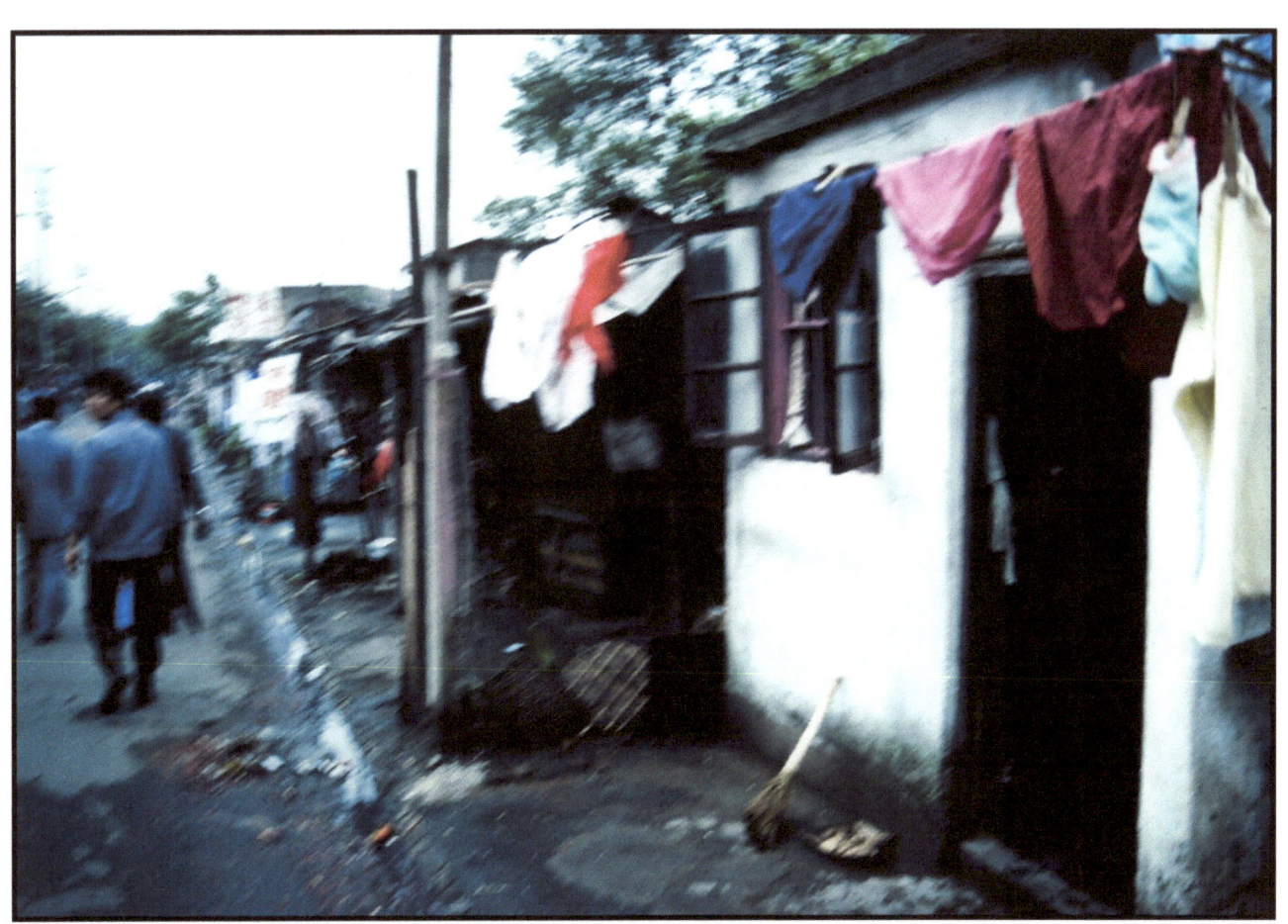

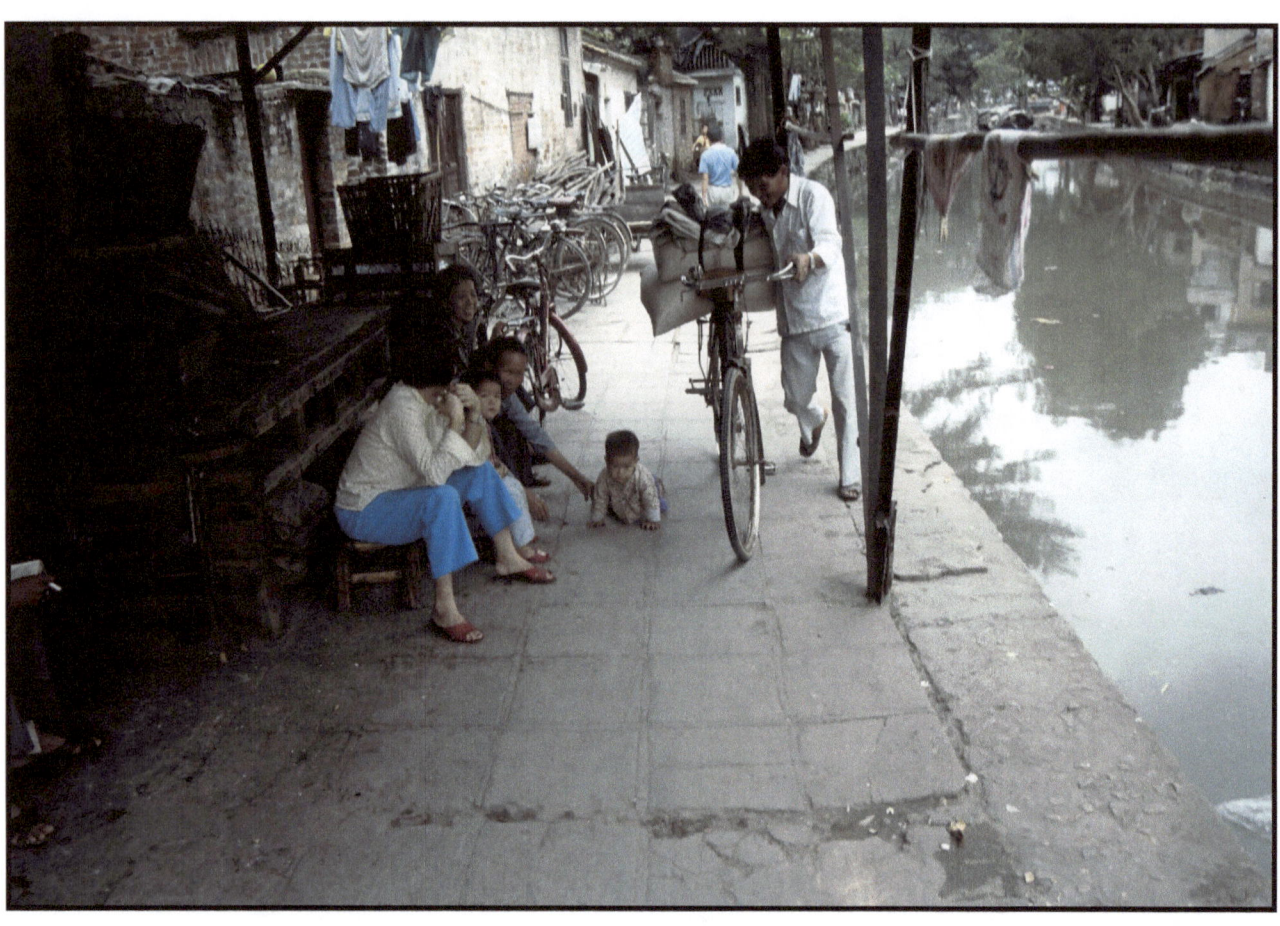

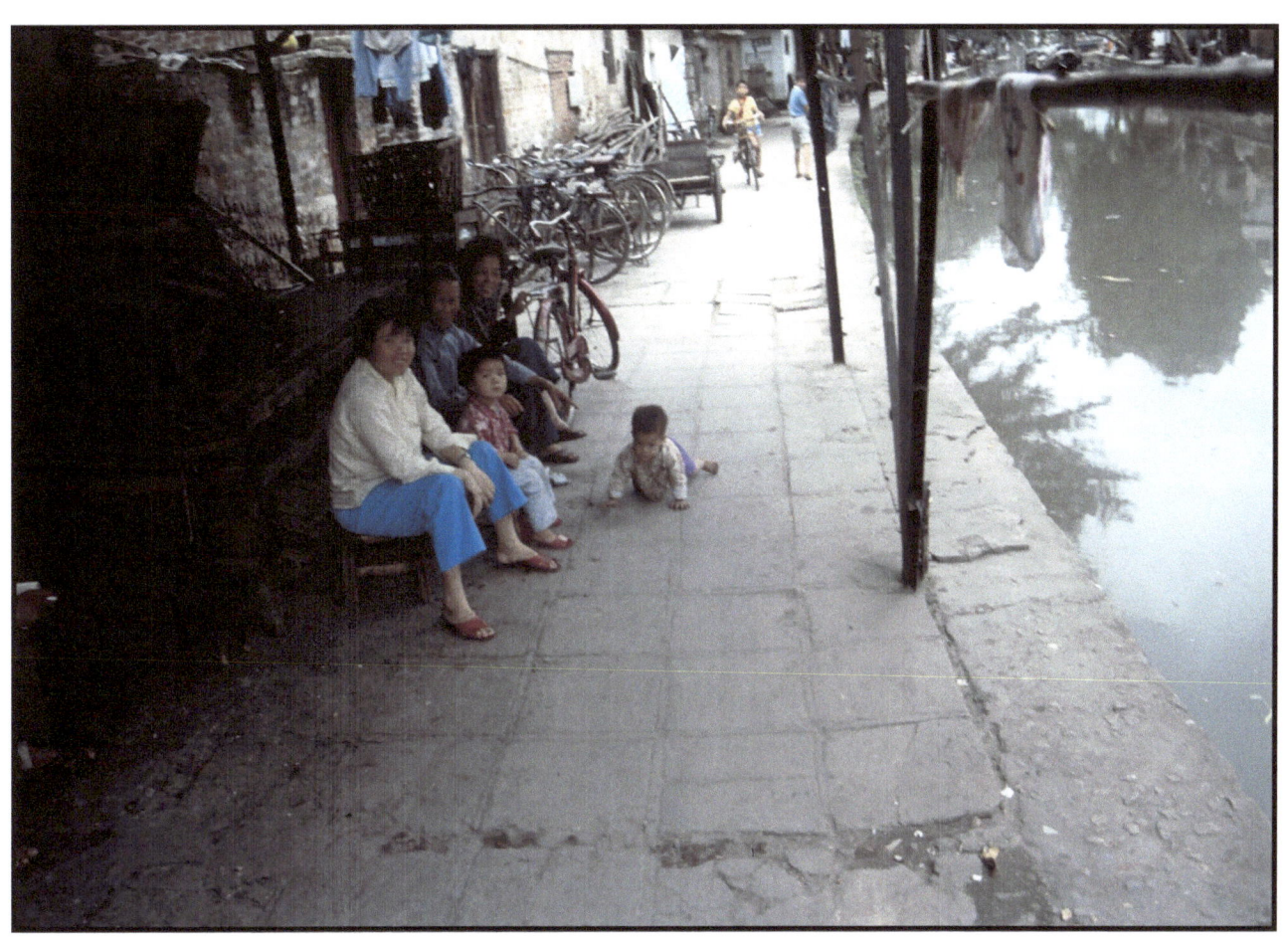

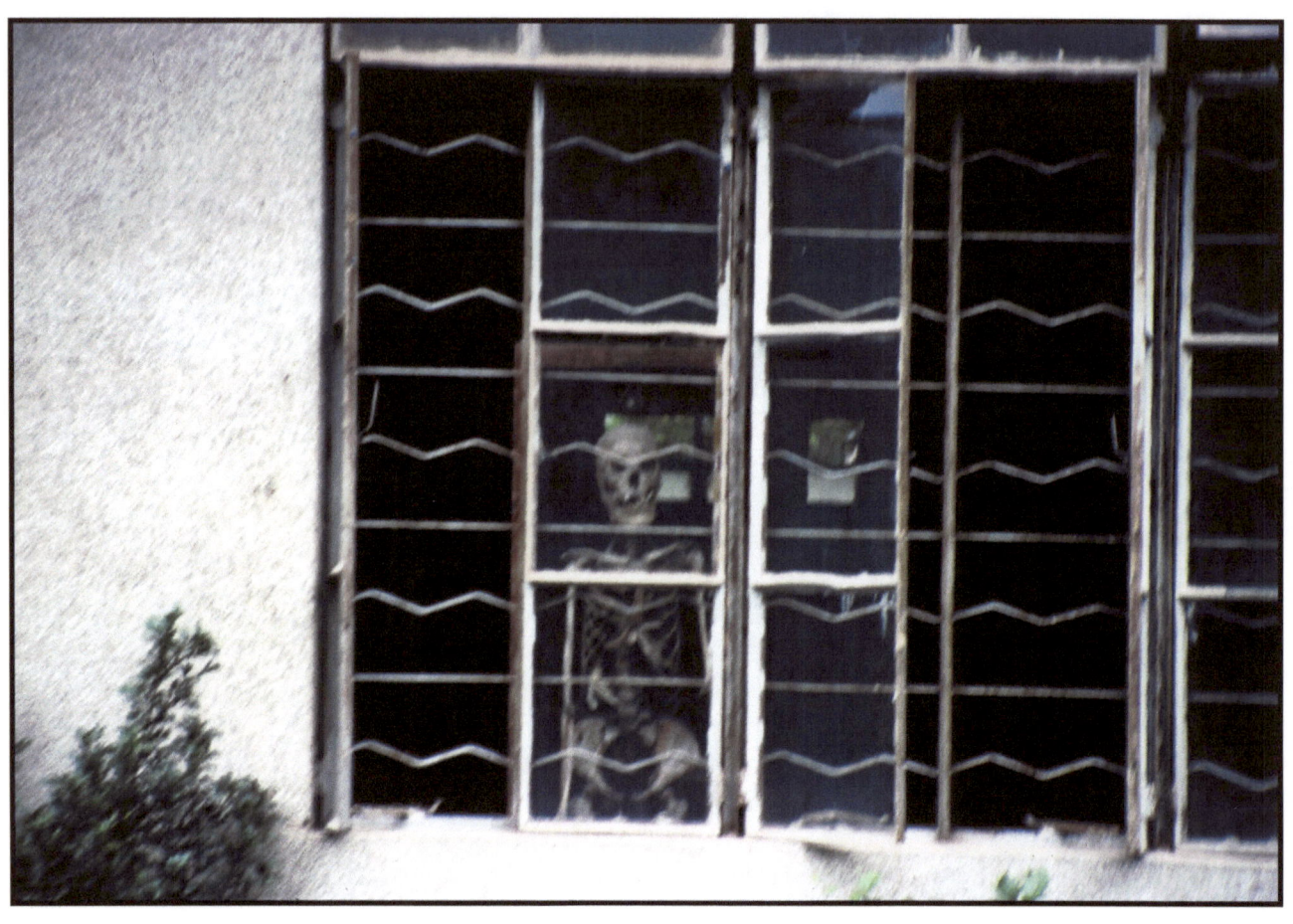

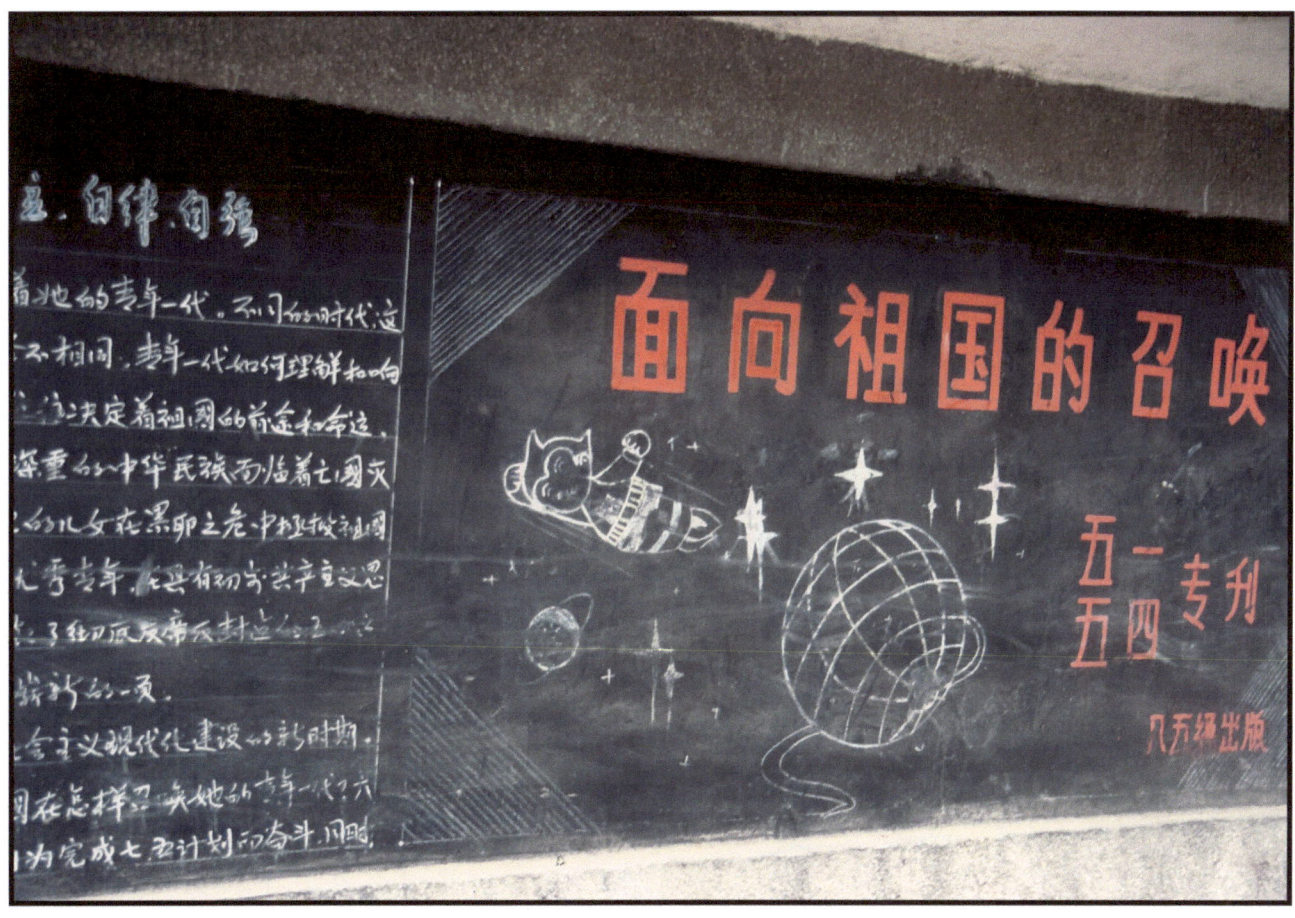

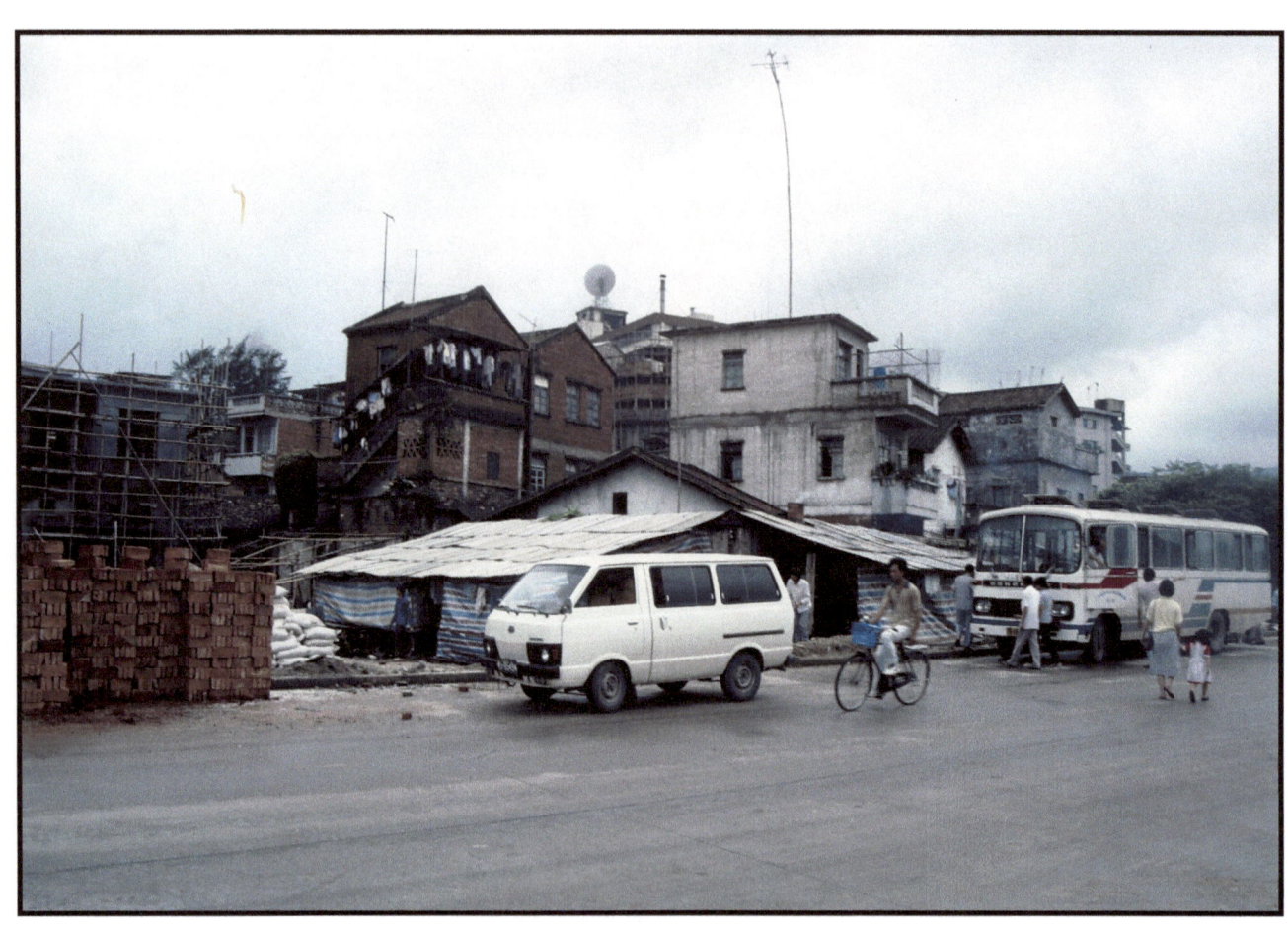

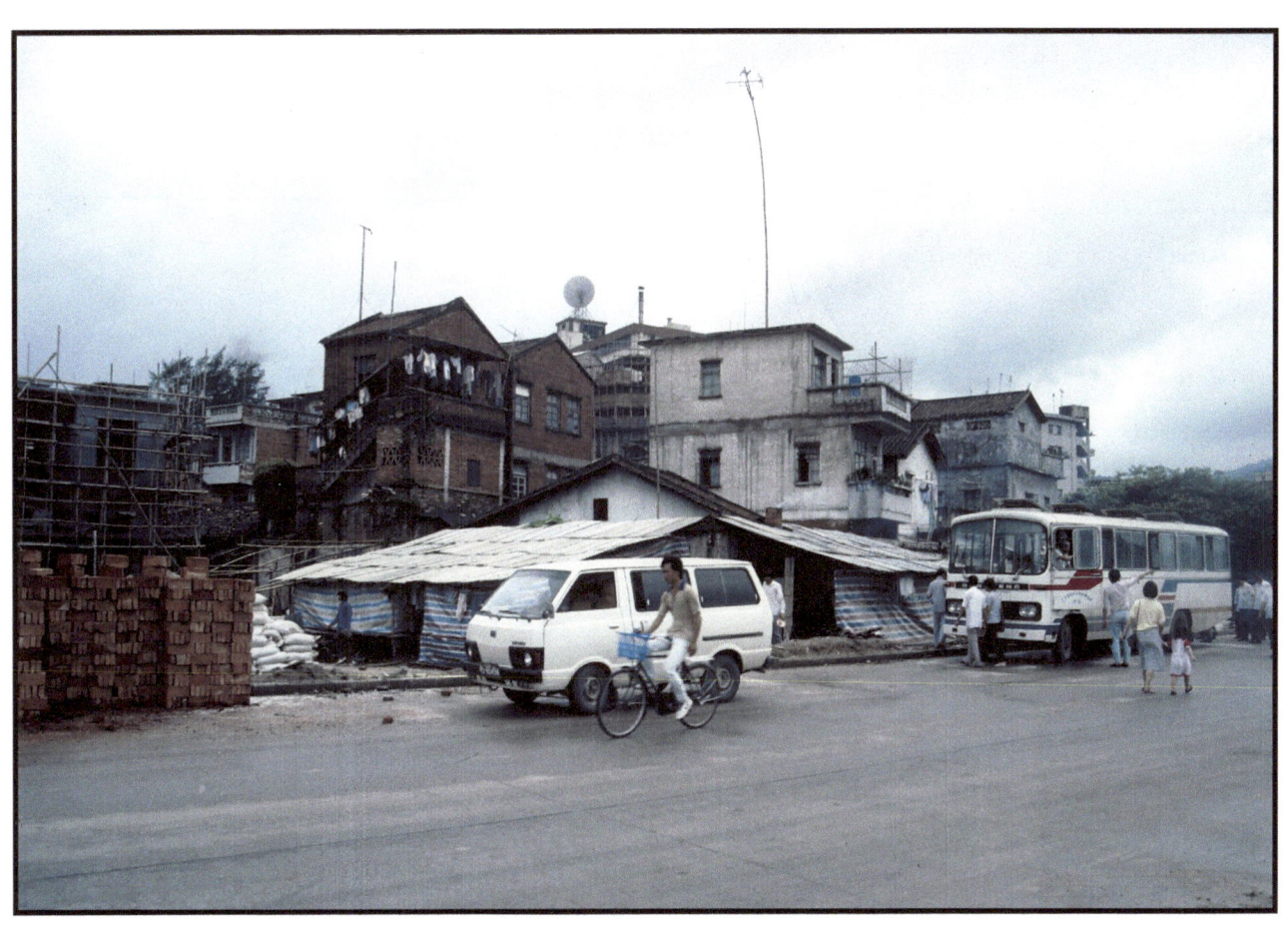

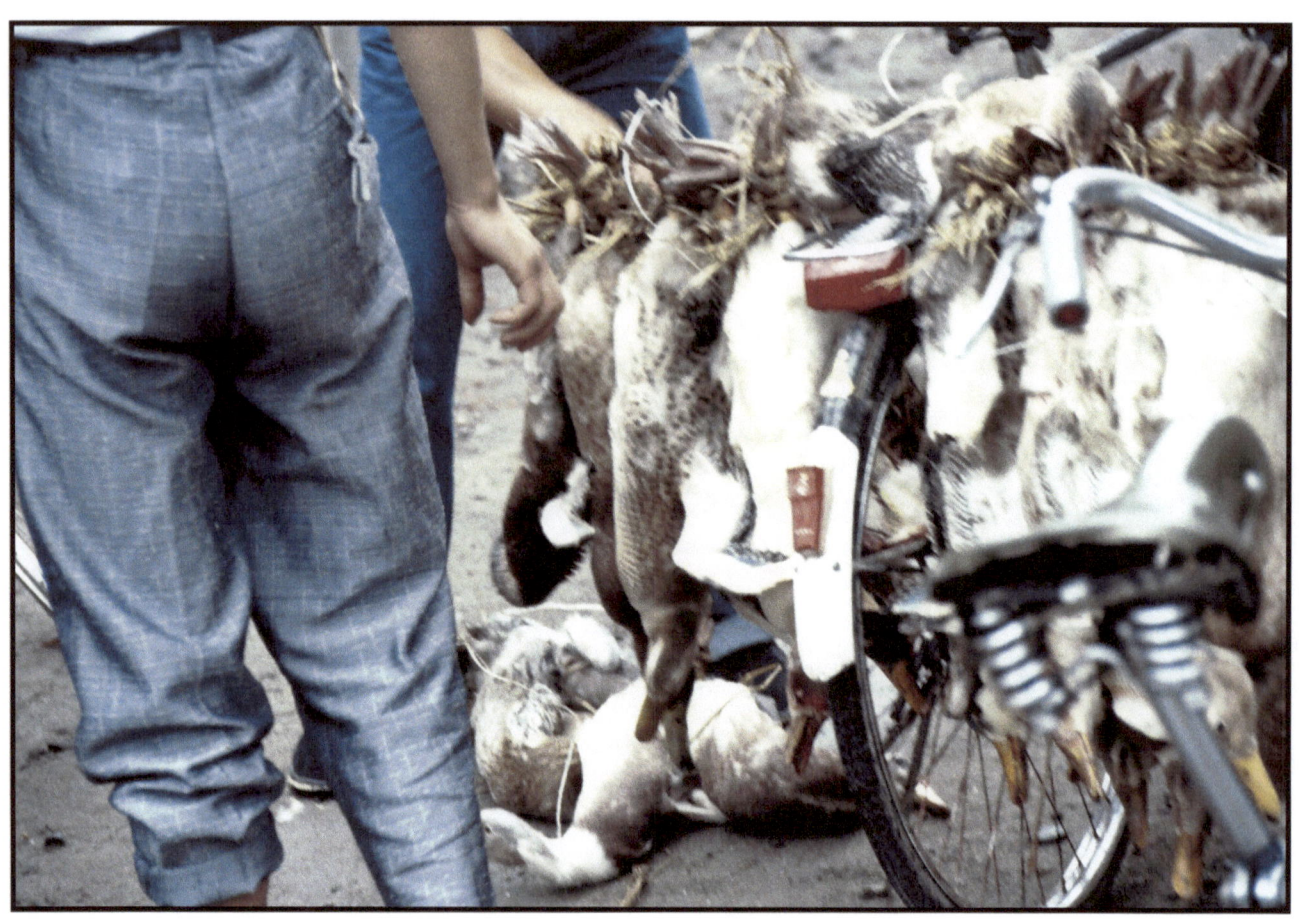

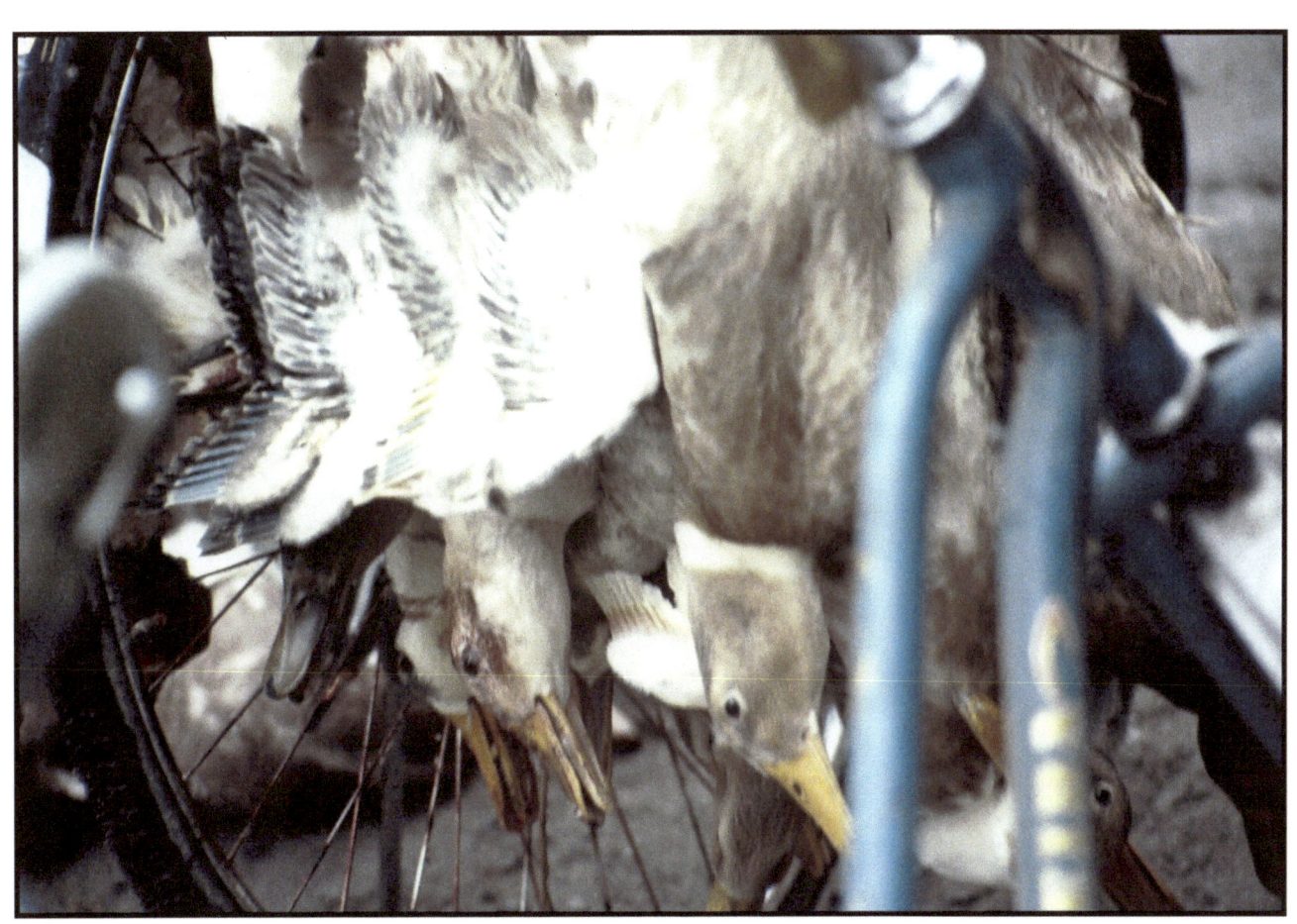

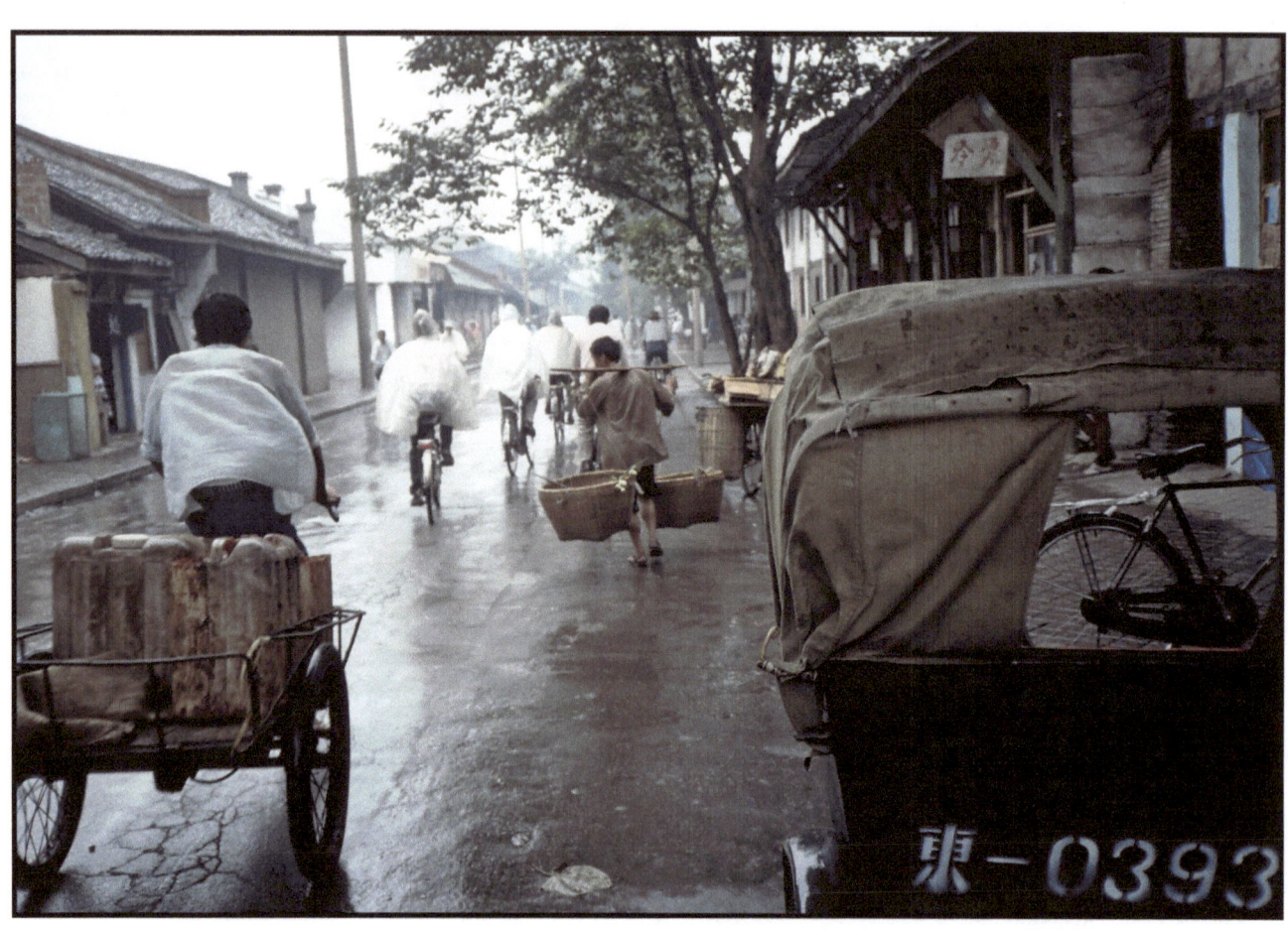

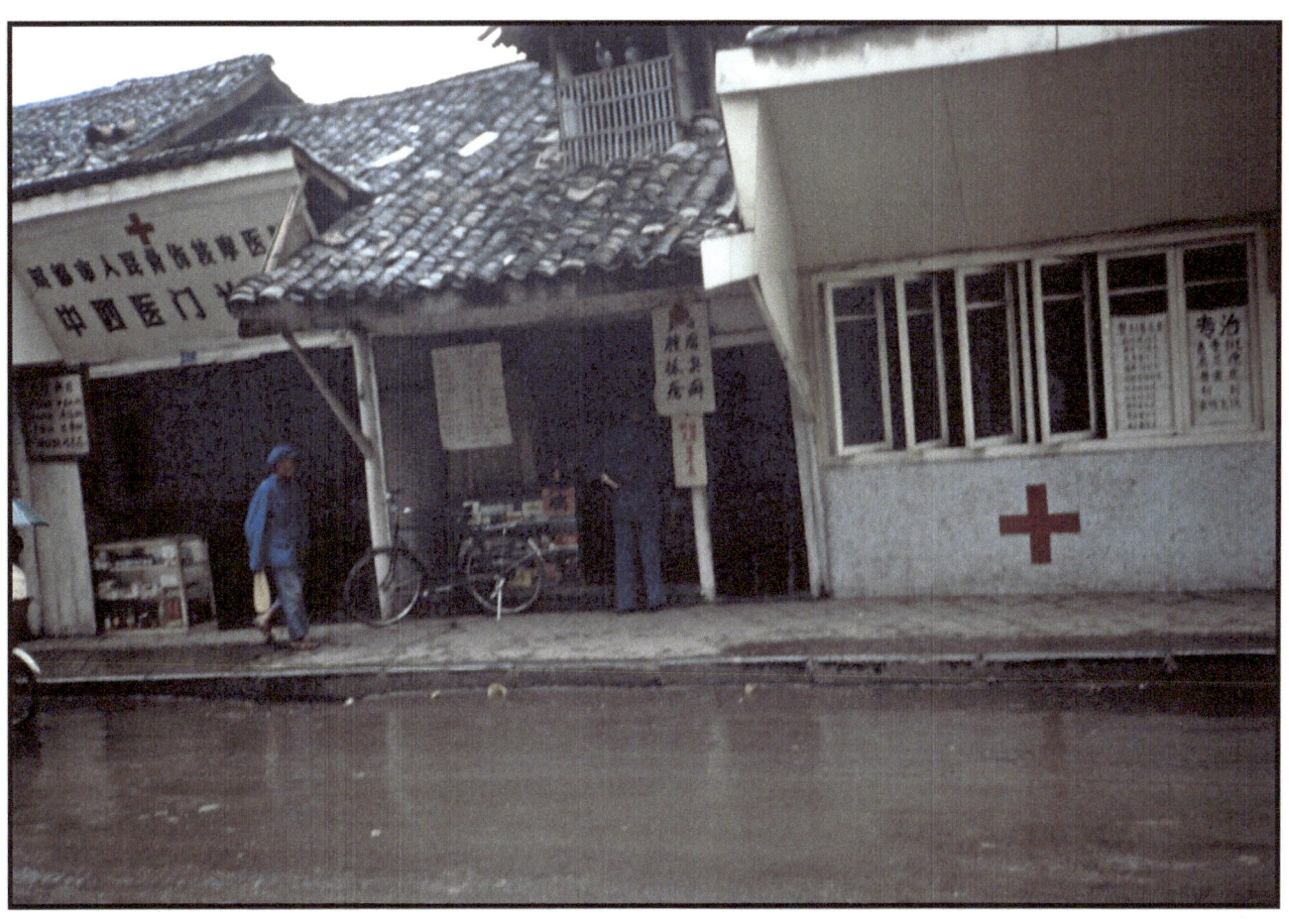

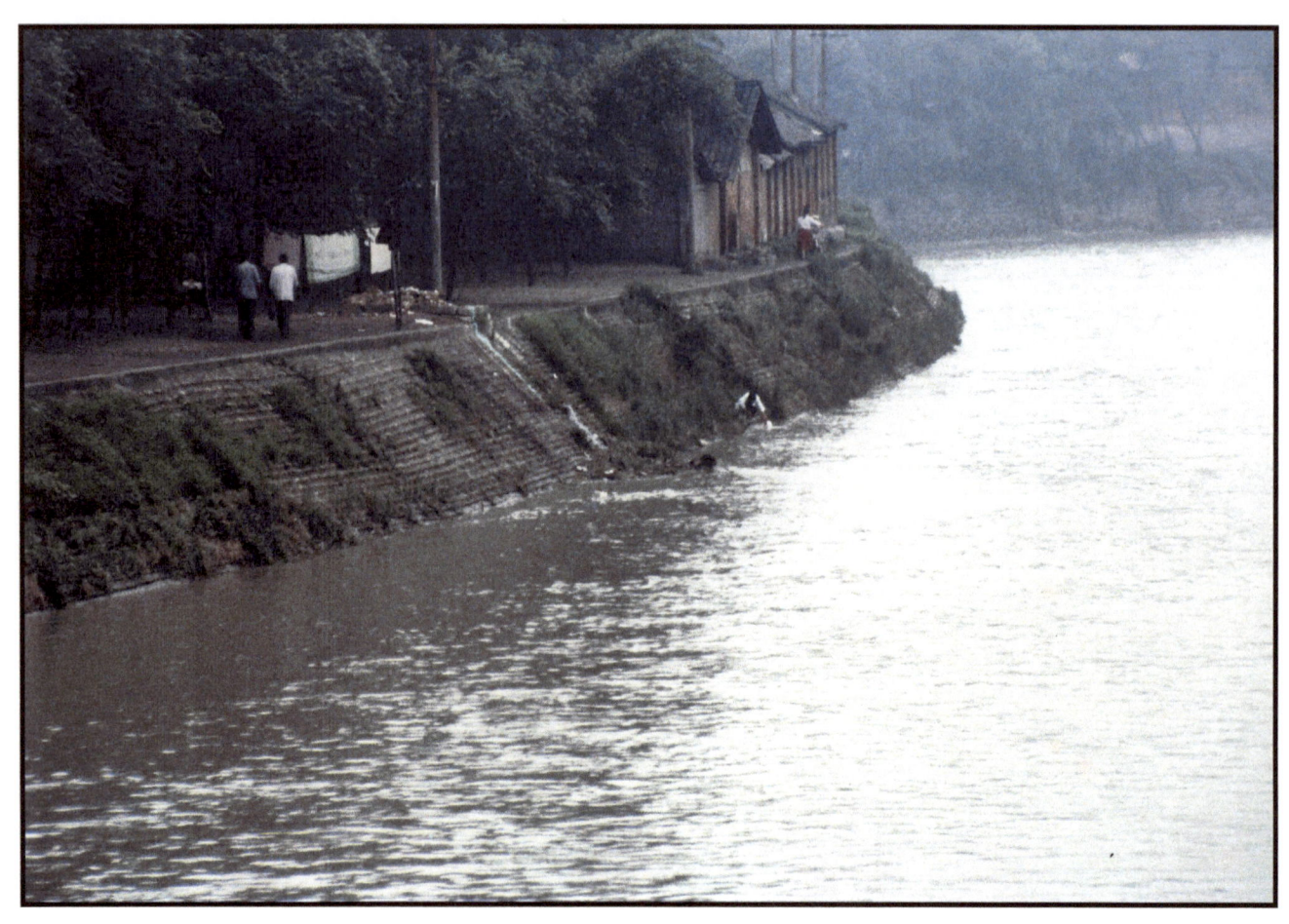

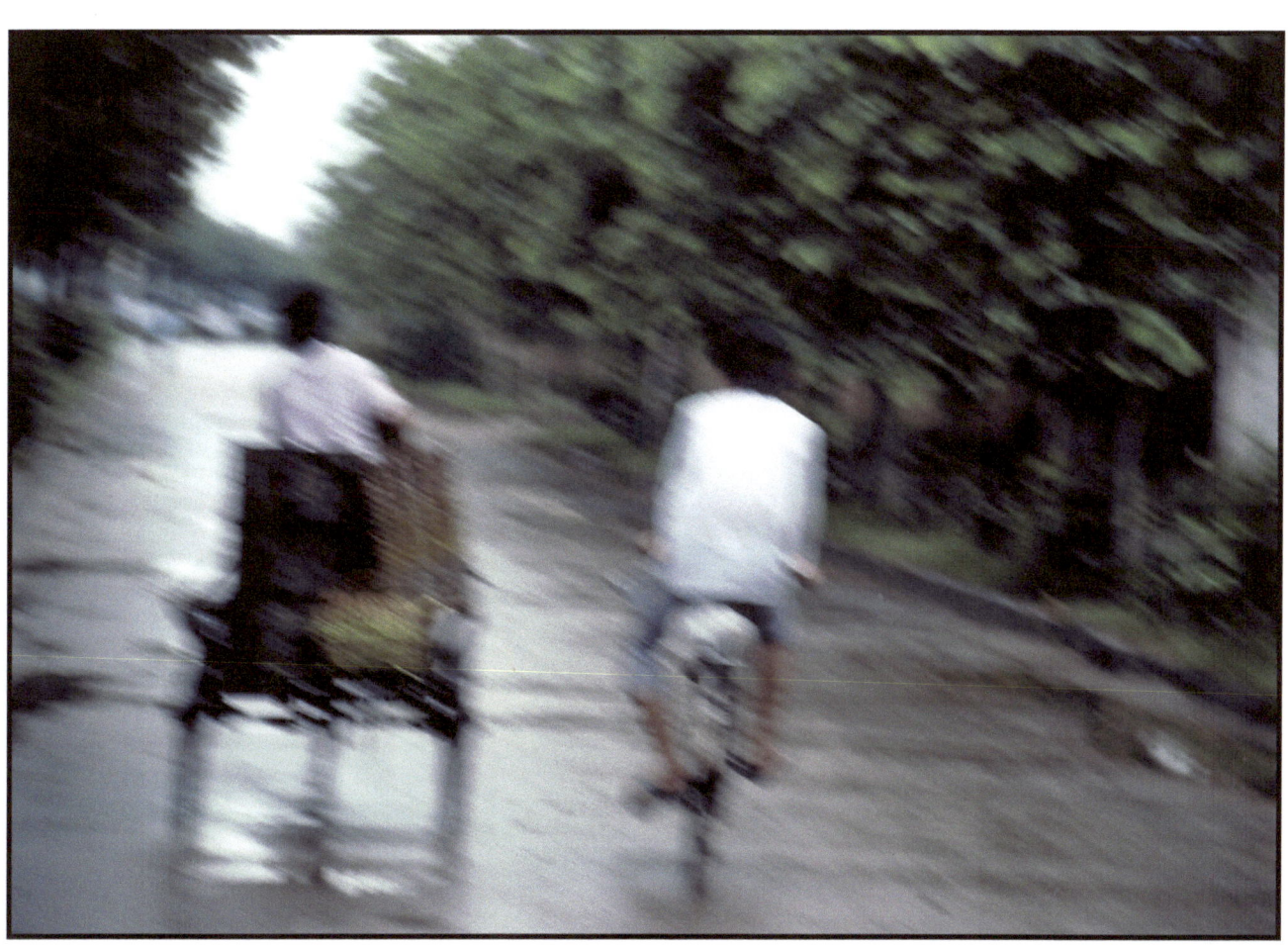

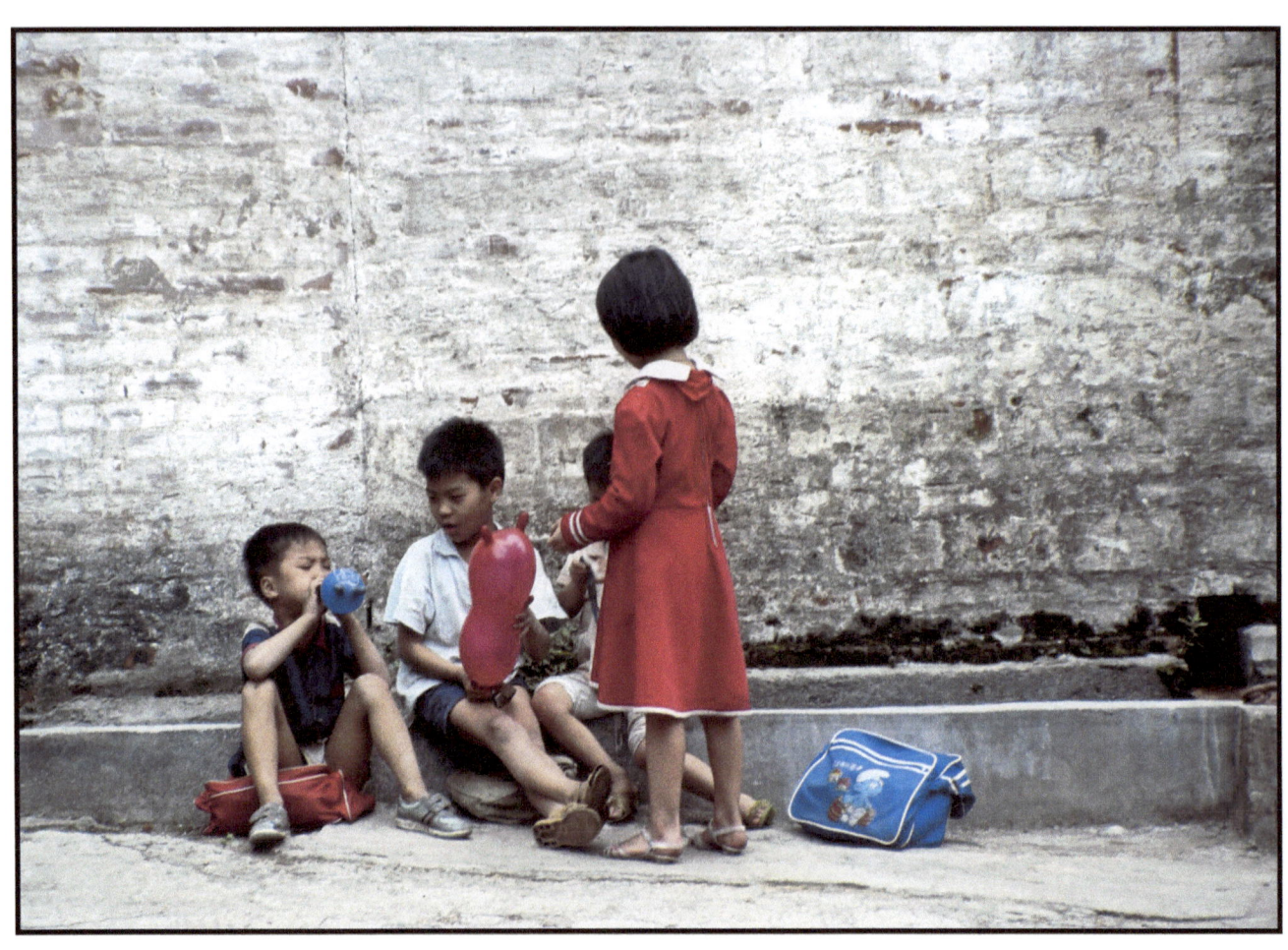

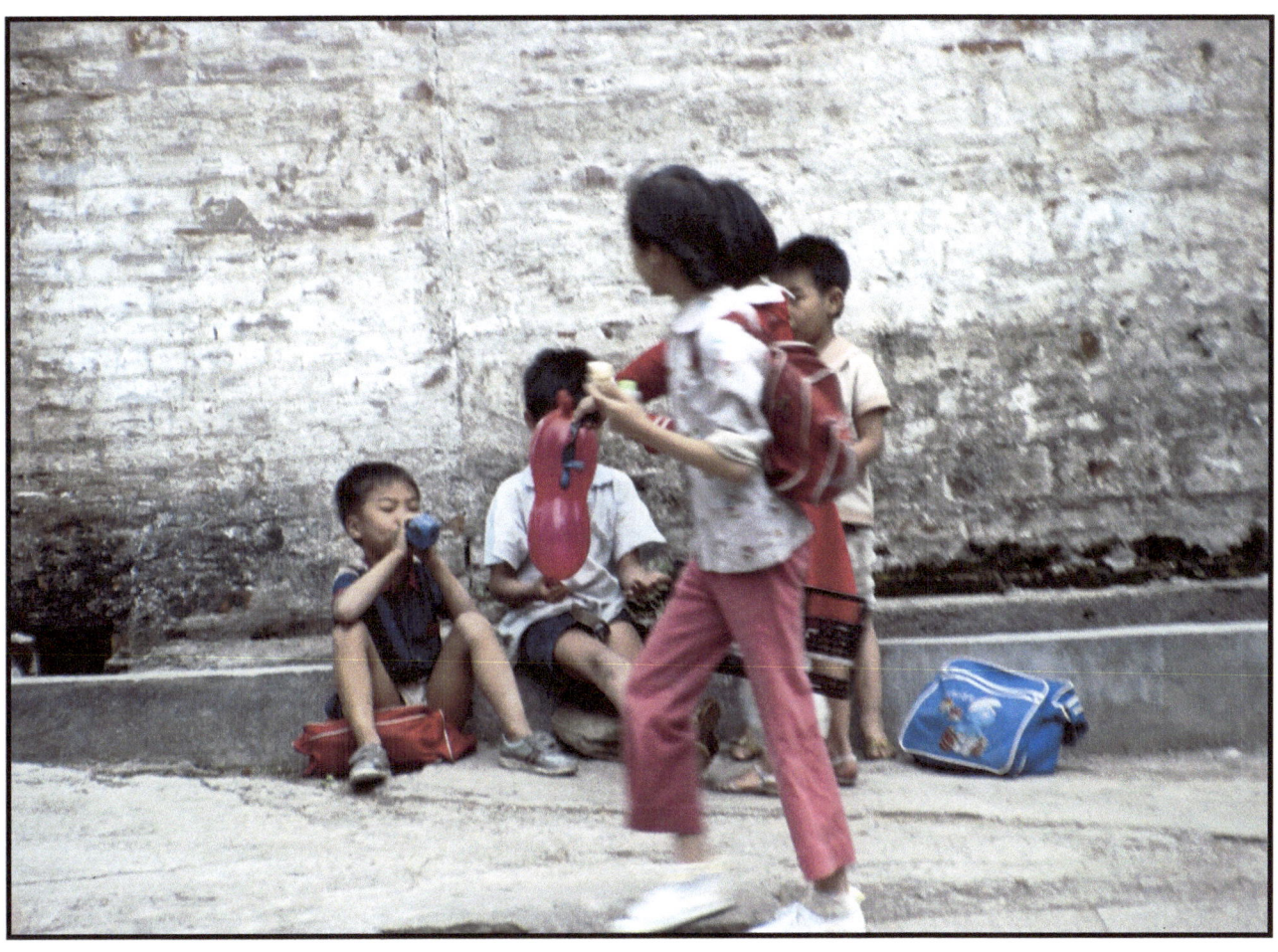

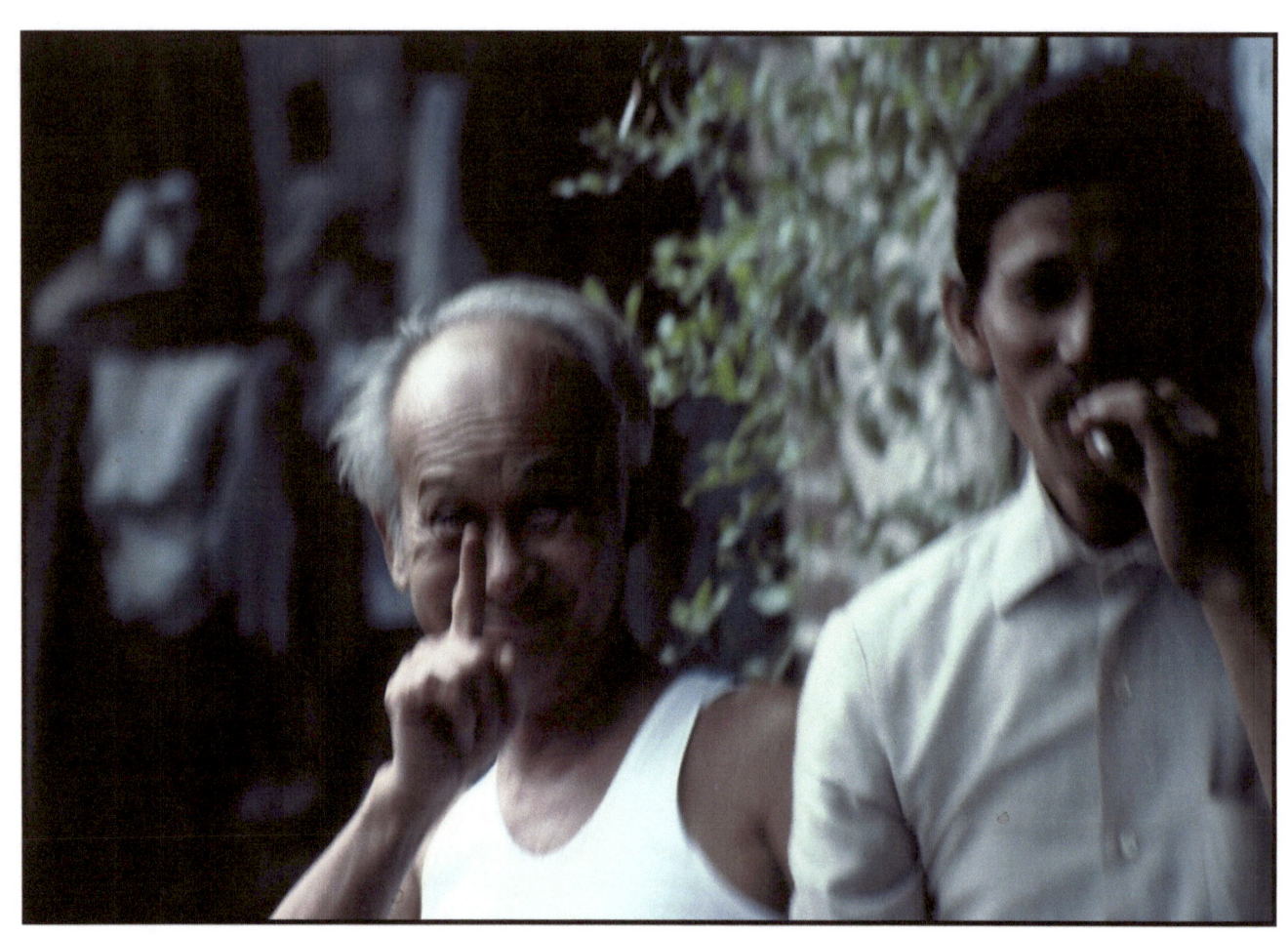

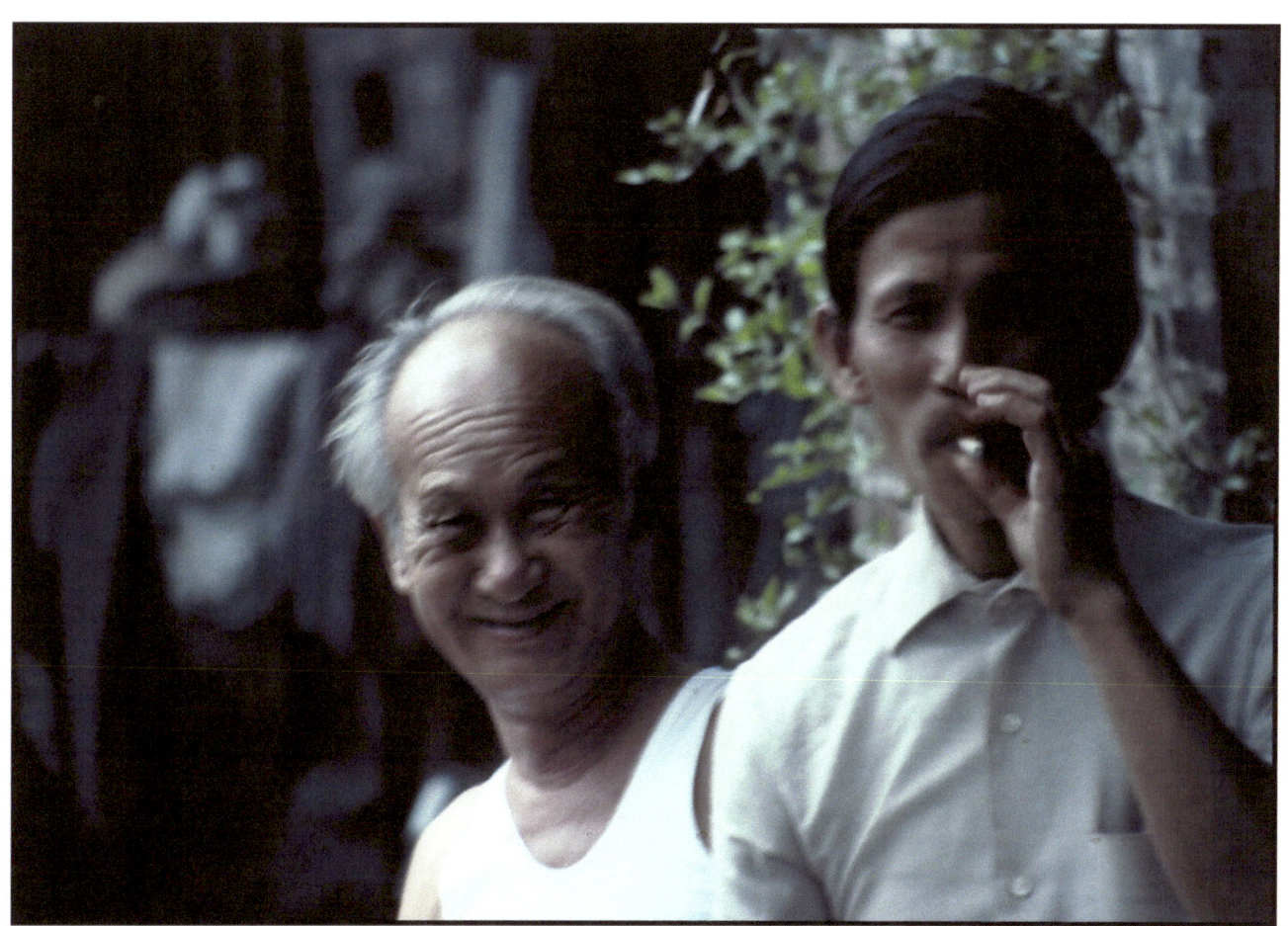

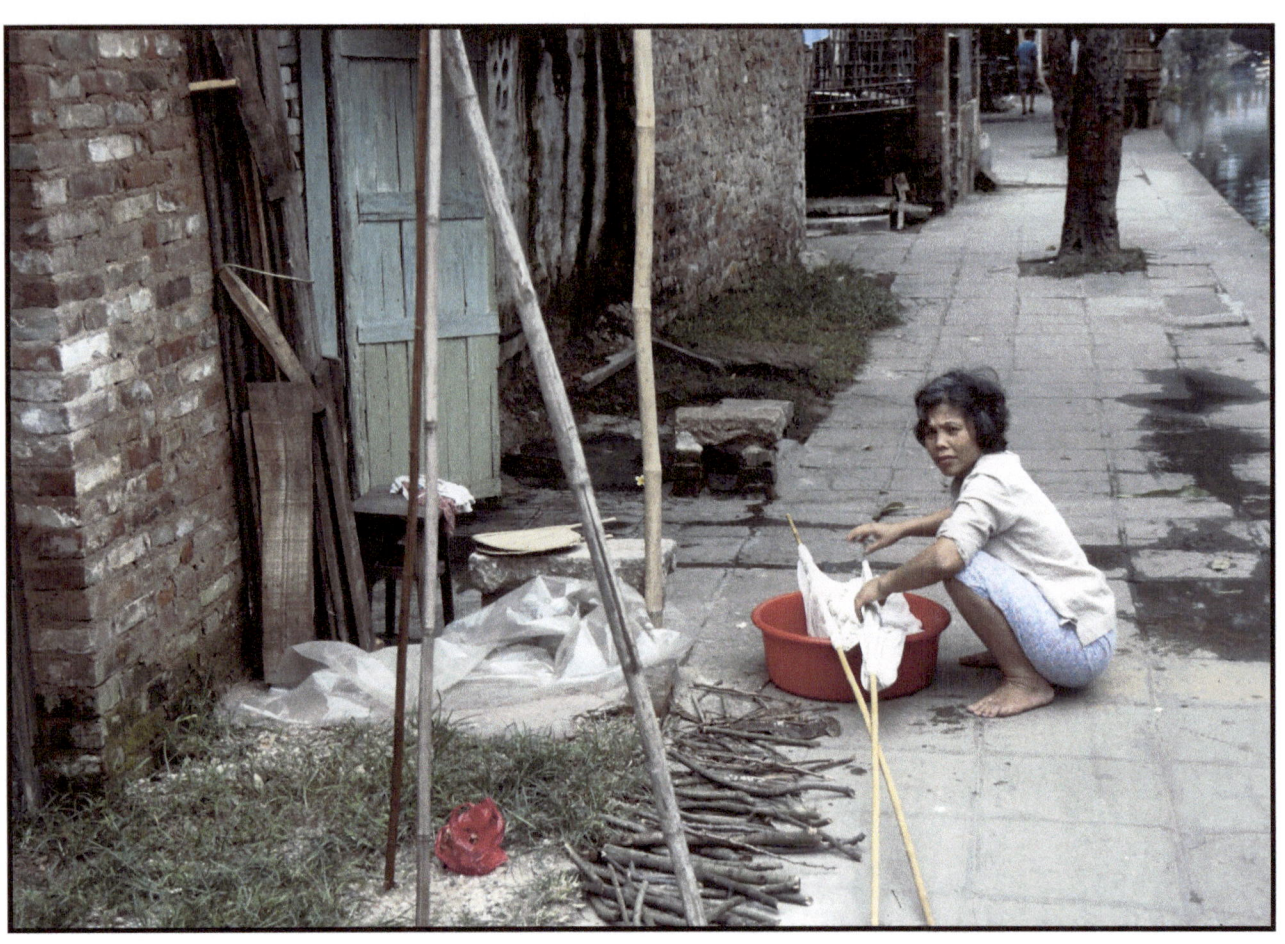

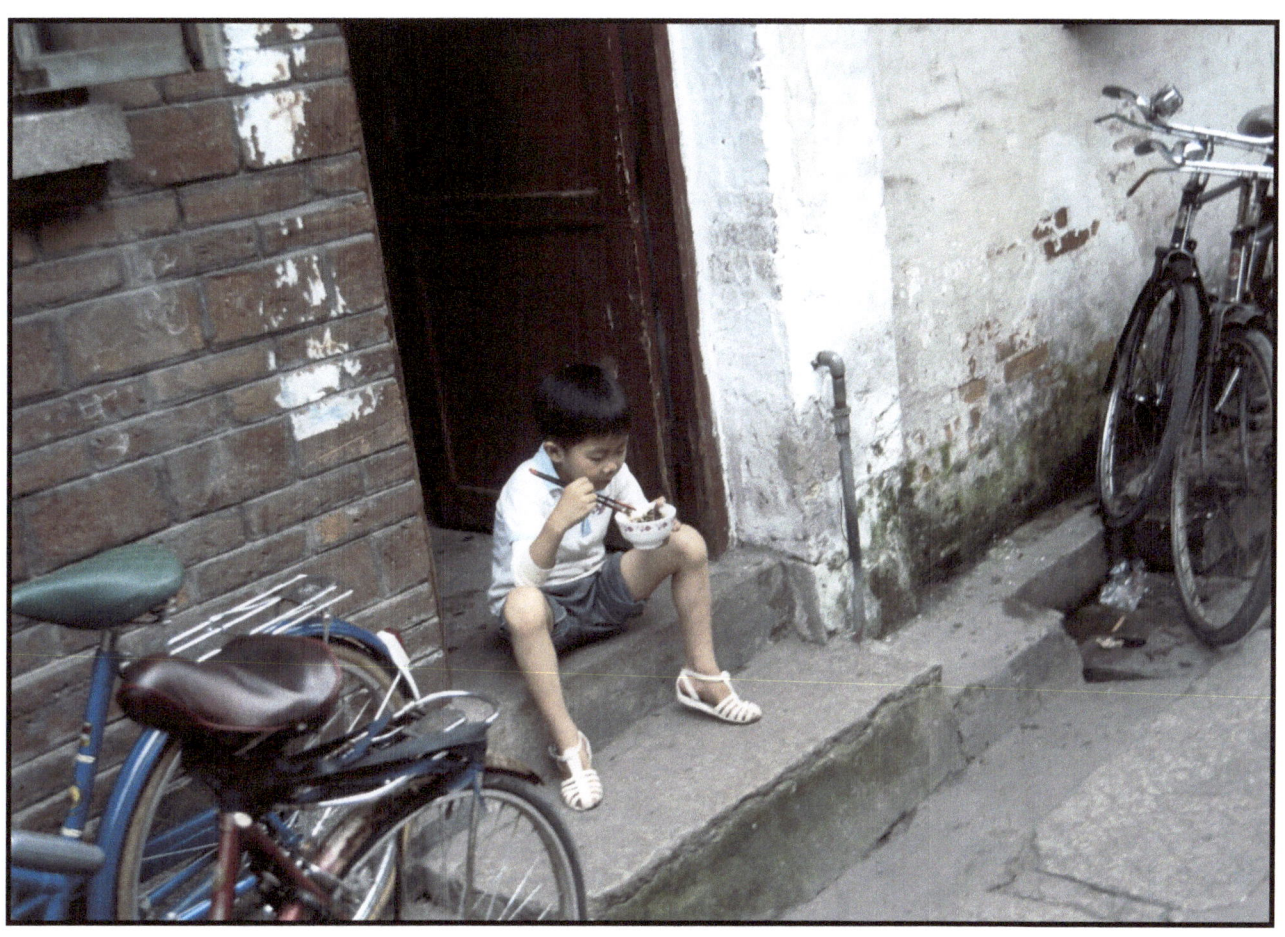

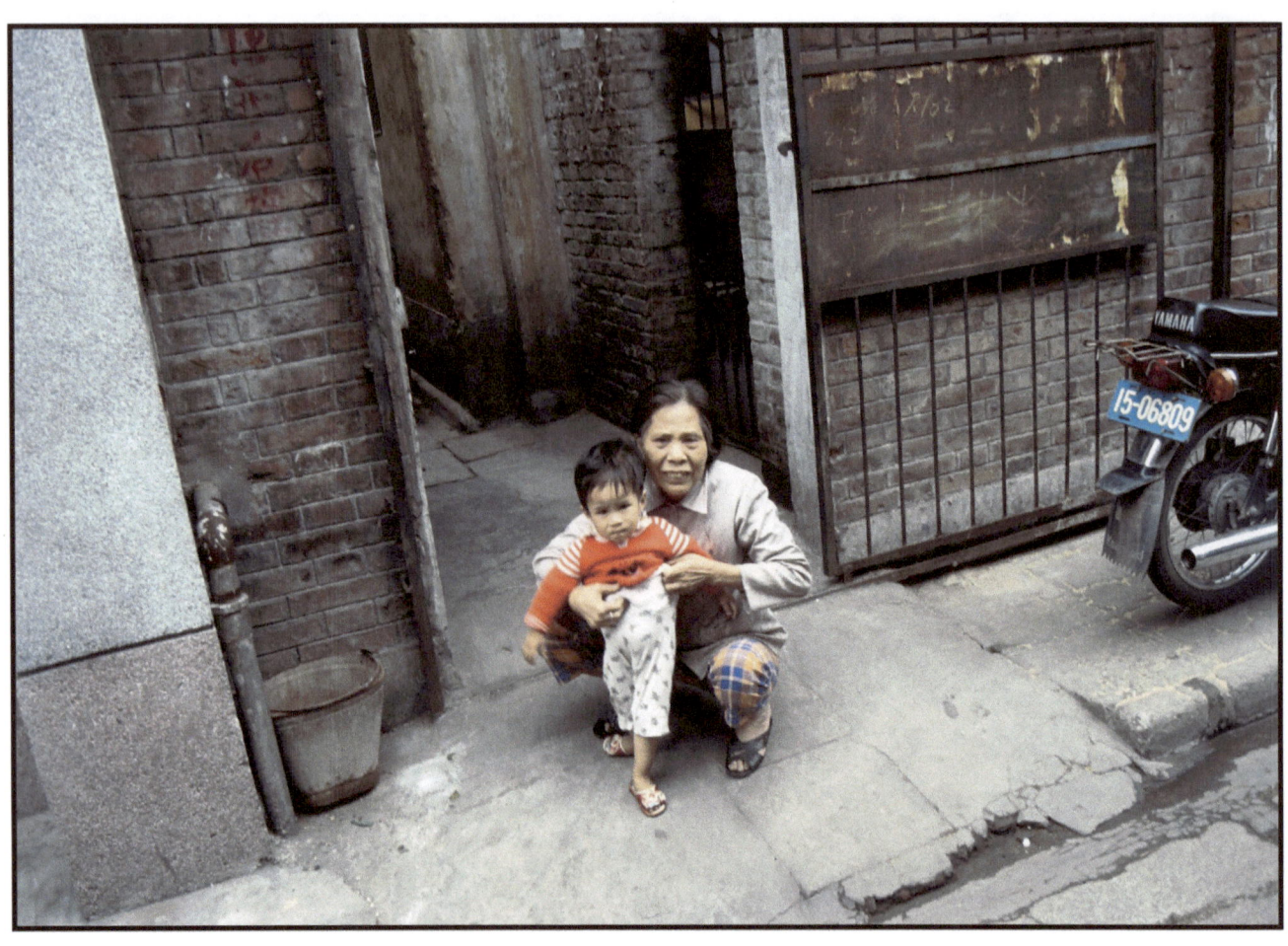

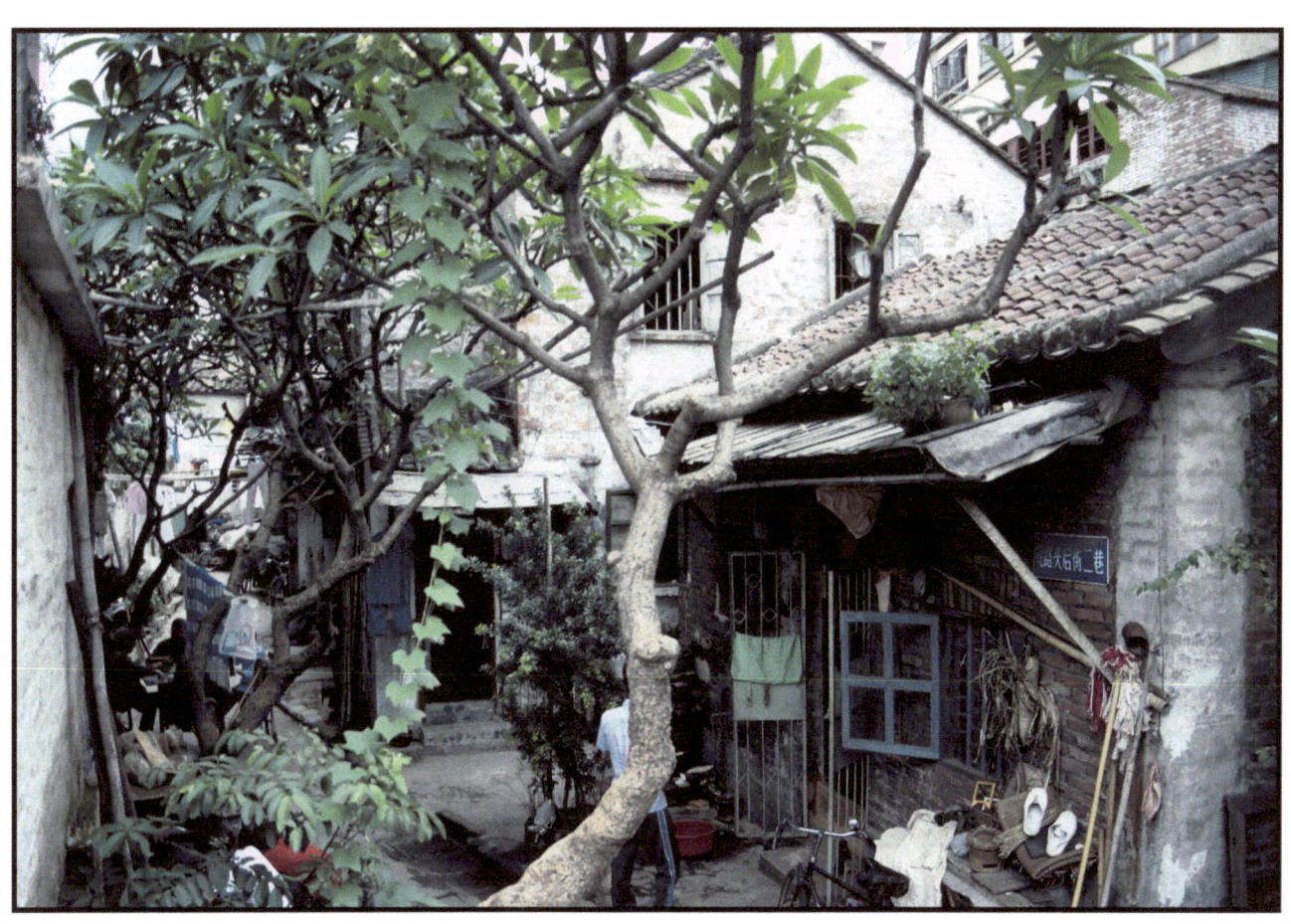

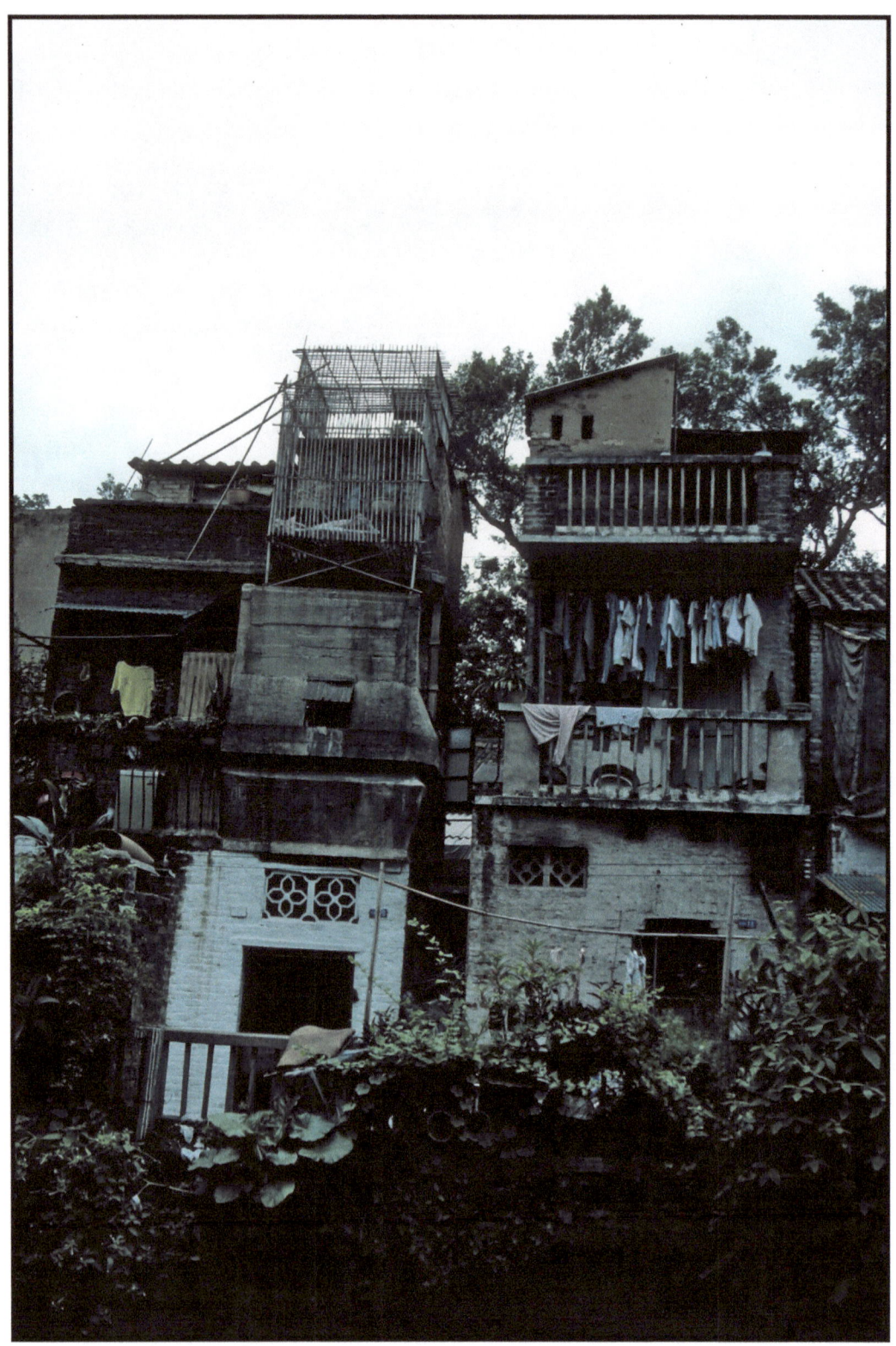

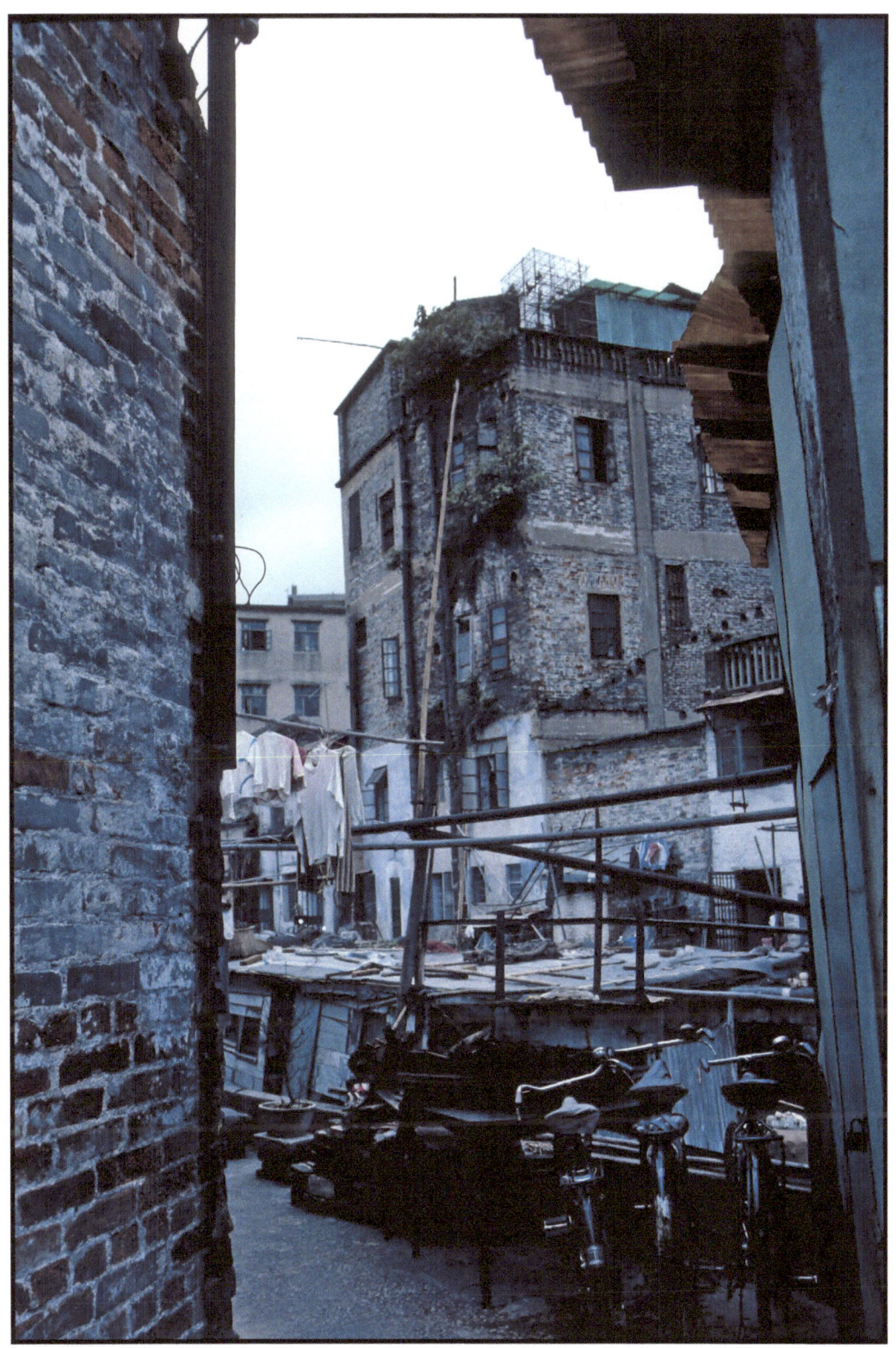

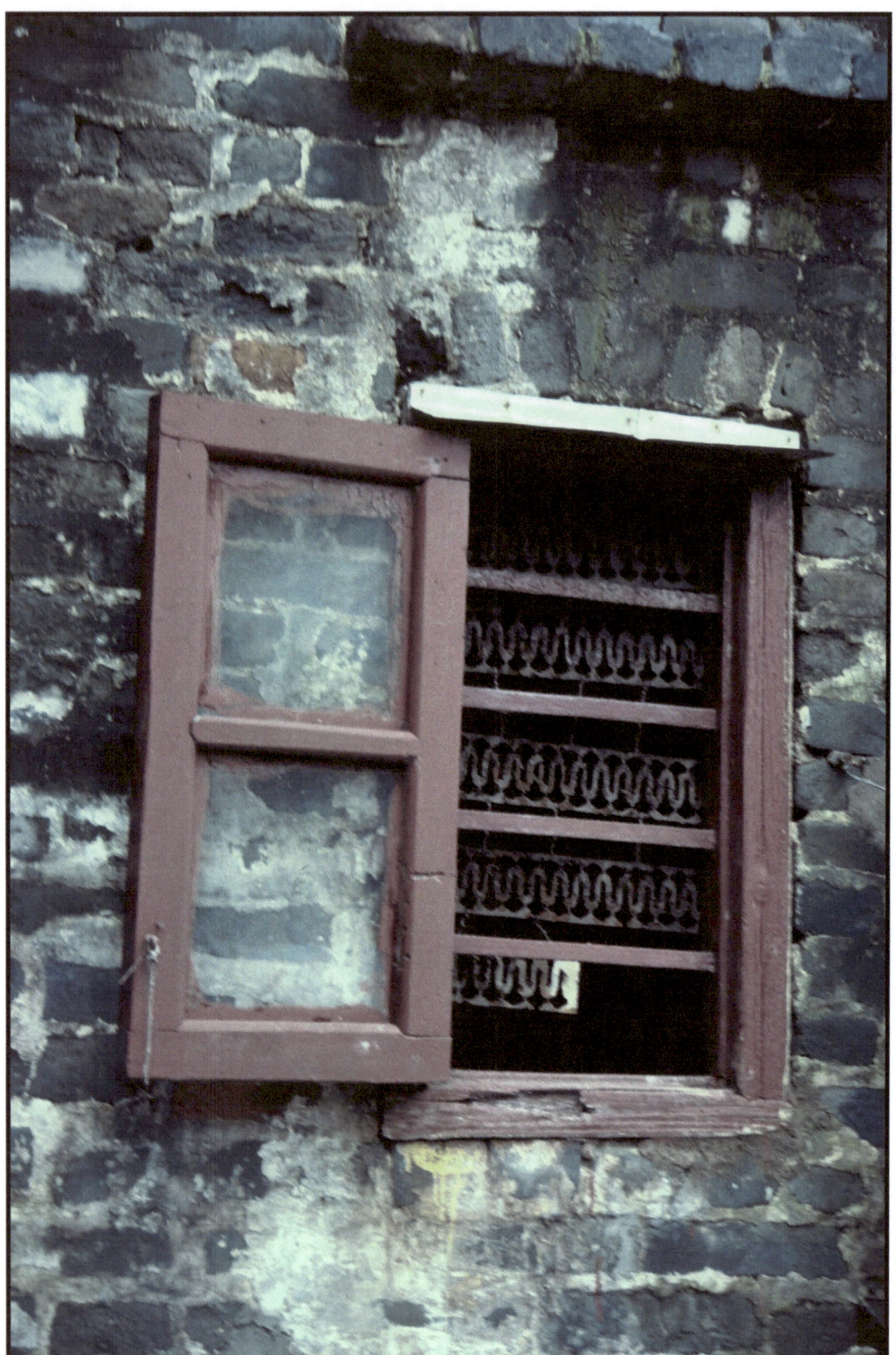

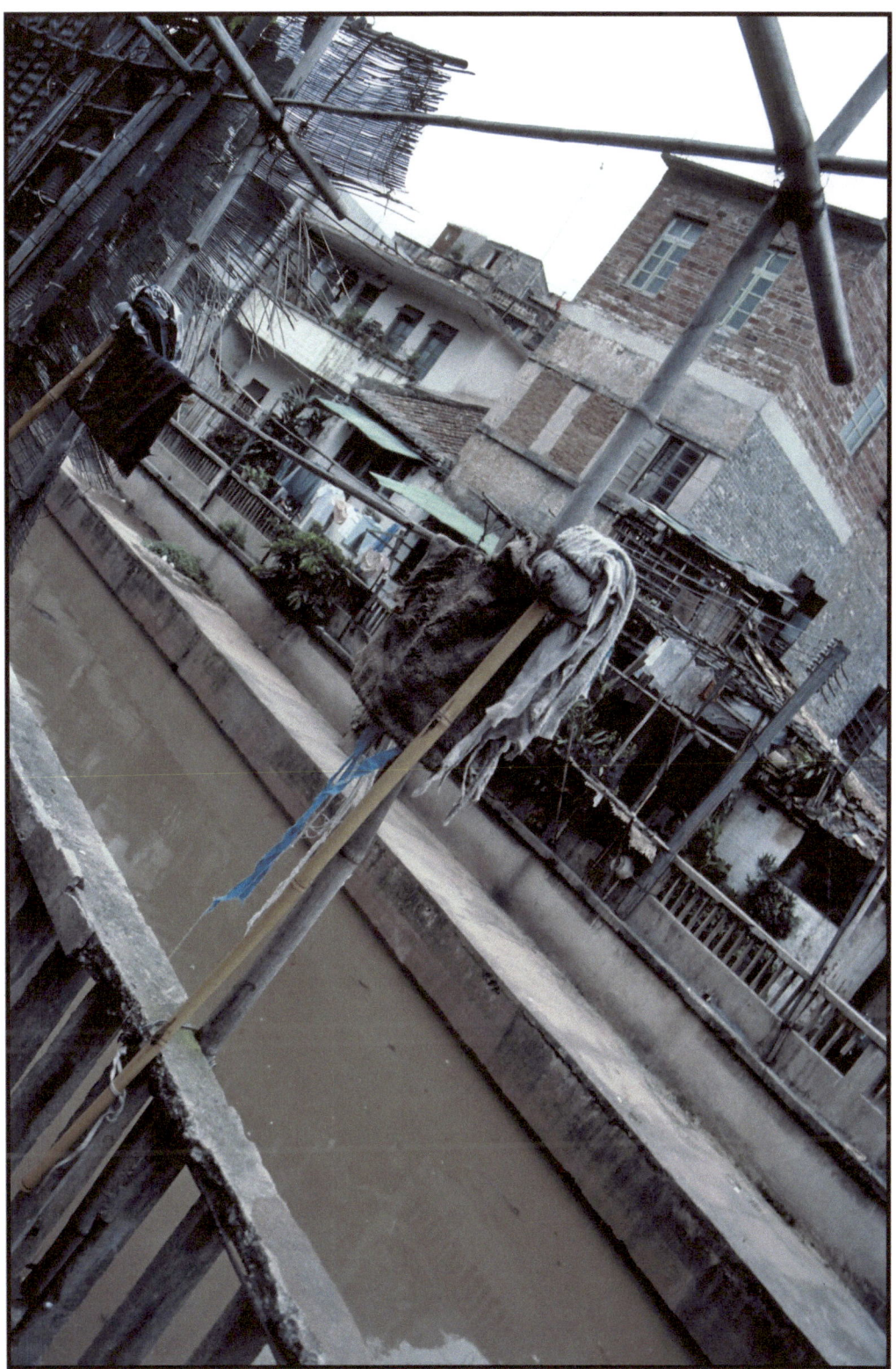

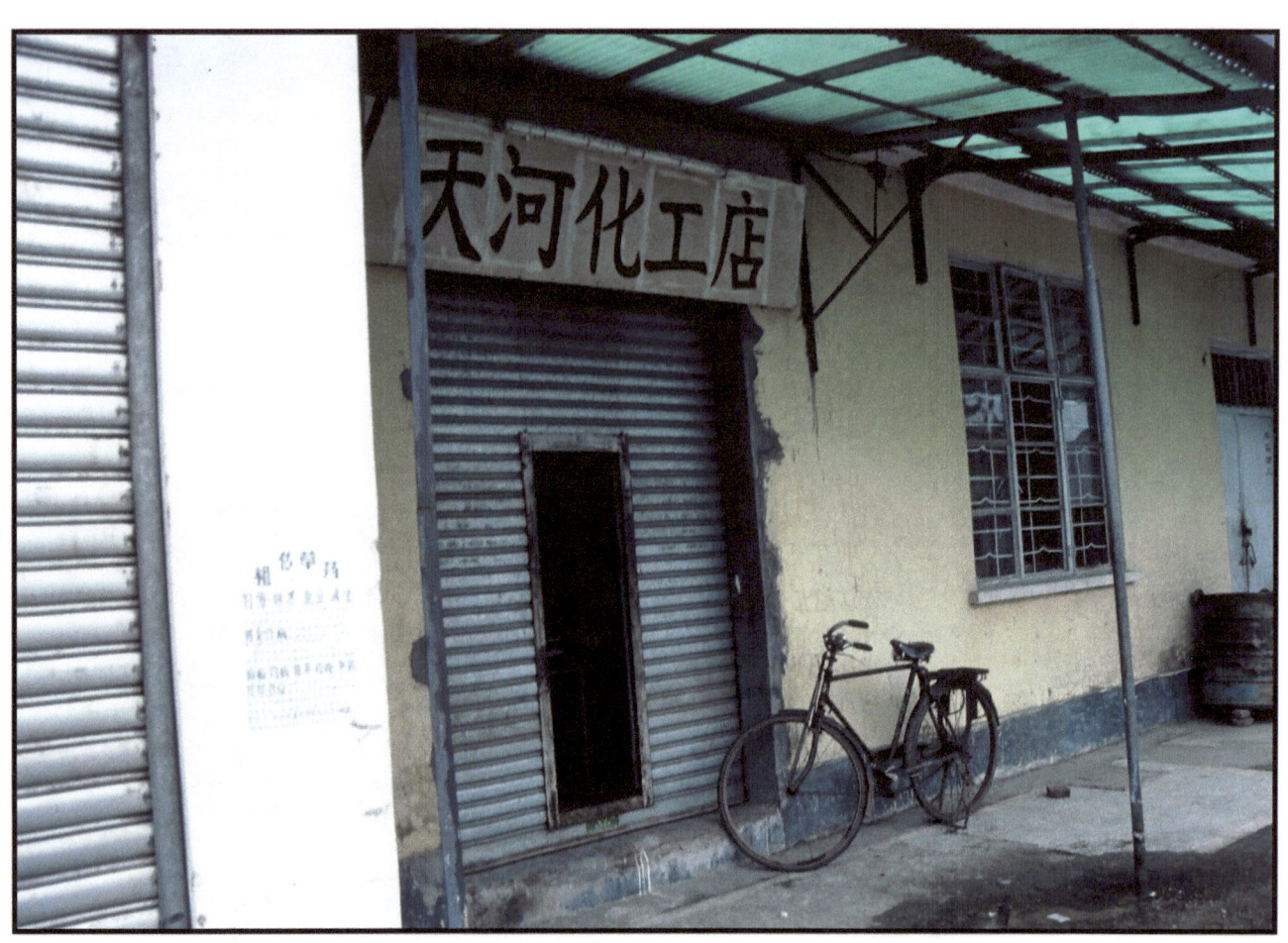

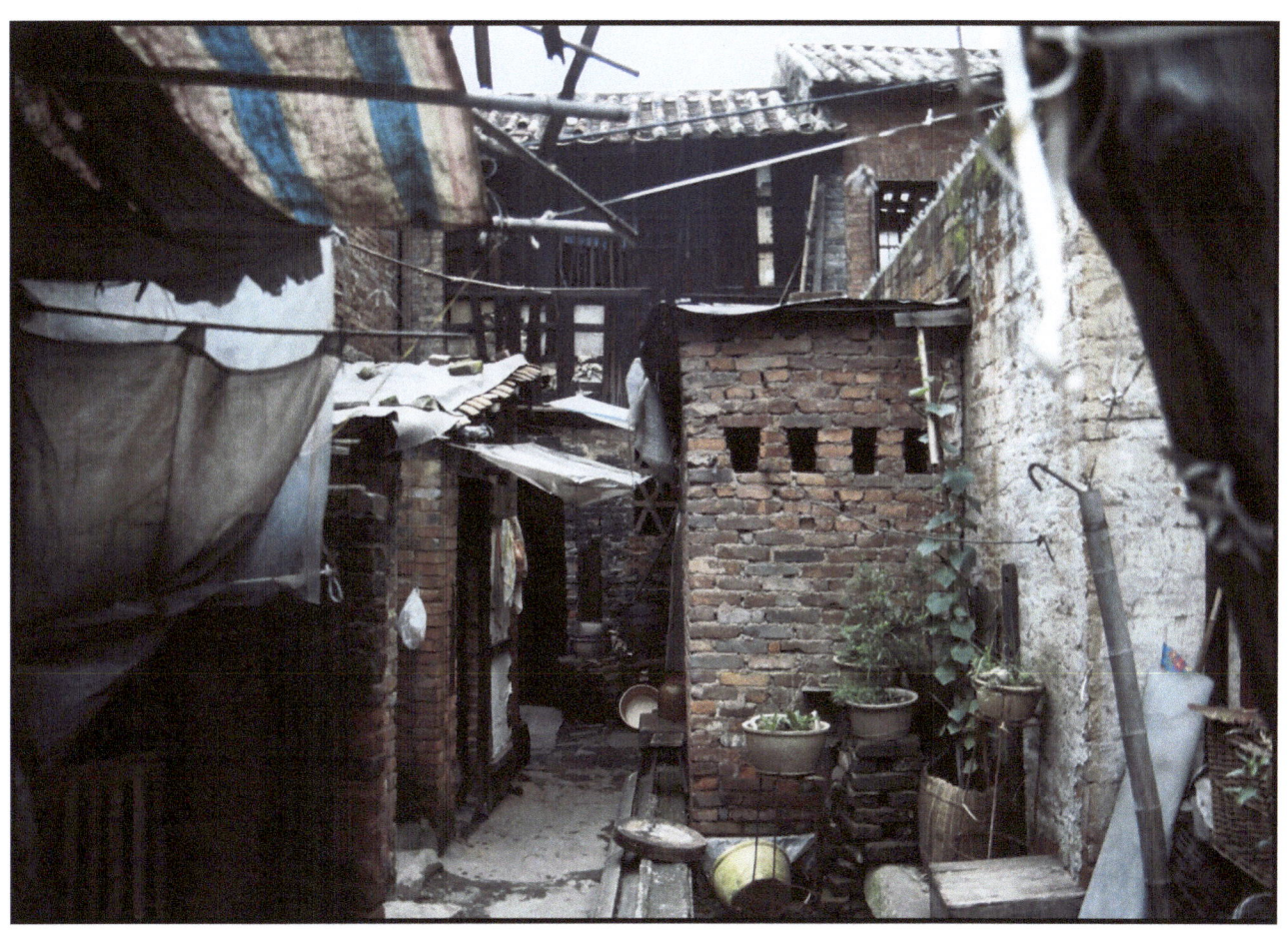

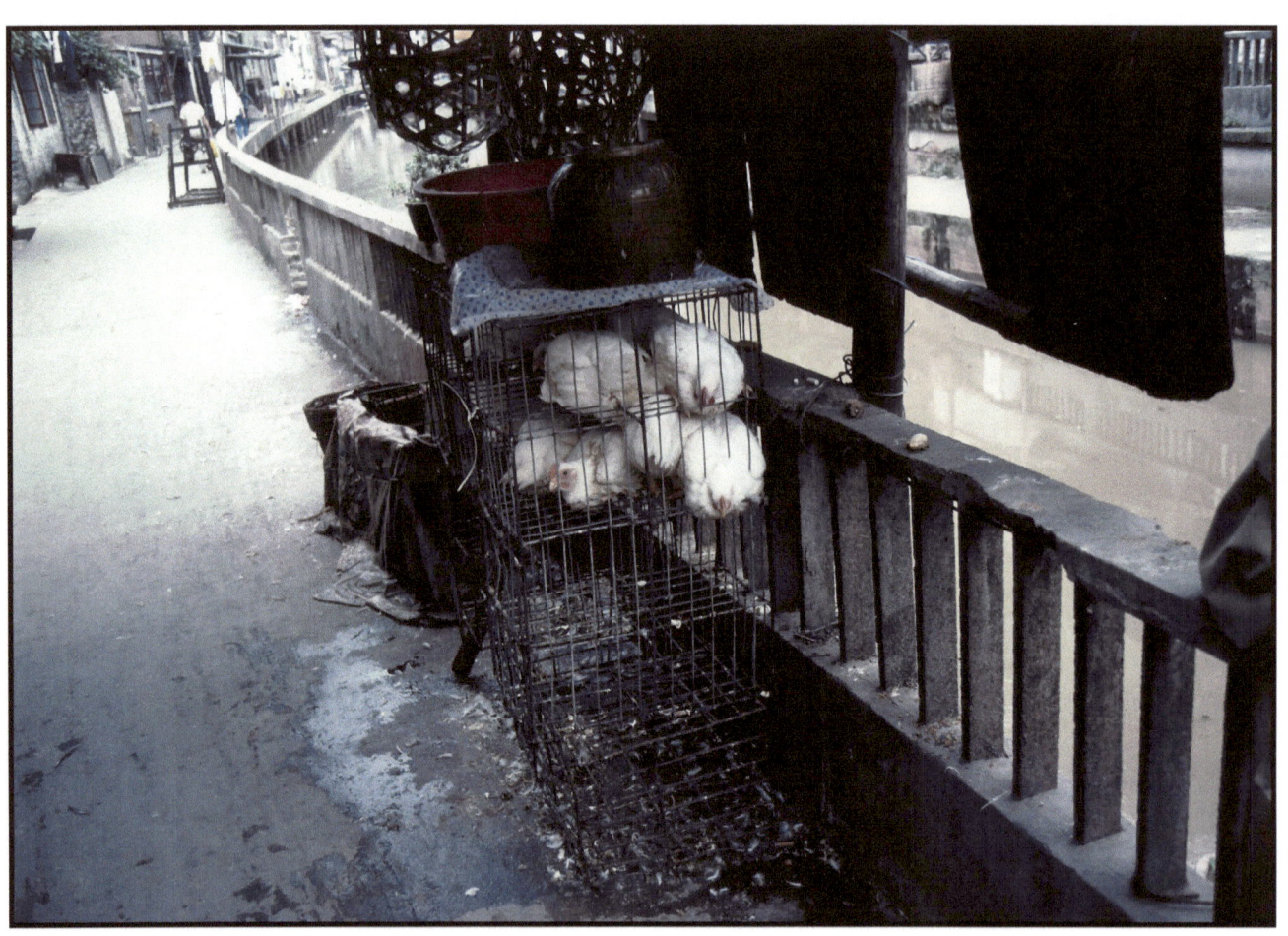

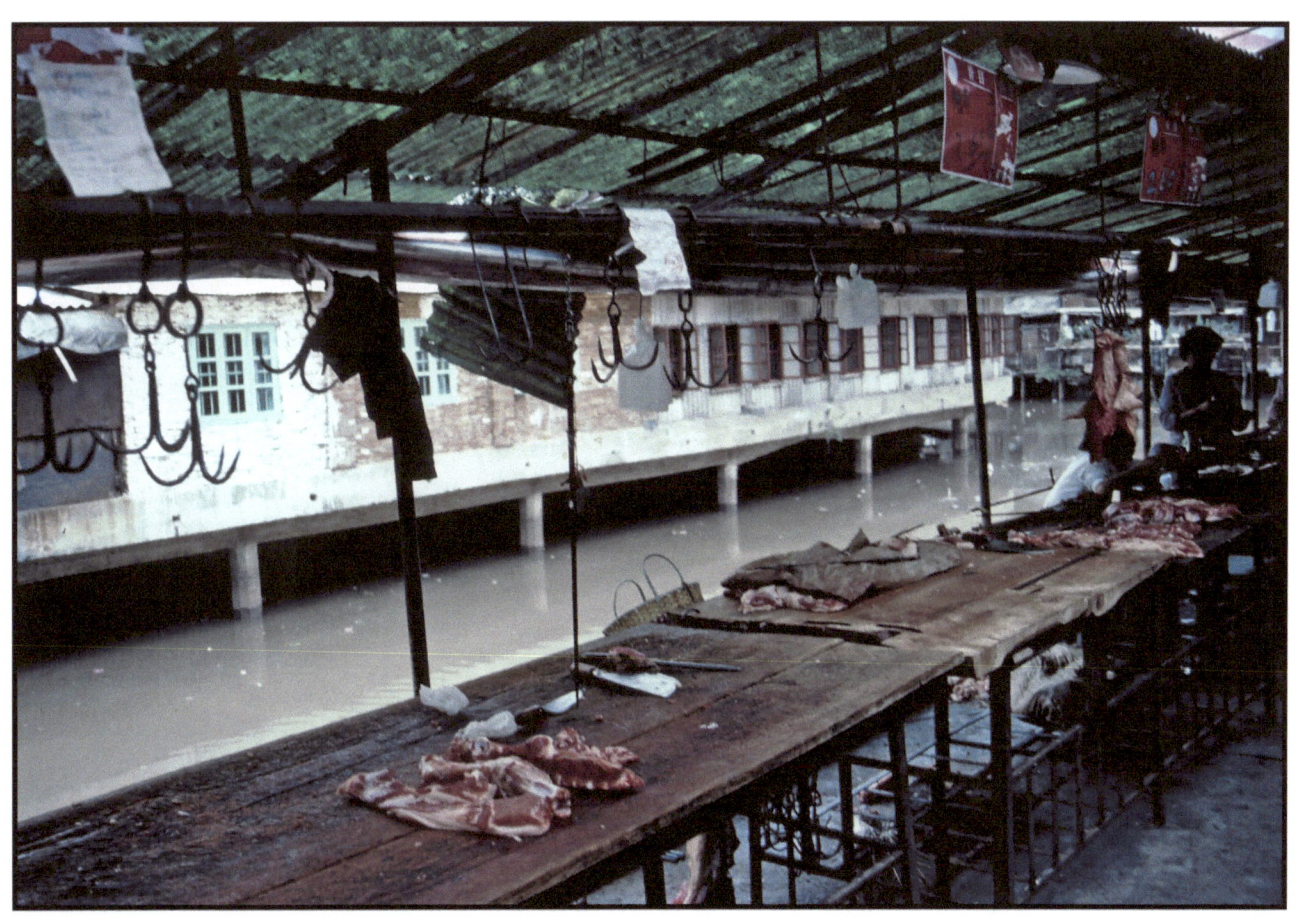

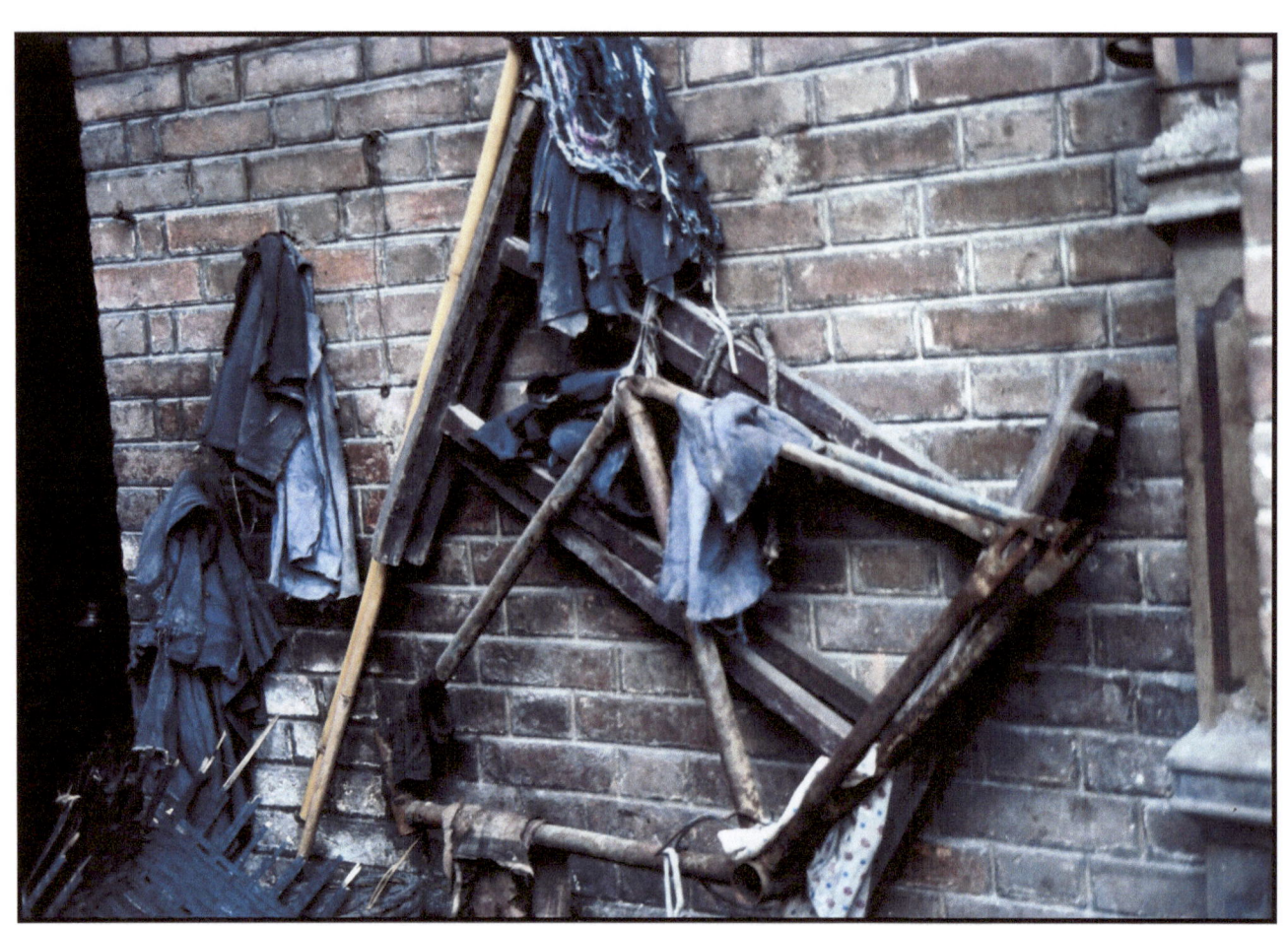

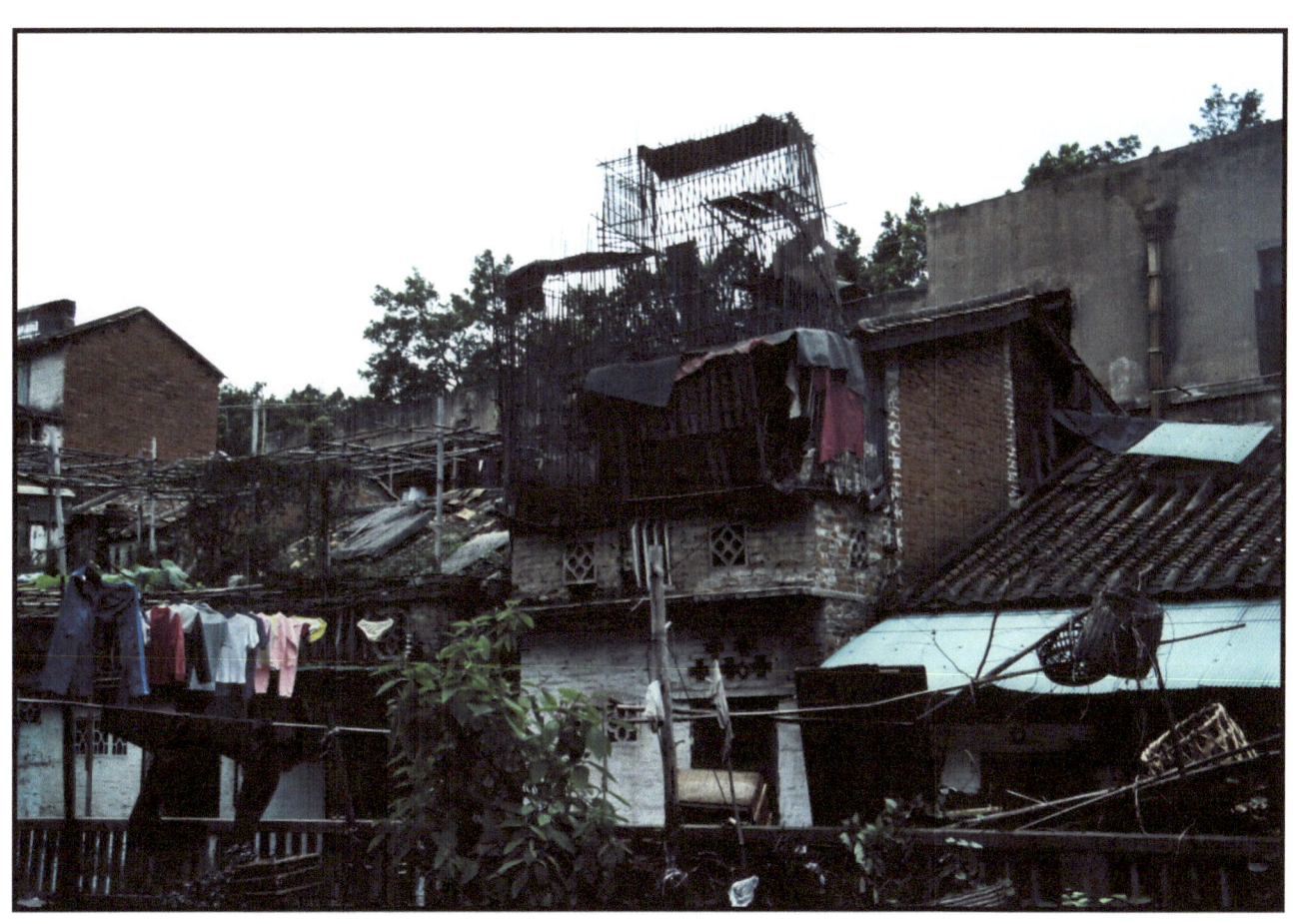

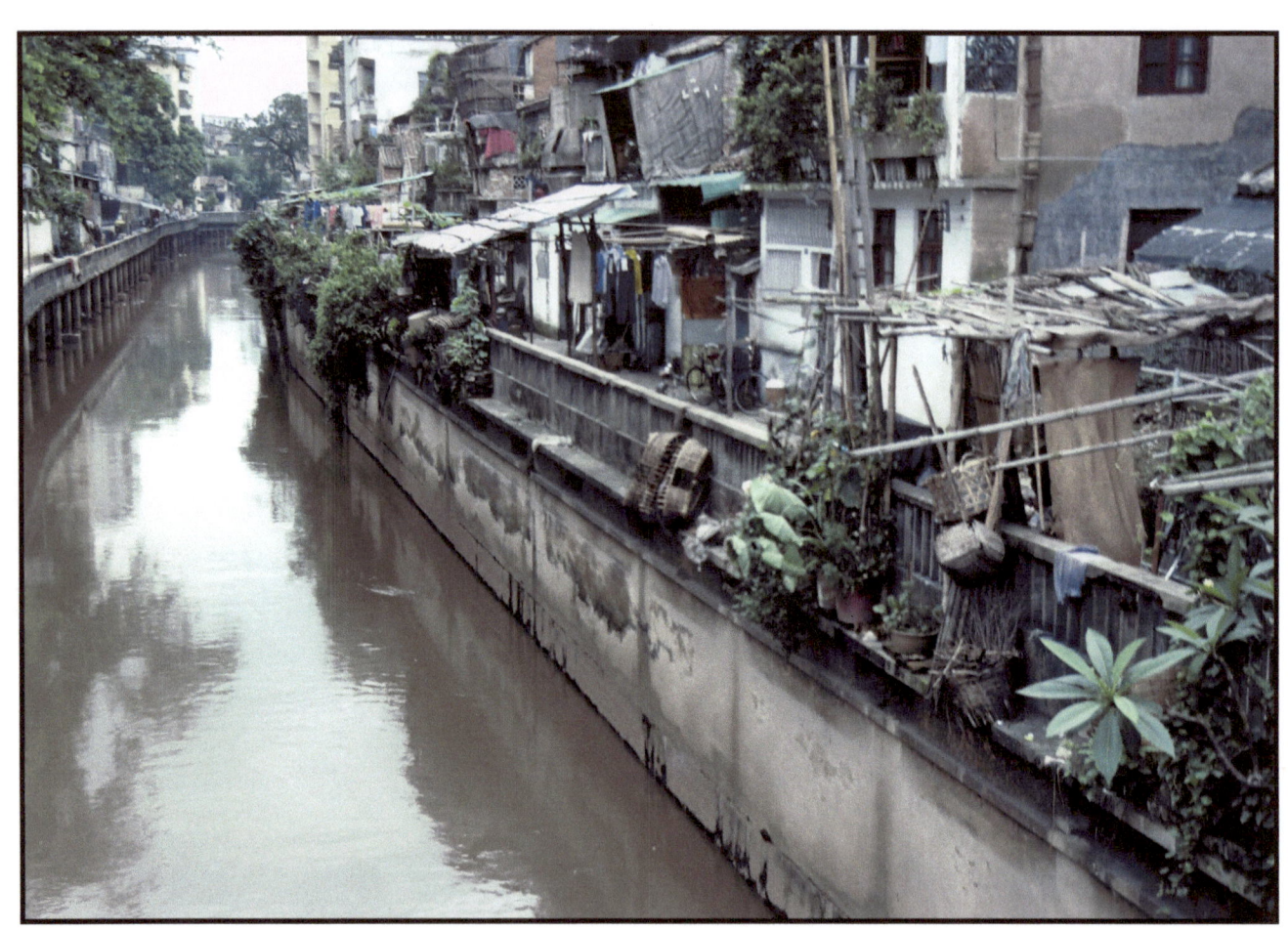

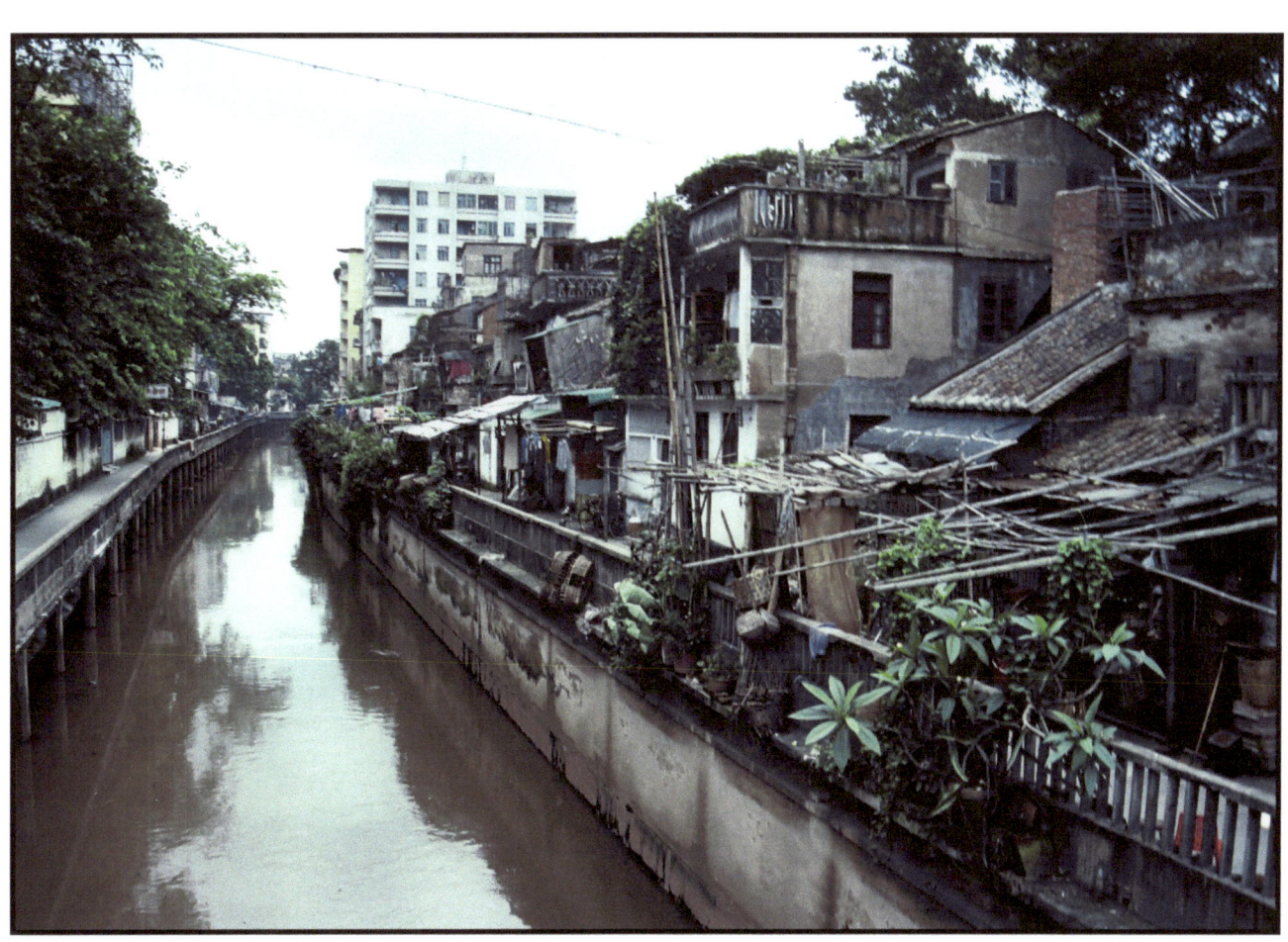

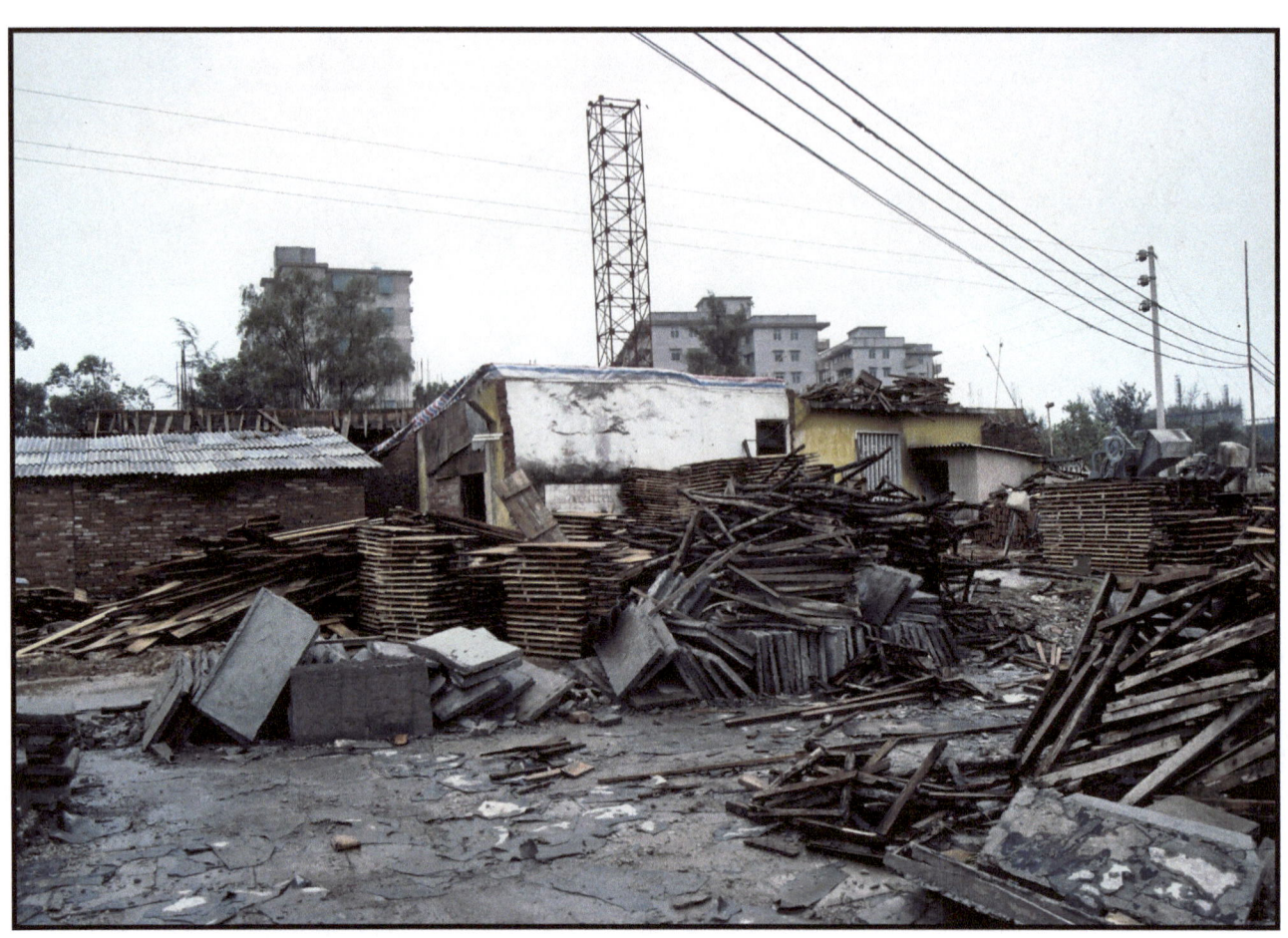

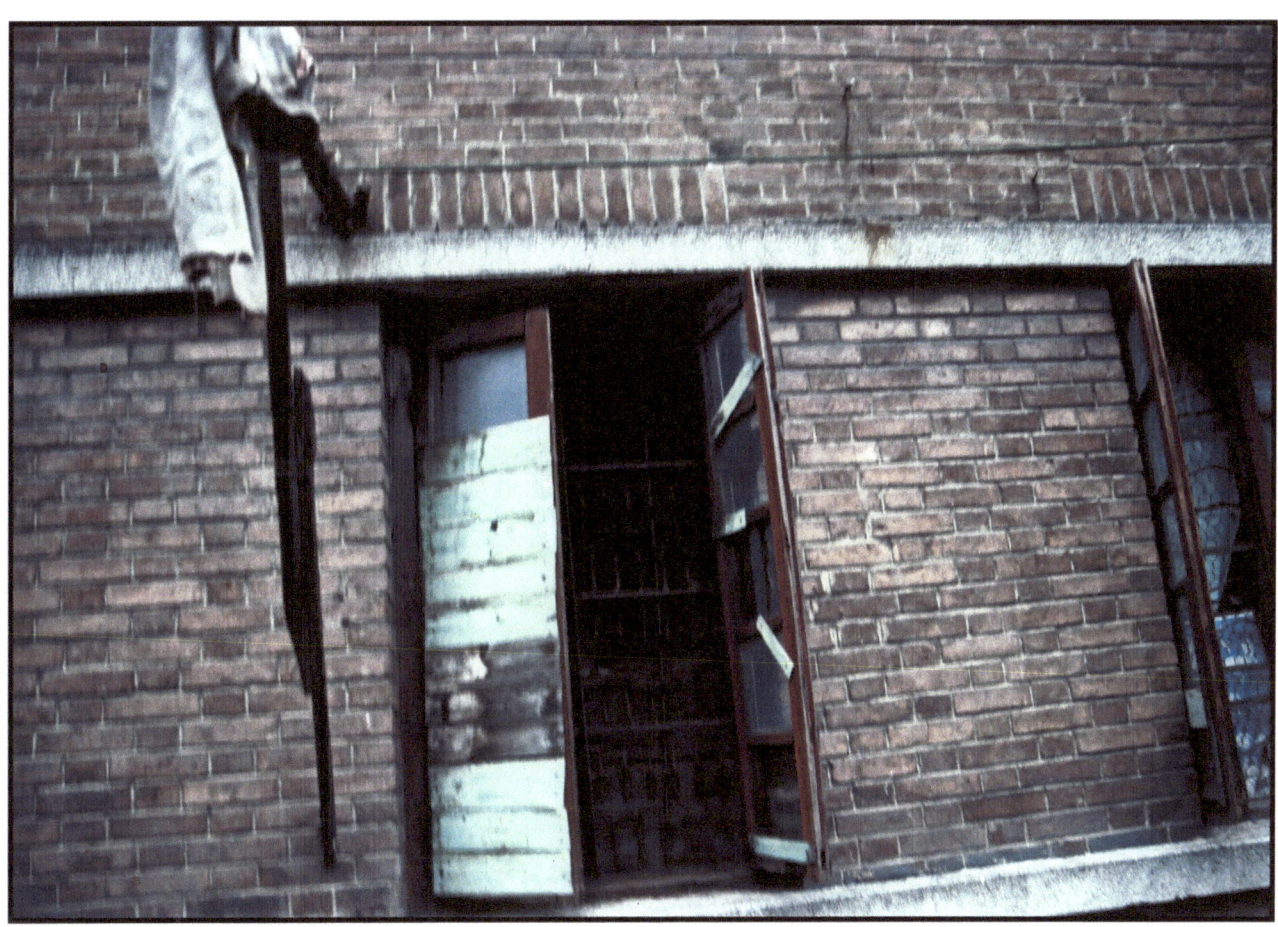

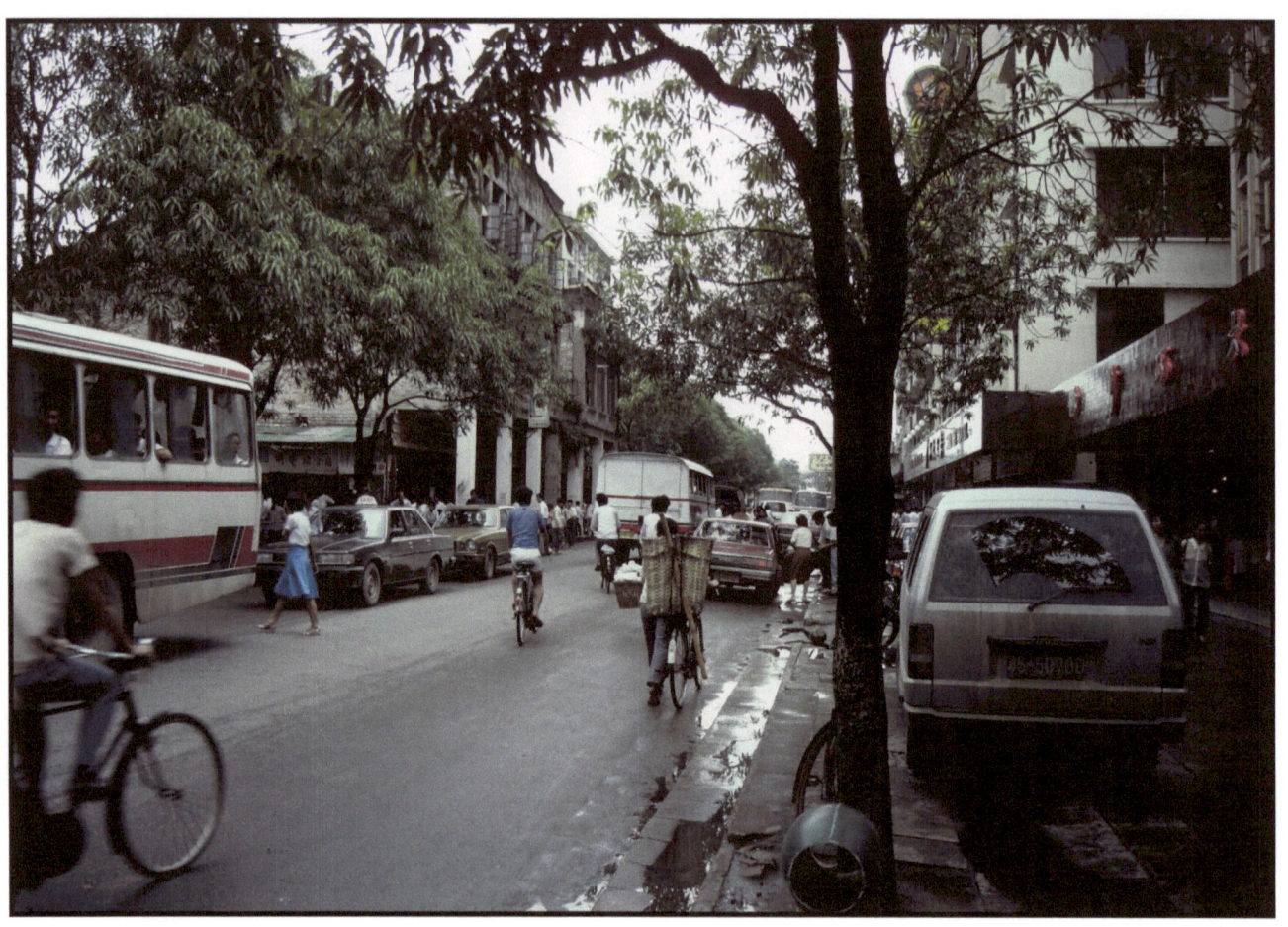

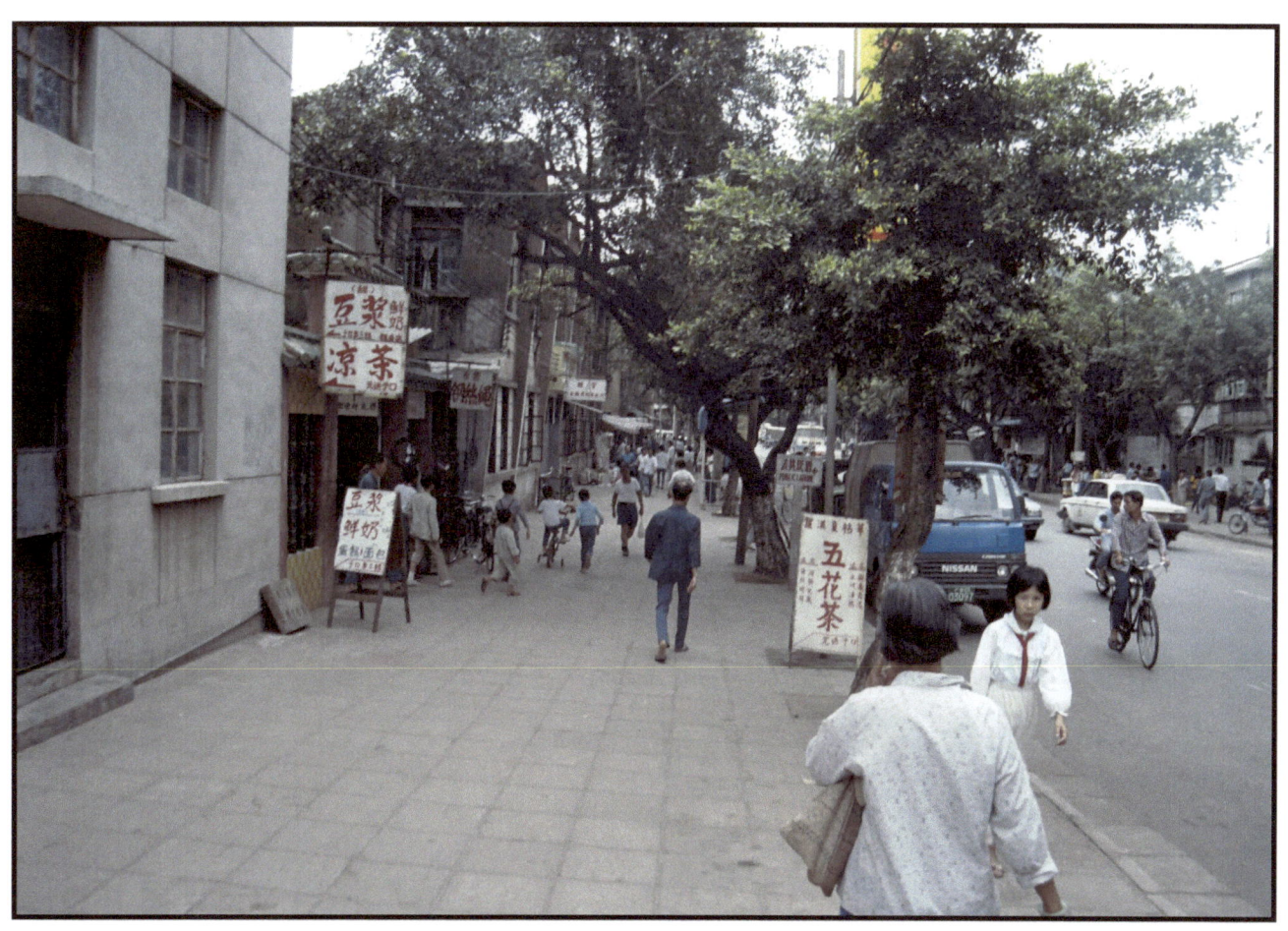

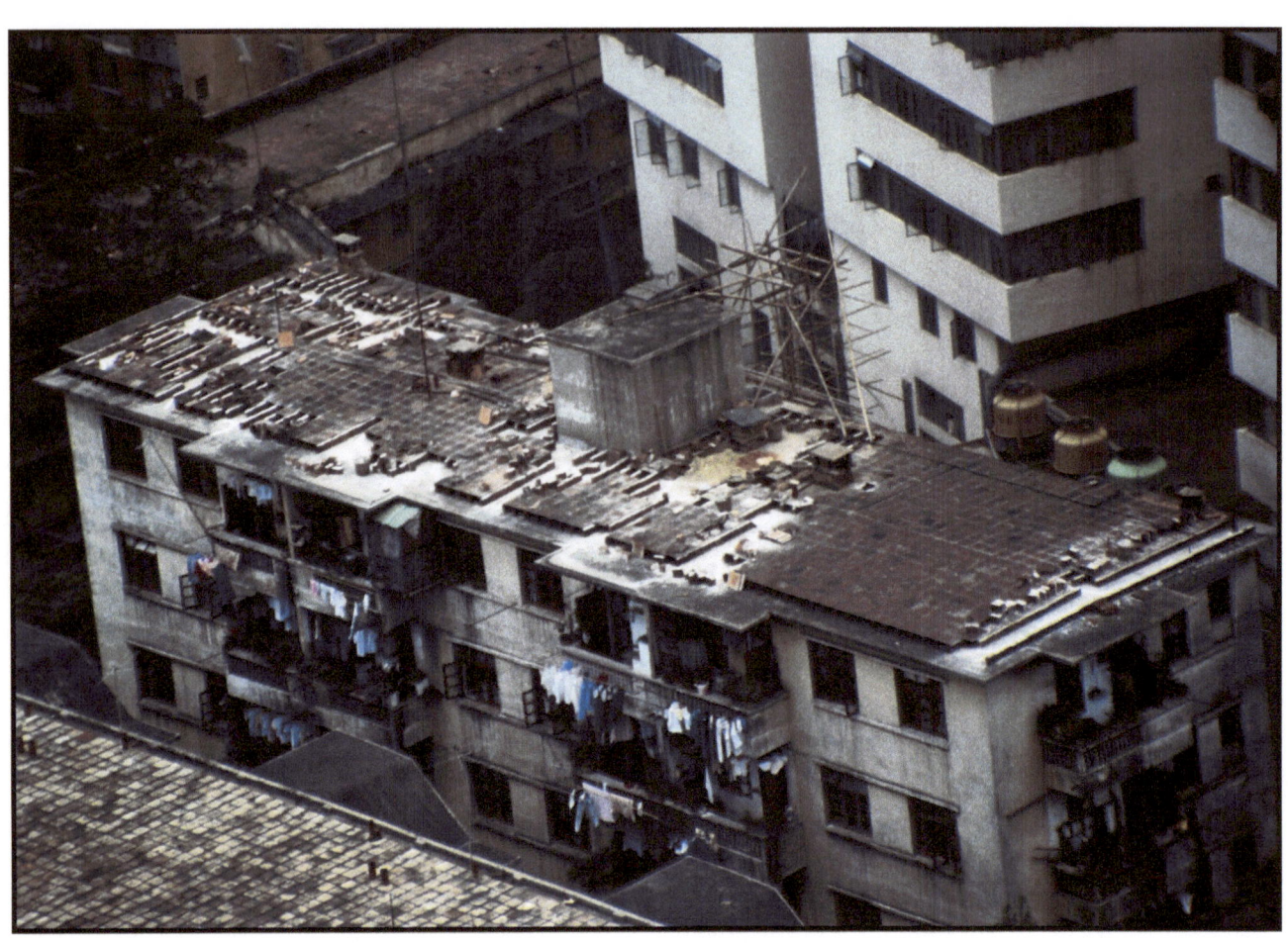

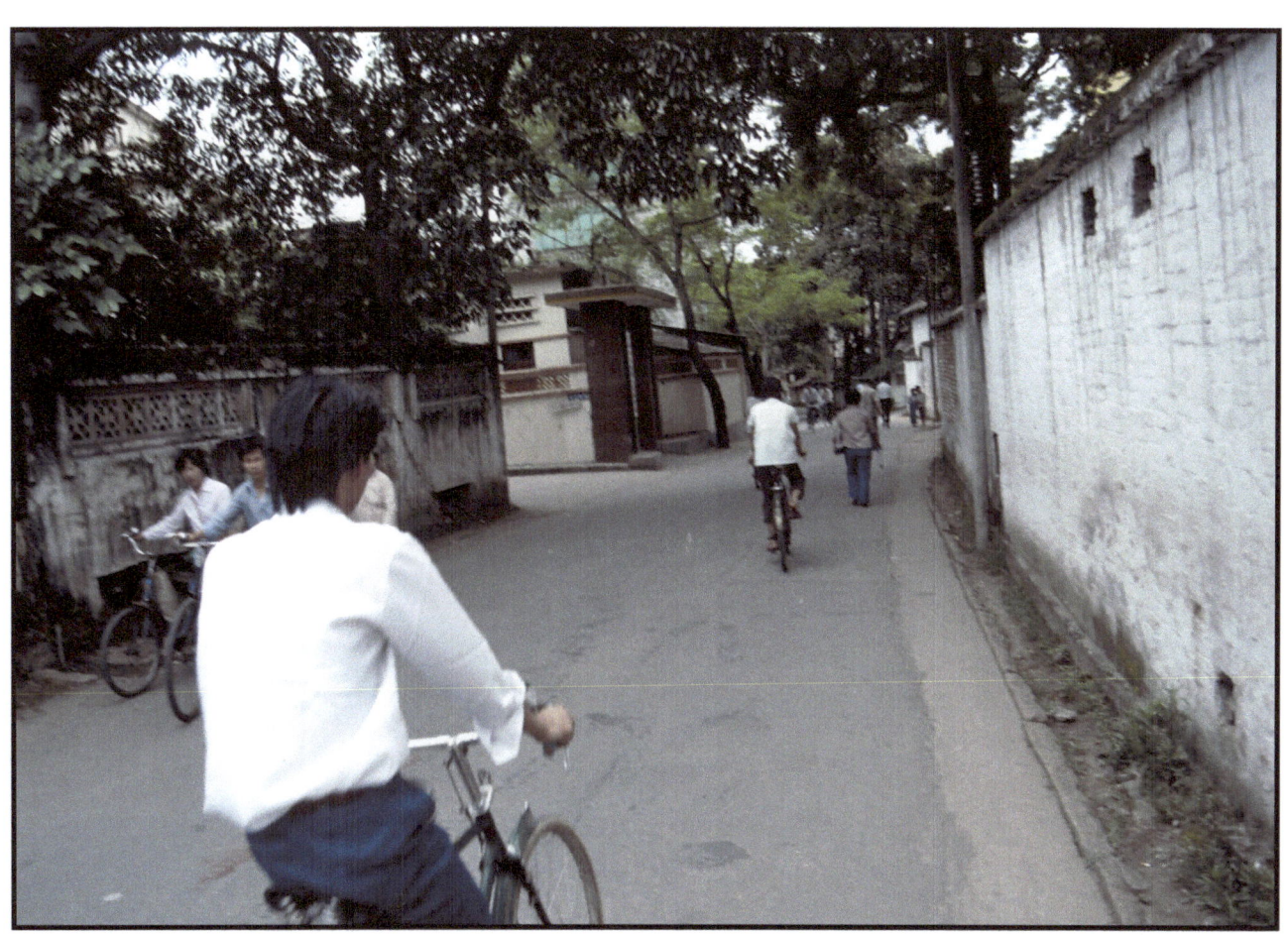

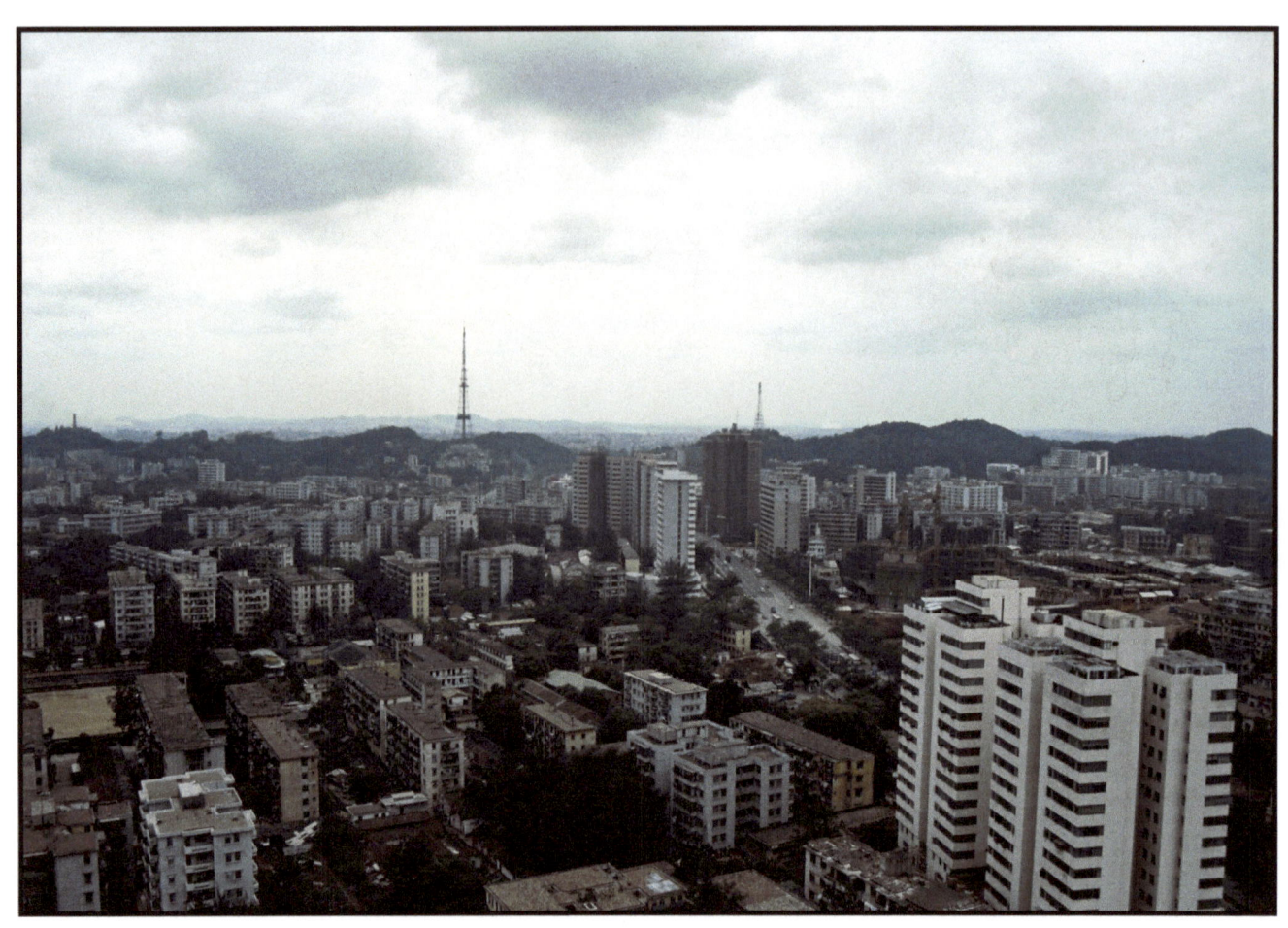

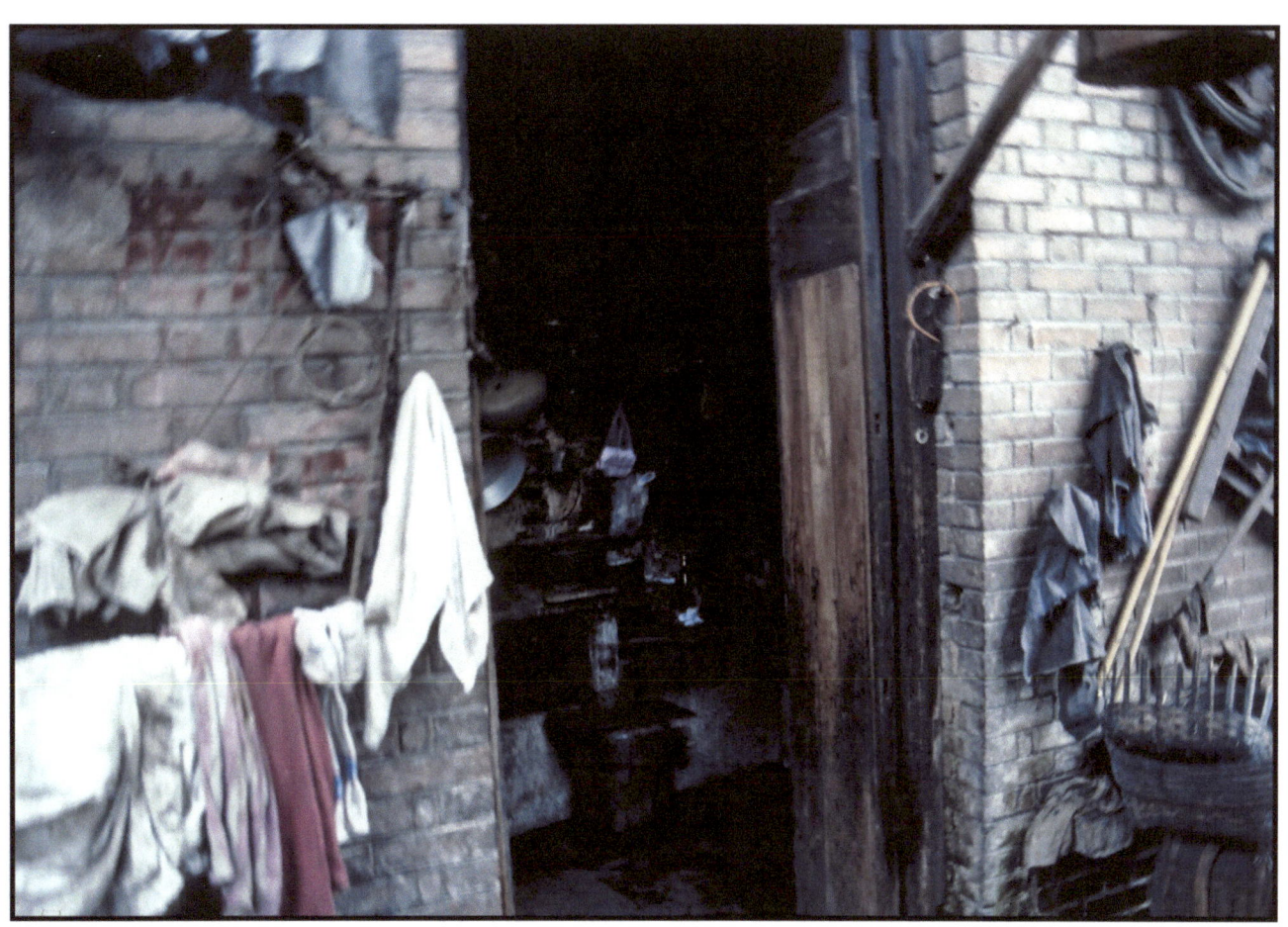

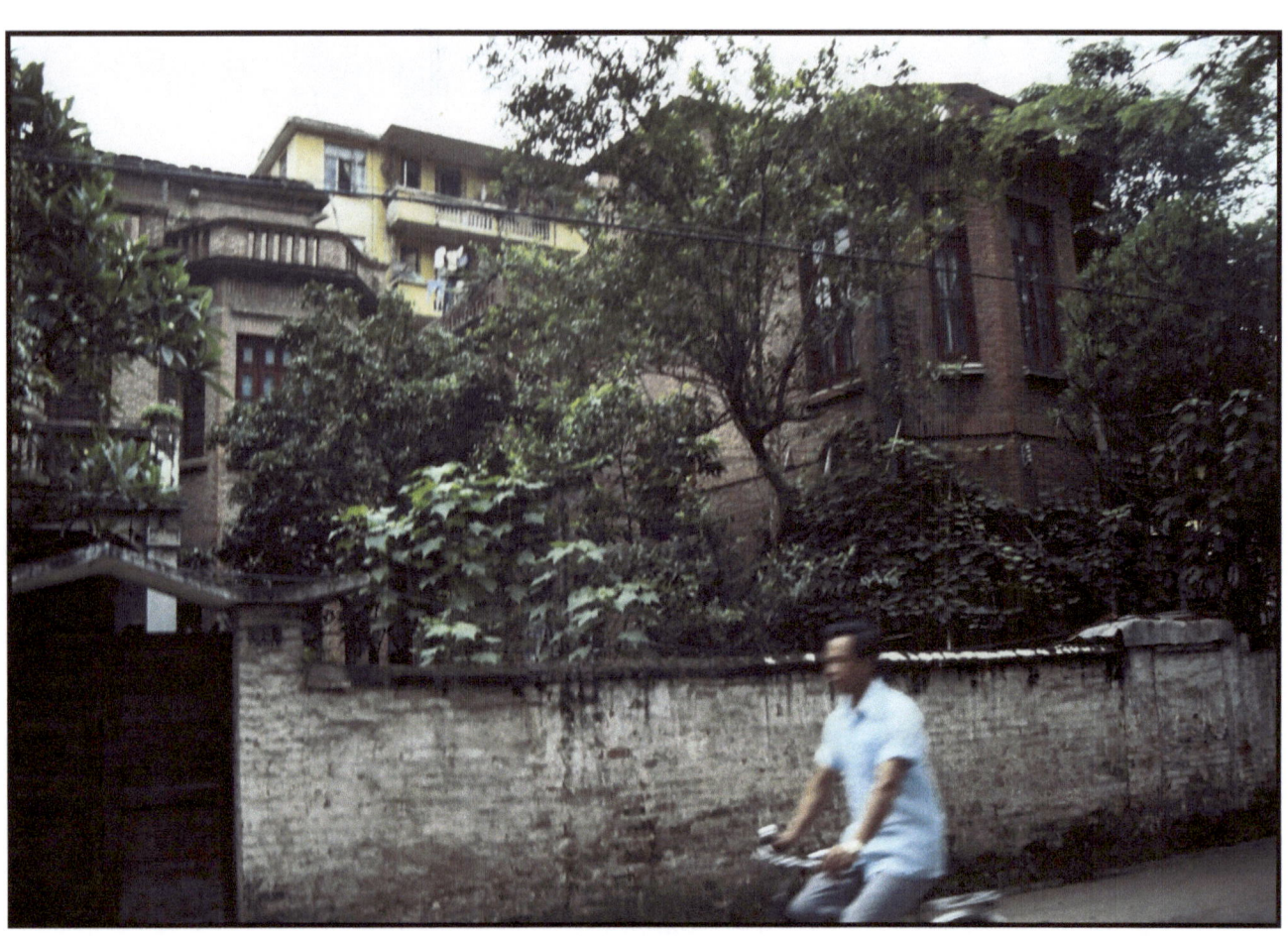

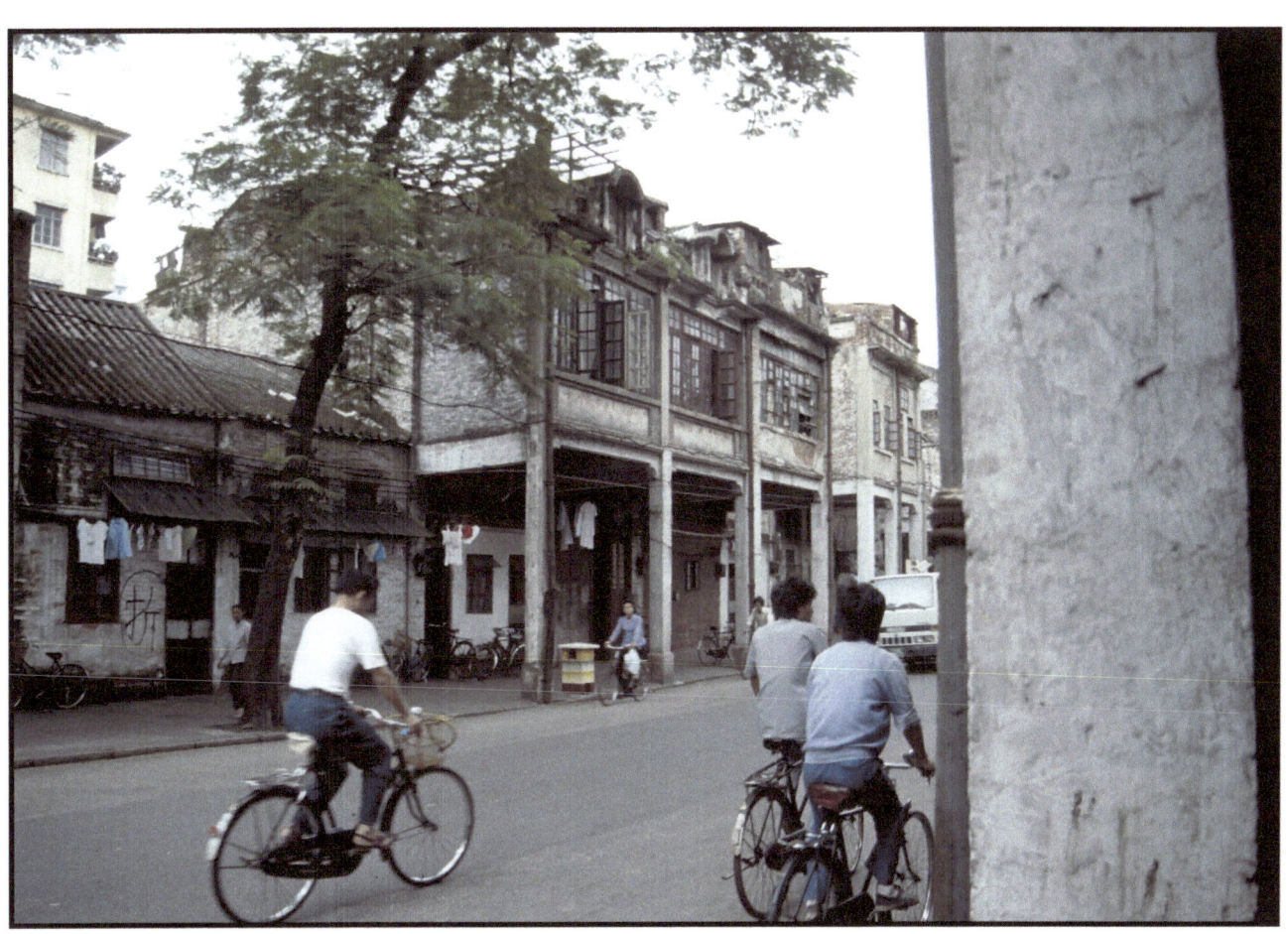

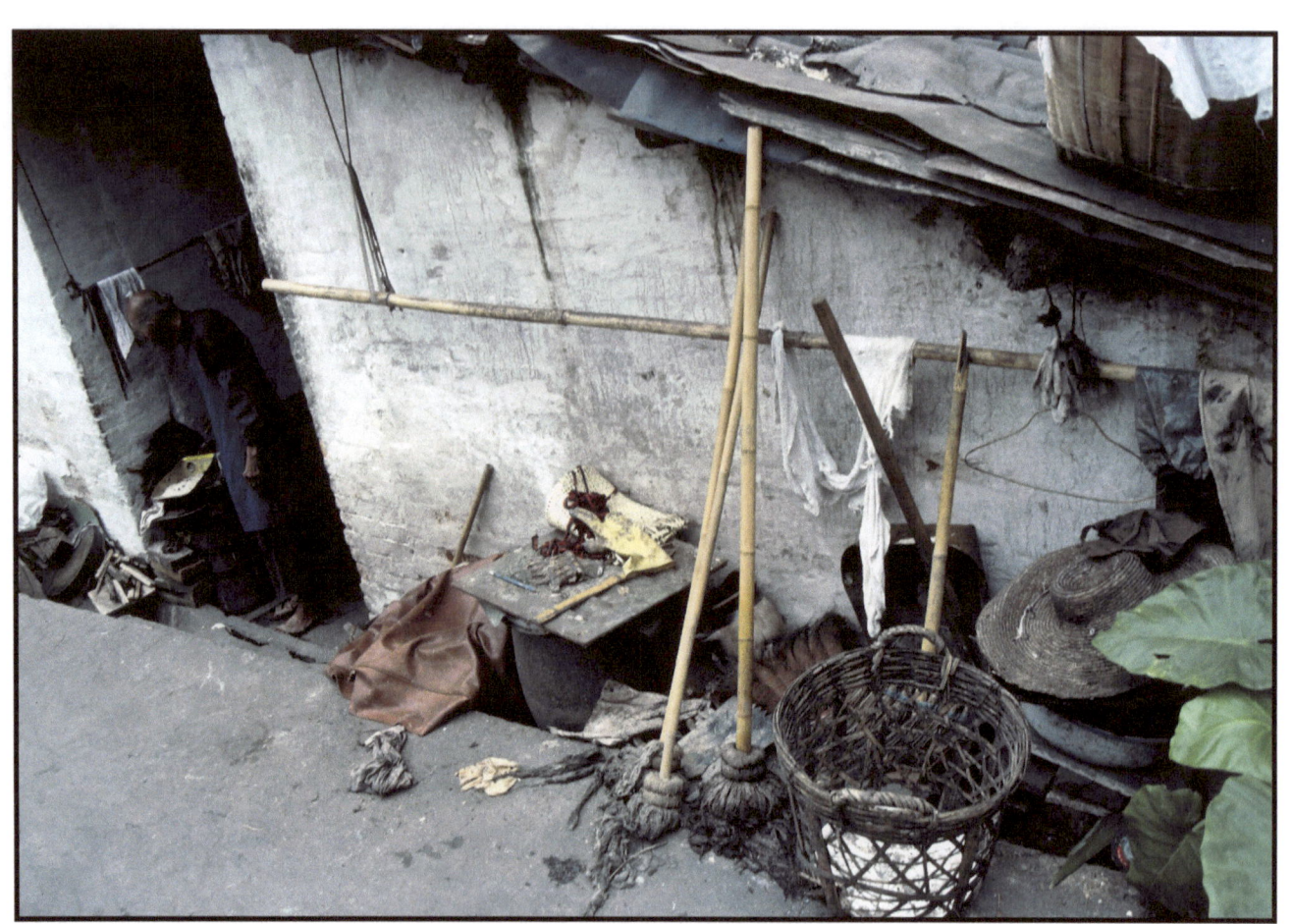

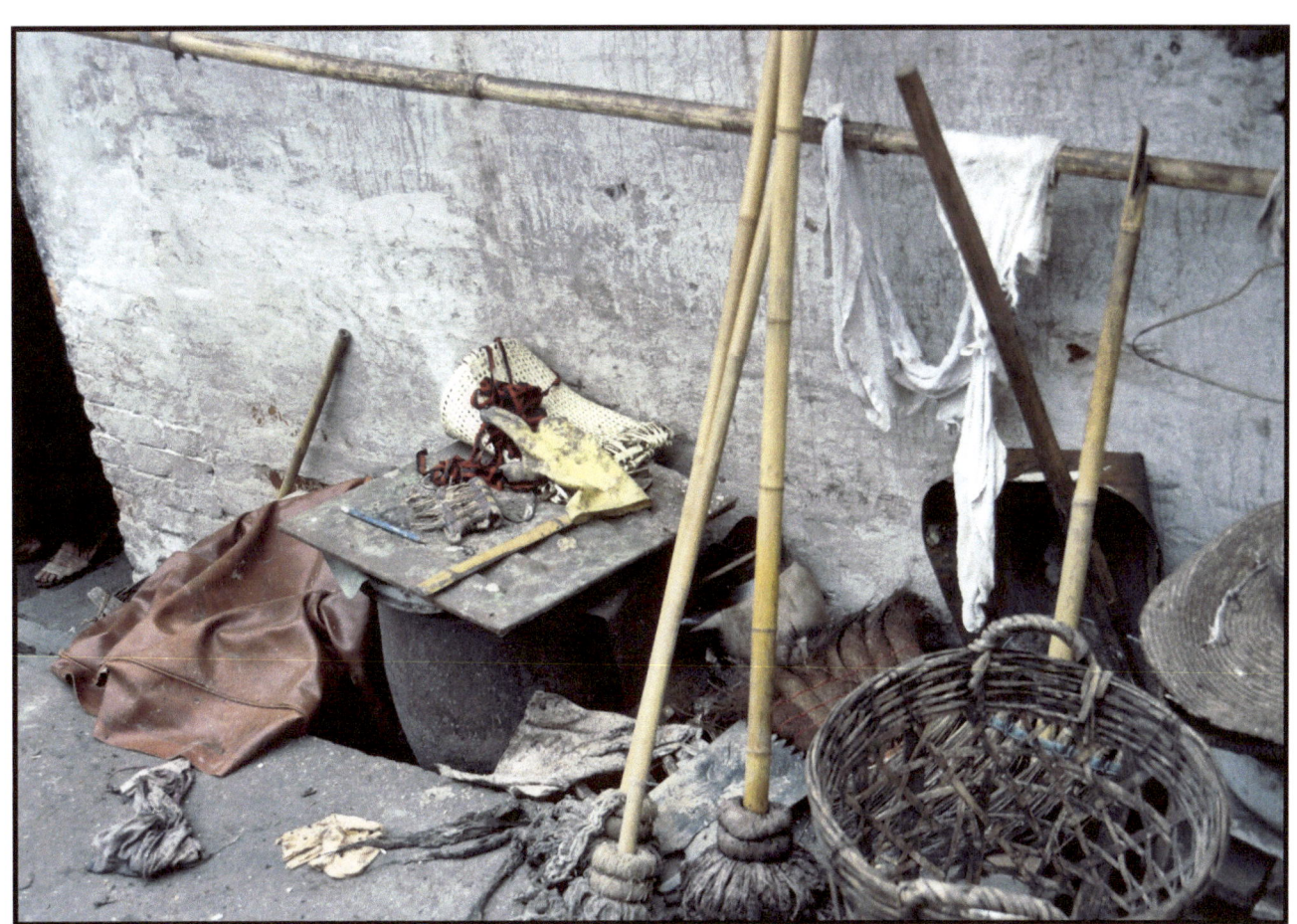

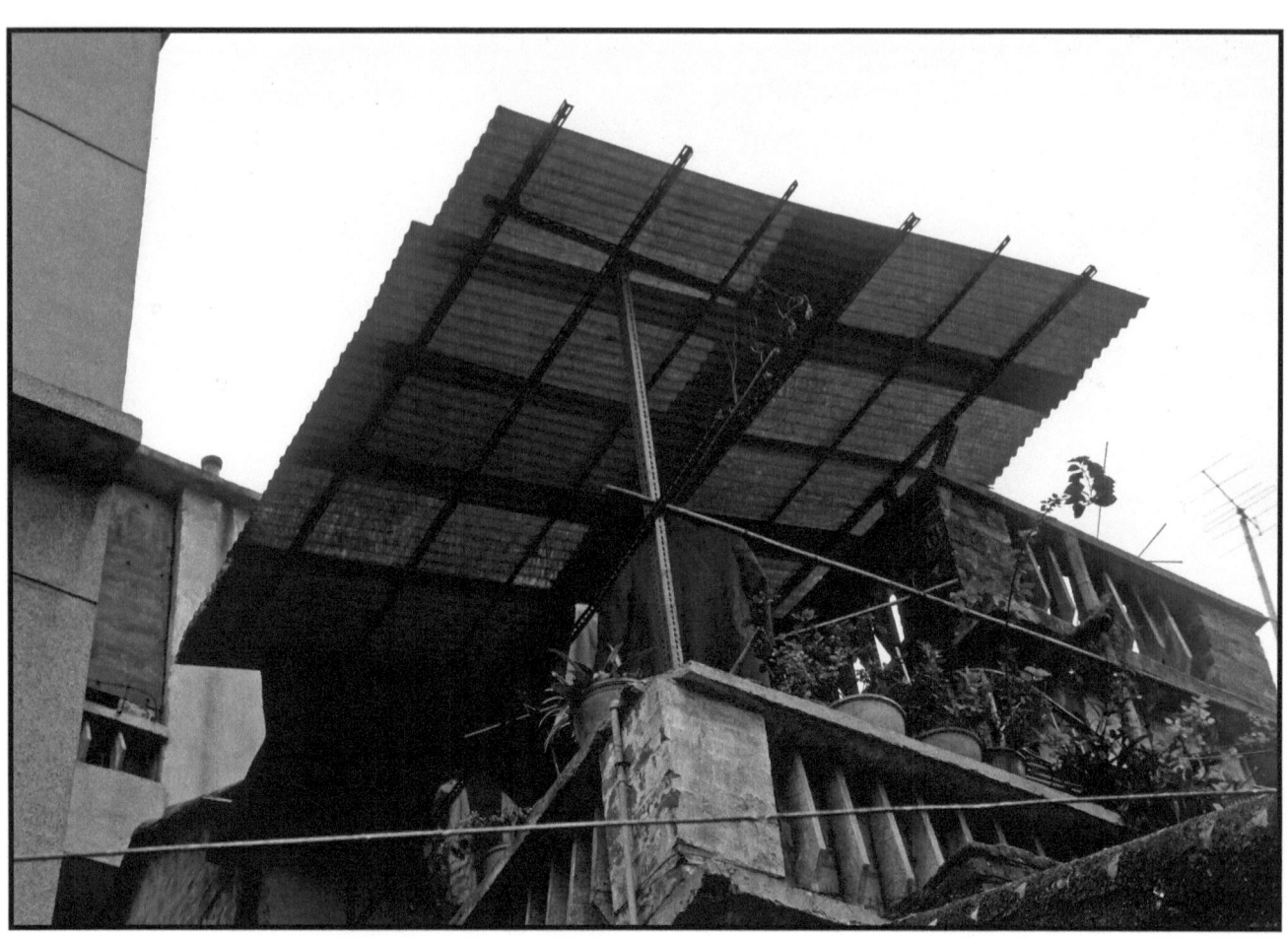

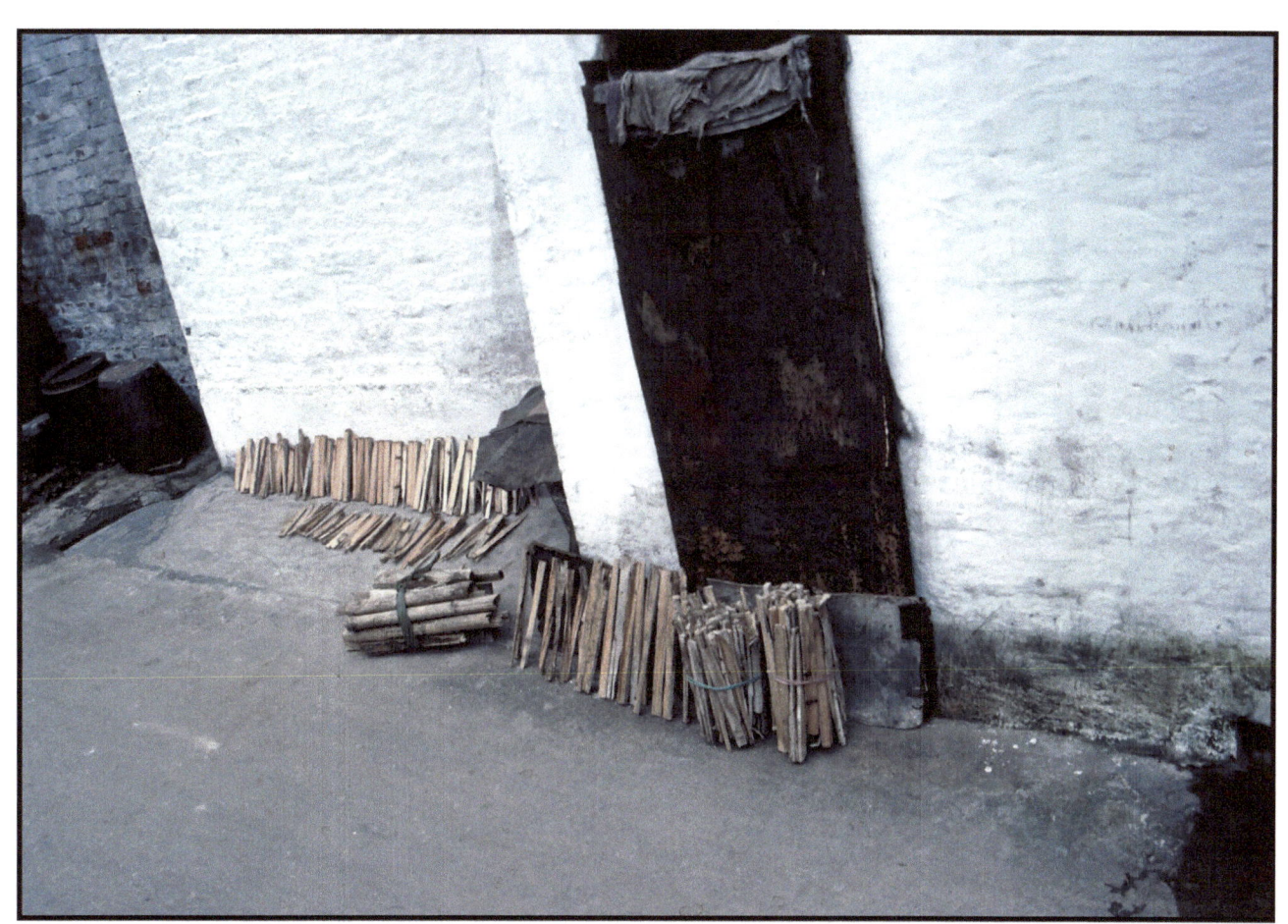

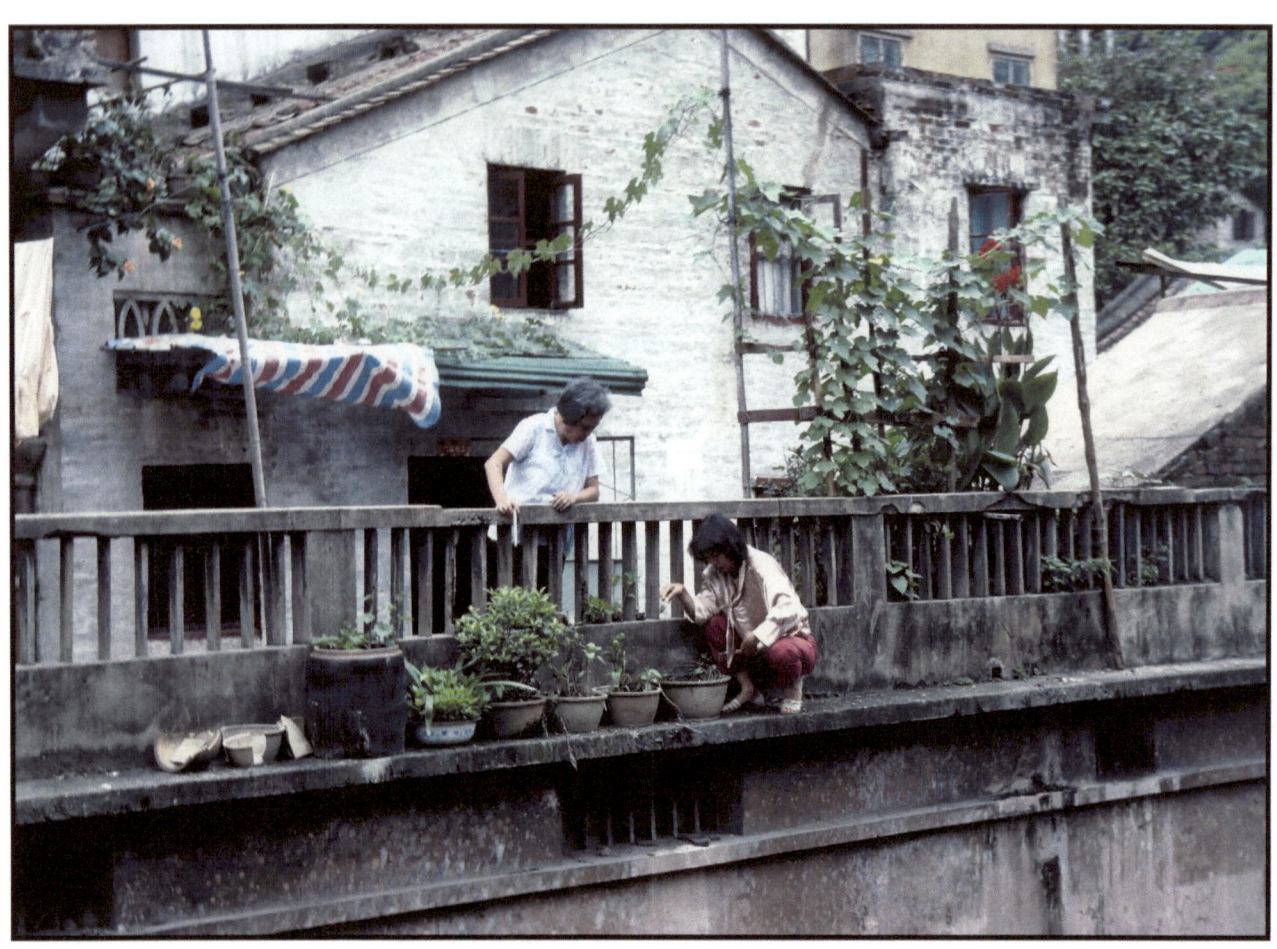

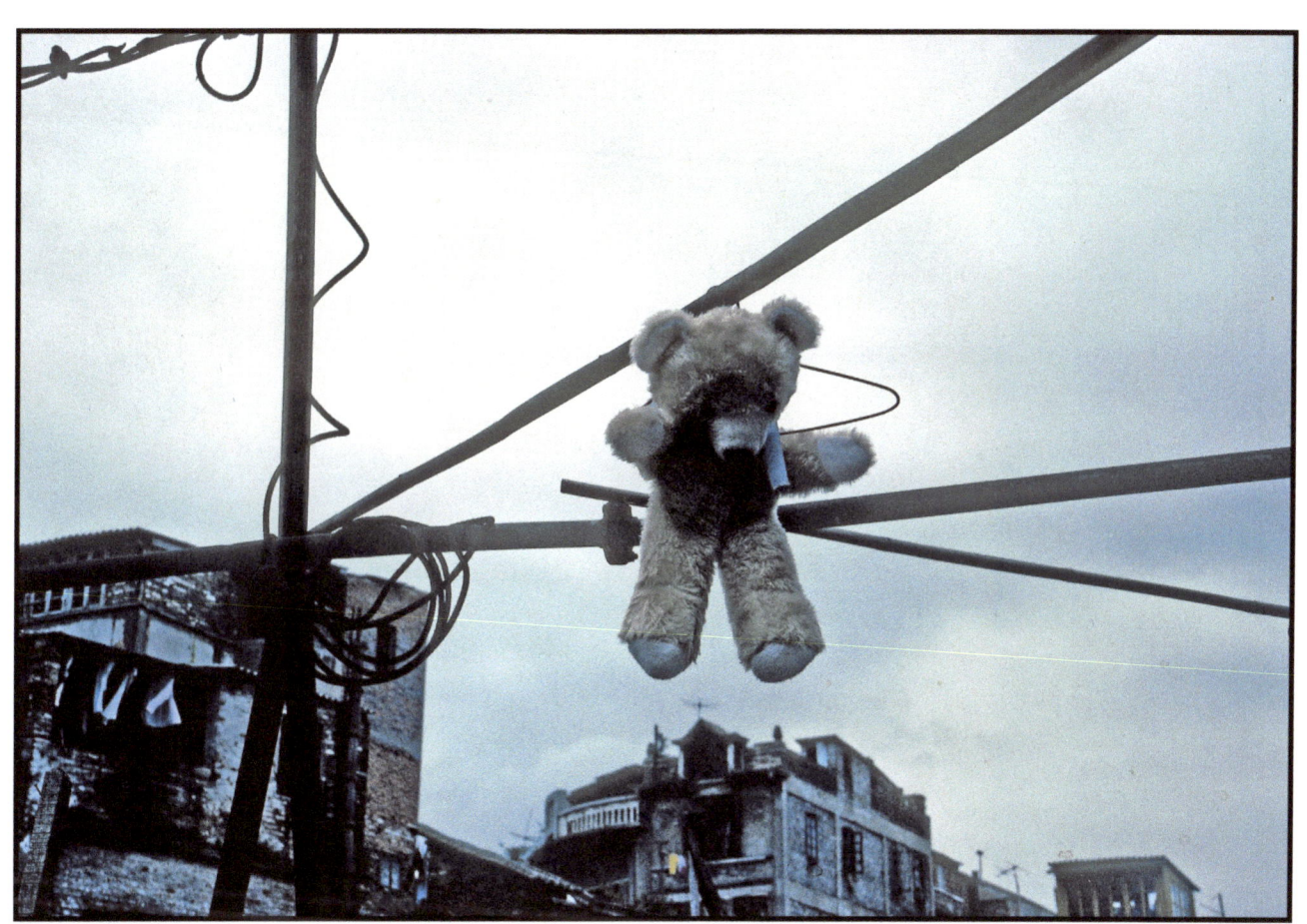

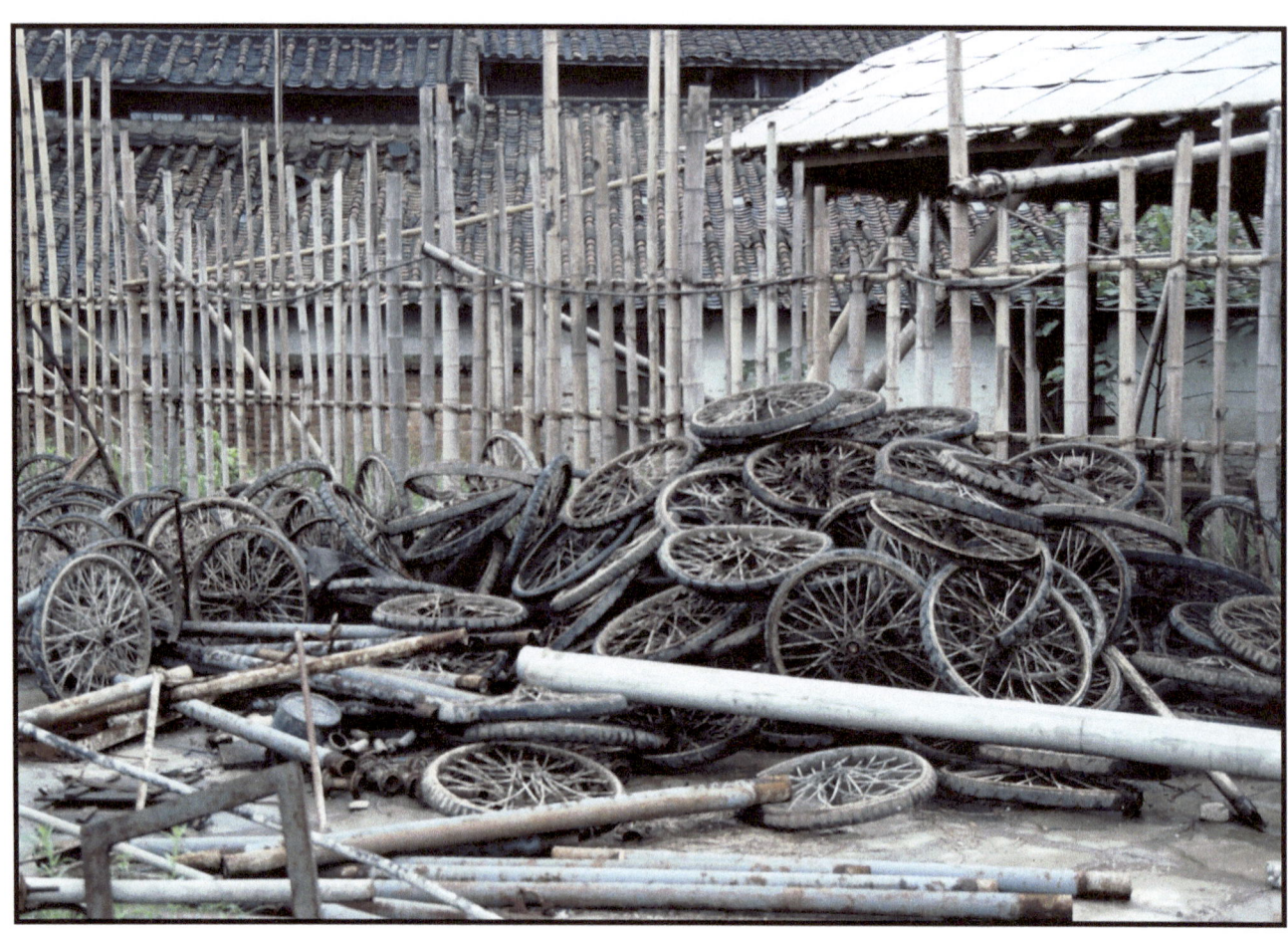

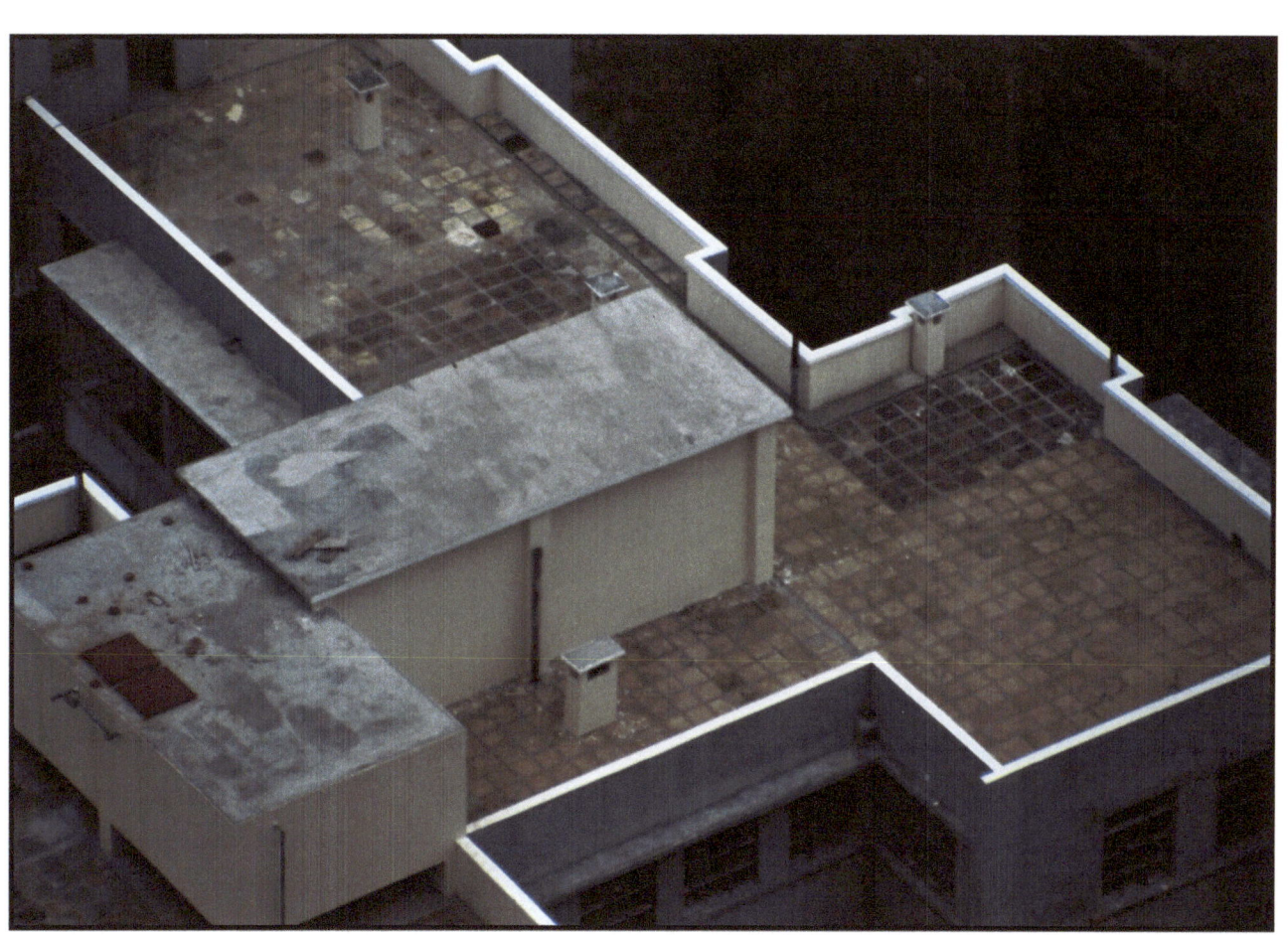

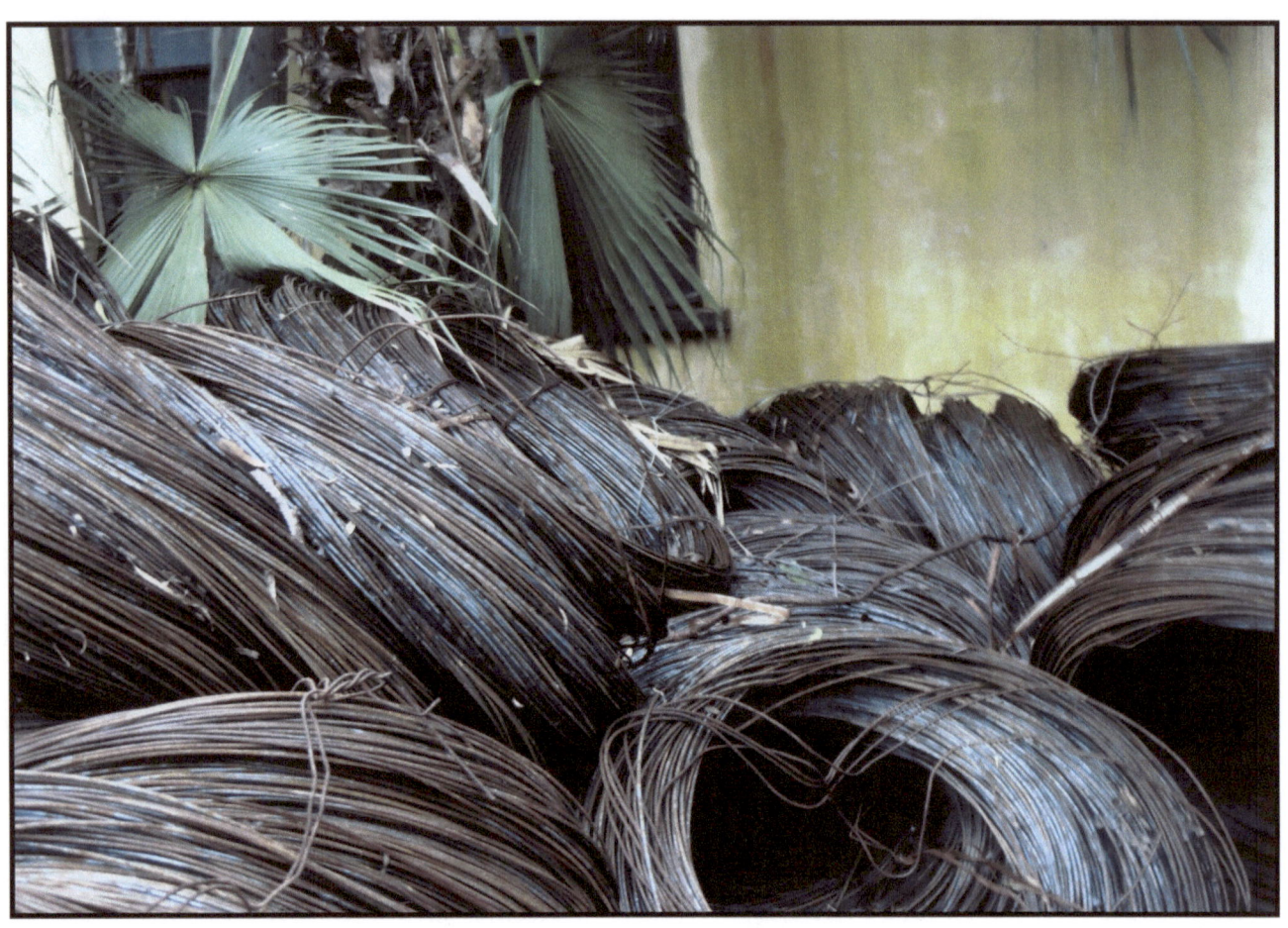

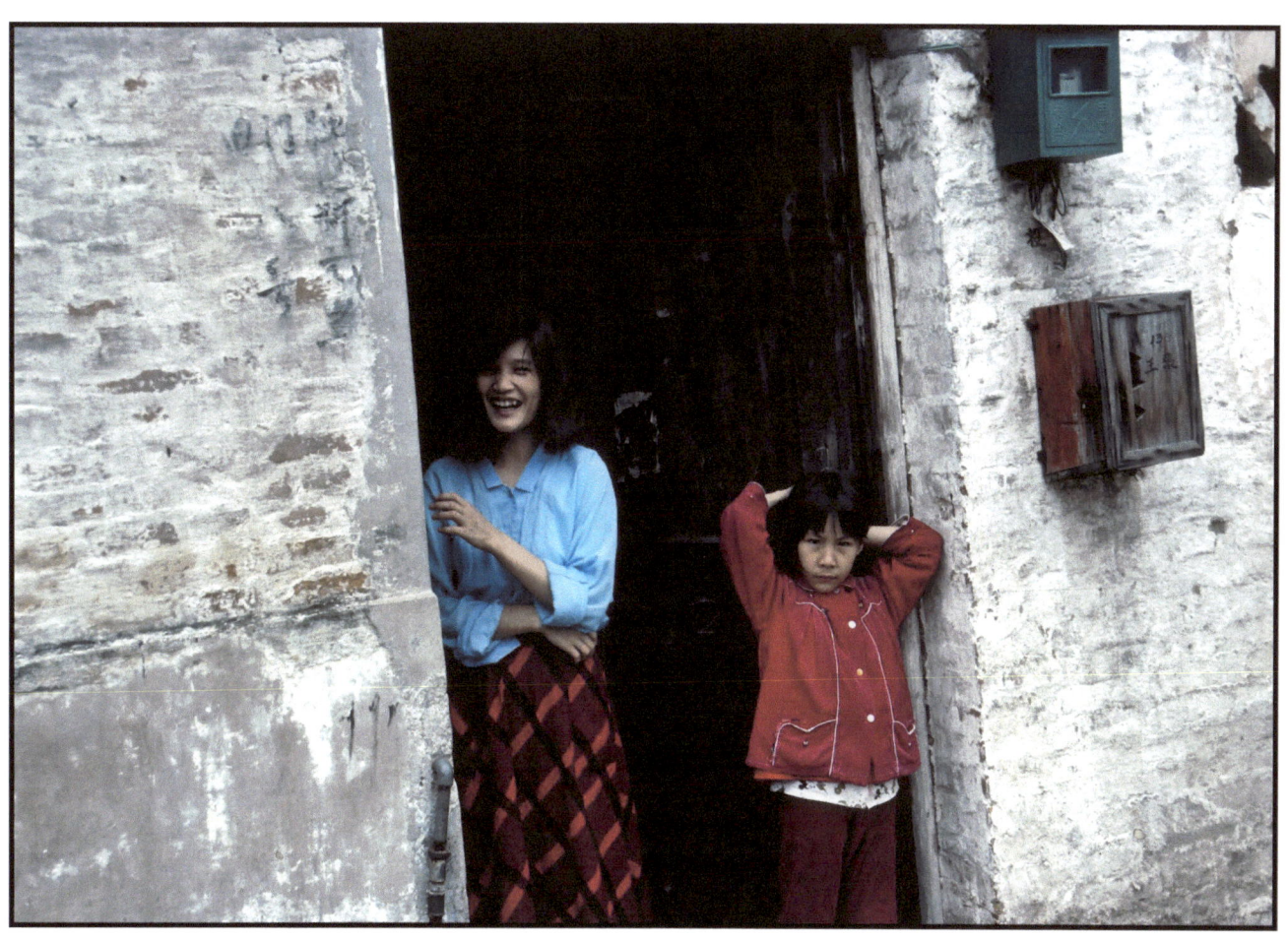

www.ingramcontent.com/pod-product-compliance
Lightning Source LLC
Chambersburg PA
CBHW051149220526
45473CB00003B/710